PUBLIC HEALTH LAW

IN A NUTSHELL®

SECOND EDITION

JAMES G. HODGE, JR.
Professor of Public Health Law and Ethics
Sandra Day O'Connor College of Law
Arizona State University

WEST ACADEMIC PUBLISHING

© 2014 LEG, Inc. d/b/a West Academic
© 2016 LEG, Inc. d/b/a West Academic
      444 Cedar Street, Suite 700
      St. Paul, MN 55101
      1-877-888-1330

Printed in the United States of America

ISBN: 978-1-63459-279-6

PREFACE / INTRODUCTION

The study or practice of public health law is challenging due largely to the breadth of the field. As defined in more detail in Chapter 1, public health law includes laws that: (1) are primarily designed to assure the conditions for people to be healthy, or (2) entail rights-based or structural limits on efforts of public or private sectors to protect, promote, or preserve community health.

Public health laws extend to traditional areas such as the prevention and control of communicable diseases (e.g., HIV/AIDS, measles, mumps), chronic conditions (e.g., heart disease, cancers, diabetes, Alzheimers), injuries (e.g., gunshot wounds, vehicular crashes, domestic incidents), and other health threats (e.g., food-borne illnesses, bioterrorism, environmental health impacts).

Related to these areas are significant legal issues arising from the use of identifiable information for public health surveillance, regulation of property to abate nuisances, inspection of commercial establishments to detect public health threats, and limitations on the dissemination of commercial or other messages that negatively impact community health.

Under even broader conceptions, public health law envelops any legal efforts that address negative effects on human health. These may include various measures to target the underlying causes of poor health outcomes, such as lack of access to health services; socio-economic, racial, ethnic, or other disparities in the distribution of services; homelessness or housing limitations; insufficient food or sustenance; and environmental factors, such as air or water pollution, or global climate change.

Though its scope is comprehensive, the field of public health law also has boundaries for the purposes of this text (and also to avoid duplication of material in other NUTSHELL series texts, notably ADMINISTRATIVE LAW, BIOETHICS & LAW, CONSTITUTIONAL LAW, DISABILITY LAW, ENVIRONMENTAL LAW, HEALTH CARE LAW & ETHICS, and MENTAL HEALTH LAW). In the interests of presenting a cohesive vision of public health law concentrated on core aspects of the field, this text does not include significant coverage of several legal issues that directly or tangentially affect the public's health. These include laws concerning access and delivery of health care services; national health care reform; disability law; environmental protection (except as related to environmental health); mental health law; and the licensure or regulation of public health or health care workers and entities.

A. Sources of Public Health Law

The primary sources of U.S. public health law are diverse. Given the heavy role of government in protecting the public's health, constitutional issues often arise (*see* the U.S. Constitution Bill of Rights and 14th Amendment, restated hereafter, for reference throughout the text). One of the central themes of the field is the consummate need to balance public and private interests in effectuating public health objectives and programs. Federal, tribal, state, and local lawmakers are responsible for public health statutes or other legislative enactments. Some of these legislative efforts are based on model public health acts or provisions produced via academic or other entities. Legislatures also empower public health and other executive branch agencies to create and enforce regulatory or administrative laws or issue executive orders to advance public health goals.

Courts at all levels of government contribute to the breadth and limits of public health powers through pivotal decisions on constitutional or other challenges. Collectively these cases constitute what is known as the "common law." Finally, public health law includes "soft law" examples, such as memoranda of understanding, departmental policies, letters of clarification, or other initiatives. While these examples do not carry the same legal weight as statutes, regulations, or cases, law- and policy-makers may defer to soft law sources in assessing public health legal issues.

B. Teaching & Practicing Public Health Law

Not long ago, core courses in public health law were taught in just a handful of largely graduate-level institutions. Few practitioners nationally identified themselves as "public health lawyers." In the past few decades, however, public health law has emerged as a distinct field of practice and a formal course of academic study. Thousands of practitioners working in public and private sector positions have received comprehensive or select training in public health legal topics. Hundreds of core courses in public health law are taught annually in lecture, seminar, and clinical formats across the country.

Based on my 2012 survey of public health law academics, core courses in public health law (coupled often with ethics or policy) are offered routinely at virtually all accredited schools of public health, over one-third of American Bar Association (ABA)-accredited law schools, multiple schools of medicine, and even some undergraduate institutions. In addition to these core classes, many undergraduate and graduate schools offer courses in health law, bioethics, or other areas that include prominent public health law topics. James G. Hodge, Jr., *A Modern Survey on Teaching Public Health Law in the U.S.,* 40 J.L. MED. & ETHICS 1034 (2013).

Students across the country may find this NUTSHELL valuable as a complement to existing texts used in these courses. Among others, these texts include:

- LAWRENCE O. GOSTIN, PUBLIC HEALTH LAW AND ETHICS: A READER (2d ed. 2010) (used in my own courses);

- RICHARD J. BONNIE & RUTH GAARE BERNHEIM, PUBLIC HEALTH LAW, ETHICS, AND POLICY (2015);

- LAW IN PUBLIC HEALTH PRACTICE (Richard A. Goodman et al. eds., 2d ed. 2007); and

- KENNETH R. WING ET AL., PUBLIC HEALTH LAW (2007).

Major topics in this NUTSHELL include many of the issues addressed in these texts and courses, although under varied organizational patterns or levels of coverage. For example, while Professor Gostin disperses emergency legal preparedness issues throughout his READER, these issues are combined in the final chapter of the NUTSHELL. The text's Table of Contents or Index facilitates a quick comparison and examination of relevant passages based on study assignments or interest areas.

For public health or legal practitioners seeking a solid introduction or enhanced understanding of the field outside formal coursework, this text provides a helpful tool for self-study, as well as a practical guide on core topics in a condensed format. Some of the practice guidance stems from ongoing efforts of the Network for Public Health Law to assist public health officials and their legal counsel (among others) through specific guidance on legal issues arising in their own practice.

C. Acknowledgments

Many thanks to outstanding colleagues at institutions and locations across the country who provided their input, research, or reviews for the 1st or 2nd editions of this text. They include (in alphabetical order): Leila F. Barraza, J.D., M.P.H., Jennifer Bernstein, J.D., M.P.H., Scott Burris, J.D., Veda Collmer, J.D., Alicia Corbett, J.D., Brooke Courtney, J.D., M.P.H., Corey Davis, J.D., M.P.H.,

Lance A. Gable, J.D., M.P.H., Richard A. Goodman, M.D., J.D., M.P.H., Monica Hammer, J.D., Kathleen Hoke, J.D., Peter D. Jacobson, J.D., M.P.H., Nancy Kaufman, R.N., M.S., Stacie Kershner, J.D., Kellie Manders, J.D., Greg Measer, J.D., Chase Millea, Rose Meltzer, Daniel G. Orenstein, J.D., Wendy E. Parmet, J.D., Tia Powell, M.D., Clifford M. Rees, J.D., Susan Russo, J.D., Lainie Rutkow, J.D., M.P.H., Ph.D., Stephen P. Teret, J.D., M.P.H., Jon S. Vernick, J.D., M.P.H., Kim Weidenaar, J.D., and Lexi White, J.D.

Special thanks to Asha M. Agrawal, Sarah A. Wetter, and Brenna Carpenter, J.D. candidates at the Sandra Day O'Connor College of Law, and Matthew R. Saria, whose contributions were indispensable to the production of the text.

Finally, I dedicate this 2nd edition of the text to Andrea, Maria, Avery, and Collin for their constant support for its preparation and publication. Thank you.

JAMES G. HODGE, JR., J.D., LL.M.

August 31, 2015

The U.S. Constitution
Bill of Rights & 14th Amendment

Amendment I. Congress shall make no law respecting an establishment of religion, or prohibiting the free exercise thereof; or abridging the freedom of speech, or of the press; or the right of the people peaceably to assemble, and to petition the Government for a redress of grievances.

Amendment II. A well regulated Militia, being necessary to the security of a free State, the right of the people to keep and bear Arms, shall not be infringed.

Amendment III. No Soldier shall, in time of peace be quartered in any house, without the consent of the Owner, nor in time of war, but in a manner to be prescribed by law.

Amendment IV. The right of the people to be secure in their persons, houses, papers, and effects, against unreasonable searches and seizures, shall not be violated, and no Warrants shall issue, but upon probable cause, supported by Oath or affirmation, and particularly describing the place to be searched, and the persons or things to be seized.

Amendment V. No person shall be held to answer for a capital, or otherwise infamous crime, unless on a presentment or indictment of a Grand Jury, except in cases arising in the land or naval forces, or in the Militia, when in actual service in time of War or public danger; nor shall any person be subject for the same offence to be twice put in jeopardy of life or limb; nor shall be compelled in any criminal case to be a witness against himself, nor be deprived of life, liberty, or property, without due process of law; nor shall private property be taken for public use, without just compensation.

Amendment VI. In all criminal prosecutions, the accused shall enjoy the right to a speedy and public trial, by an impartial jury of the State and district wherein the crime shall have been committed, which district shall have been previously ascertained by law, and to be informed of the nature and cause of the accusation; to be confronted with the witnesses against him; to have compulsory process for obtaining witnesses in his favor, and to have the Assistance of Counsel for his defence.

Amendment VII. In Suits at common law, where the value in controversy shall exceed twenty dollars, the right of trial by jury shall be preserved, and no fact tried by a jury, shall be otherwise re-examined in any Court of the United States, than according to the rules of the common law.

Amendment VIII. Excessive bail shall not be required, nor excessive fines imposed, nor cruel and unusual punishments inflicted.

Amendment IX. The enumeration in the Constitution, of certain rights, shall not be construed to deny or disparage others retained by the people.

Amendment X. The powers not delegated to the United States by the Constitution, nor prohibited by it to the States, are reserved to the States respectively, or to the people.

Amendment XIV. Section 1. All persons born or naturalized in the United States, and subject to the jurisdiction thereof, are citizens of the United States and of the State wherein they reside. No State shall make or enforce any law which shall abridge the privileges or immunities of citizens of the United States; nor shall any State deprive any person of life, liberty, or property, without due process of law; nor deny to any person within its jurisdiction the equal protection of the laws.

Section 2. Representatives shall be apportioned among the several States according to their respective numbers, counting the whole number of persons in each State, excluding Indians not taxed. But when the right to vote at any election for the choice of electors for President and Vice-President of the United States, Representatives in Congress, the Executive and Judicial officers of a State, or the members of the Legislature thereof, is denied to any of the male inhabitants of such State, being twenty-one years of age, and citizens of the United States, or in any way abridged, except for participation in rebellion, or other crime, the basis of representation therein shall be reduced in the proportion which the number of such male citizens shall bear to the whole number of male citizens twenty-one years of age in such State.

Section 3. No person shall be a Senator or Representative in Congress, or elector of President and Vice-President, or hold any office, civil or military, under the United States, or under any State, who, having previously taken an oath, as a member of Congress, or as an officer of the United States, or as a member of any State legislature, or as an executive or judicial officer of any State, to support the Constitution of the United States, shall have engaged in insurrection or rebellion against the same, or given aid or comfort to the enemies thereof. But Congress may by a vote of two-thirds of each House, remove such disability.

Section 4. The validity of the public debt of the United States, authorized by law, including debts incurred for payment of pensions and bounties for services in suppressing insurrection or rebellion, shall not be questioned. But neither the United States nor any State shall assume or pay any debt or obligation incurred in aid of insurrection or rebellion against the United States, or any claim for the loss or emancipation of any slave; but all such debts, obligations and claims shall be held illegal and void.

Section 5. The Congress shall have the power to enforce, by appropriate legislation, the provisions of this article.

OUTLINE

PREFACE / INTRODUCTION III
THE U.S. CONSTITUTION BILL OF RIGHTS & 14TH
    AMENDMENT IX
TABLE OF CASES XVII
GLOSSARY OF ACRONYMS XXIII

PART 1. CORE STRUCTURE & BASES OF PUBLIC HEALTH LAW

Chapter 1. The Field of Public Health Law 3
A.   Public Health Law: Then & Now 4
B.   Defining Public Health Law 7
C.   Building Evidence for Public Health Law 13
D.   The Role of Public Health Ethics 16

**Chapter 2. Source & Scope of Public Health
    Legal Powers 25**
A.   The Constitutional Fountain of Public
    Health Powers 27
    1.   Federalism.. 28
    2.   Separation of Powers 32
B.   Federal Public Health Powers 36
C.   State Public Health Powers 38
    1.   Police Powers.. 38
    2.   Parens Patriae Powers 39
D.   Local Public Health Powers 41
E.   Tribal Public Health Powers 43

Chapter 3. Constitutional Rights & the Public's Health 47
A. Foundations of Rights-Based Limitations 47
B. Brief Overview of Specific Rights 51
C. Voluntary, Mandatory & Compulsory Powers 62
D. Balancing Individual & Community Interests 65

PART 2. LEGAL AUTHORITY TO PREVENT & CONTROL PUBLIC HEALTH CONDITIONS

Chapter 4. Preventing & Treating Communicable Conditions 77
A. Communicable Conditions—Defined 78
B. Testing & Screening 82
C. Treatment & Related Therapies 87
    1. Directly-observed Therapy 89
    2. Expedited Partner Therapy 90
    3. Forced Treatment 91
D. Partner Notification 93
E. Vaccination 95
F. Social Distancing Measures 101
    1. State & Local Quarantine & Isolation.... 102
    2. Federal Quarantine & Isolation.............. 105
    3. Curfews & Closures 106
    4. Personal Liberties 107

Chapter 5. Addressing Chronic Conditions 111
A. Chronic Conditions—Defined 112
B. Causes of Chronic Conditions......................... 115

C.   Legal Authorities.............................. 119
    1.   The Power to Tax 121
    2.   The Power to Spend.................. 124
    3.   The Power to Regulate 128
    4.   Addressing Disability Bias...................... 132

Chapter 6. Mitigating the Incidence &
    Severity of Injuries & Other Harms 139
A.   Primary Sources of Injuries, Harms &
    Deaths 141
B.   Addressing Harms Through Tort Law.......... 147
    1.   Negligence 148
    2.   Intentional Acts 151
    3.   Strict Liability........................... 153
    4.   Products Liability 153
C.   Criminal Law & Public Health...................... 162

PART 3. LAW & THE PROMOTION OF
THE PUBLIC'S HEALTH

Chapter 7. Public Health Information
    Management, Privacy & Security 171
A.   Surveillance & Reporting.............................. 172
B.   Balancing Individual Privacy & Communal
    Interests.. 176
C.   Privacy, Confidentiality & Security 178
    1.   Federal Privacy Laws 180
    2.   HIPAA Privacy Rule 183
    3.   State & Local Privacy Laws 188
D.   Privacy & the Right to Know.......................... 190
E.   Distinguishing Practice & Research 193

Chapter 8. Regulating Communications....... 201
A.   Public Health Education.................................. 202
B.   Required Disclosures of Public Health
     Information... 206
     1.   Warnings & Advisories............................ 207
     2.   Menu Labeling 213
C.   Controlling Commercial Communications.... 217
D.   Commercial Speech & Tobacco...................... 223

**Chapter 9. Monitoring Property & the Built
     Environment 229**
A.   Inspections & Oversight 230
B.   Search & Seizure... 232
C.   Nuisance Abatement..................................... 237
     1.   Public Nuisance 237
     2.   Private Nuisance..................................... 241
D.   Takings... 243
E.   Zoning & the Built Environment 246

**Chapter 10. Public Health Emergency
     Legal Preparedness & Response............. 255**
A.   Defining Public Health Emergencies............ 256
B.   State & Local Public Health Emergency
     Powers.. 261
C.   Federal Public Health Emergency Powers ... 265
D.   The Evolving Emergency Legal
     Environment.. 269
     1.   Interjurisdictional Roles in
          Preparedness 270
     2.   Practicing Legal Triage 272
     3.   Emergency Liability Protections............. 274
INDEX.. 281

TABLE OF CASES

References are to Pages

44 Liquormart, Inc. v. Rhode Island 222
Adarand Constructors, Inc. v. Pena 48
Agency for Int'l Dev. v. Alliance for Open Soc'y Int'l 126
Alberts v. Devine 191
Allied Structural Steel Co. v. Spannaus 39
Allno Enters., Inc. v. Baltimore Cnty. 236
American Elec. Power Co. v. Connecticut 240
Ames v. Sears, Roebuck & Co. 158
Anspach ex rel. Anspach v. City of Phila. 88
Arcara v. Cloud Books, Inc. 246
Arlington Heights, Village of v. Metropolitan Hous. Dev.
    Corp. 57
Bearder v. State 85
Bellas v. Planning Bd. of Weymouth 252
Bellingham, City of v. Chin 239
Benning v. State 166
Bess Eaton Donut Flour Co., Inc. v. Zoning Bd. of Review
    of Town of Westerly 252
Blue v. Koren 236
Boldt v. Jostens, Inc. 151
Bolling v. Sharpe 56
Boone v. Boozman 99
Boreali v. Axelrod 34
Boyd v. Louisiana Med. Mut. Ins. Co. 97
Bronco Wine Co. v. Jolly 212
Brown v. Plata 25
Brown v. Stone 99
Brusewitz v. Wyeth 101, 157
Brzoska v. Olson 192
Buckley v. American Constitutional Law Found., Inc. ... 51
Bullitt Fiscal Ct. et. al v. Bullitt Cnty. Bd. of Health 34
Burman v. Streeval 55
California v. Monster Beverage Corp. 211
Camara v. Municipal Court of the City & Cnty. of
    S.F. 233, 234
Canterbury v. Spence 88

Castle Rock v. Gonzales.. 26
Central Hudson Gas & Elec. Corp. v. Public Serv. Comm'n
   of N.Y. 52, 220
Chevron, U.S.A., Inc. v. NRDC, Inc. 33
Chicago, City of v. Beretta U.S.A. 240
Chicago, City of v. Taylor 42
Citizens United v. Federal Election Comm'n 51
City-Wide Coal. Against Childhood Lead Paint Poisoning
   v. Philadelphia Hous. Auth. 147
Clark v. Cohen 40
Clark v. Community for Creative Non-Violence...... 53, 219
Cleburne, City of v. Cleburne Living Ctr., Inc. 50
Cleveland, City of v. State... 132
Congress Care Ctr. Assoc. v. Chicago Dep't of Health.... 40
Contreras v. City of Chicago... 236
Copart Indus. Inc. v. Consolidated Edison Co. 239
Cruzan v. Director, Mo. Dep't of Health 92
Darby, United States v. 29, 30
Daubert v. Merrell Dow Pharmaceuticals, Inc. 36
De Gidio v. Pung 90
Dempsey, People v. 95
Denver, City & Cnty. of, United States v. 38
DeShaney v. Winnebago Cnty. Dep't of Soc. Serv. 26
Discount Tobacco City & Lottery, Inc. v. U.S. 226
District of Columbia v. Heller 60
Doe v. Irwin.. 62
Doe v. Miller... 55
Doe v. Moore... 55
Dolan v. City of Tigard 249
EEOC v. Houston Funding... 58
Eller Media Co. v. City of Cleveland 42
Estelle v. Gamble.. 60
Euclid, Village of v. Ambler Realty 248
Everett v. Tenet Health Sys. Mem'l Med. Ctr., Inc. 275
Ferguson v. City of Charleston 86, 167
Field v. Gazette Pub. Co. 151
Fisher v. United States... 150
Foucha v. Louisiana.. 54
Gallo, People ex rel. v. Acuna.. 240
Geduldig v. Aiello... 49
Gitlow v. N.Y. 66
Glover v. Eastern Neb. Cmty. Office of Retardation 87

Gonzales v. Oregon 39
Gordon v. City of Moreno Valley 236
Greene v. Edwards.. 108
Gregory v. Ashcroft... 31
Grundberg v. Upjohn Co.................................... 155
Hale v. Ward Cnty. 242
Hamilton v. Beretta U.S.A. Corp. 161
Hammer v. Dagenhart....................................... 29
Harms v. City of Sibley.................................... 246
Hodgins v. USDA.. 236
Howard v. Ford Motor Co. 158
Ileto v. Glock 161
Irwindale, City of, People ex rel. v. Huy Fong Foods,
    Inc. 241
Izell v. Union Carbide Corp............................. 150
Jacobson v. Massachusetts................................... 45, 66, 70
Jensen, People v.. 192
Jew Ho v. Williamson 57, 108
Juan C., In re 106
Juveniles A, B, C, D, E, In re 84
Kehler v. Hood 278
Kelo v. City of New London 61, 244
King v. Burwell.. 32
Kirk v. Wyman... 108
L.R. Willson & Sons v. OSHRC...................... 231
Lawton v. Steele... 246
Lead Indus. Ass'n, State v.............................. 241
Lopez, United States v..................................... 31
Lorillard Tobacco Co. v. Reilly 223
Lucas v. South Carolina Coastal Council 244
Lucero v. Trosch... 243
Madsen v. Women's Health Ctr., Inc. 243
Magnuson by Mabe v. Kelsey-Hayes Co. 155
Markweise v. Peck Foods Corp. 81
Martin v. Herzog.. 150
Maryland v. King... 86
Massachusetts v. EPA...................................... 40
Mathews v. Eldridge.. 54
McCormack v. Hankscraft Co. 158
McDonald v. City of Chicago 61
Meyer v. Grant... 51
Mezick v. State.. 40

Middlebrooks v. State Bd. of Health 85
Mills v. Alabama 52
Milwaukee, City of v. Washington 90
Multimedia KSDK, Inc., In re 64
Mutual Pharm. Co., Inc. v. Bartlett 157
National Fed. of Ind. Bus. v. Sebelius 29, 31, 122, 127
New York Statewide Coal. of Hispanic Chambers of
    Commerce v. N.Y. Dep't of Health & Mental
    Hygiene 205
New York v. Burger 234
New York, City of v. Antoinette 92
New York, City of v. Milhelm Attea & Bros., Inc. 239
Newark, City of v. J.S. 90
Obergefell v. Hodges 49
Parents United for Better Sch., Inc. v. School Dist. of
    Phila. Bd. of Edu. 62
Parker v. St. Lawrence Cnty. Pub. Health Dep't 278
Pelman v. McDonald's Corp. 159
Pendergrast v. Aiken 237
Penn Central Trans. Co. v. New York City 245
Pestey v. Cushman 241
Players, Inc. v. City of New York 235
Prince v. Massachusetts 59
R.J. Reynolds Tobacco Co. v. FDA 212, 226
Randi W. v. Muroc Joint Unified Sch. Dist. 149
Rassier v. Houim 242
Reisner v. Regents of the Univ. of Cal. 192
Riggins v. Nevada 92
Roe v. Wade 166
Roper v. Simmons 60
Rose Acre Farms, Inc. v. United States 245
Rothal, State ex rel. v. Smith 240
Rush v. Obledo 236
S&S Pawn Shop Inc. v. City of Del City 236
Saenz v. Roe 55
Santosky v. Kramer 40
Schuster v. Altenberg 191
See v. City of Seattle 233, 234
Sell v. United States 93
Shilling v. Moore 37
Siegler v. Kuhlman 153
Simon v. Sargent 165

Skinner v. Railway Labor Execs. Ass'n 86
Skinner, United States v. 162
South Dakota v. Dole 125, 126
Southern Constructors, Inc. v. Loudon Cnty. Bd. of
    Educ. 43
Speaker v. CDC 106
Stanford v. Kentucky 60
Summit Cnty. Bd. of Health v. Pearson 238
Tarasoff v. Regents of the Univ. of Cal. 190
Technical Chem. Co. v. Jacobs 157
Texas v. Johnson 51
Tinker v. Des Moines Indep. Cmty. Sch. Dist. 51
Tucson Woman's Clinic v. Eden 236
United Foods, United States v. 219
United States of America for Historical Cell Site Data, In
    re Application of the 86
Vance v. Bradley 50
Virginia, United States v 49
Waller, In re v. City of New York 53
Walsh v. Stonington Water Pollution Control Auth 242
Ward v. Rock Against Racism 218
Washington, In re 92
Westbury Trombo, Inc., In re v. Board of Trs 252
Whalen v. Roe 59, 179
Wooley v. Maynard 219
Wyatt v. Stickney 41
Zemel v. Rusk 106
Zucht v. King 97

GLOSSARY OF ACRONYMS

The following acronyms are used throughout the text:

ABA—American Bar Association

ABLA—Alcoholic Beverage Labeling Act

ACA—Patient Protection & Affordable Care Act

ACIP—Advisory Committee on Immunization Practices

ADA—Americans with Disabilities Act

AMA—American Medical Association

BLS—Bureau of Labor Statistics

BPA—Bisphenol A

CBRN—Chemical, Biological, Radiological, Nuclear

CDC—Centers for Disease Control & Prevention

CMS—Centers for Medicare & Medicaid Services

COPD—Chronic Obstructive Pulmonary Disease

CPSA—Consumer Product Safety Act

CPSC—Consumer Product Safety Commission

CRA—Civil Rights Act

CSTE—Council of State & Territorial Epidemiologists

DHHS—Department of Health & Human Services

DHS—Department of Homeland Security

DOT—Directly-observed Therapy

DUI—Driving Under the Influence

EEOC—Equal Employment Opportunity Commission

EHR—Electronic Health Record

EMAC—Emergency Management Assistance Compact

EMTALA—Emergency Medical Treatment & Active Labor Act

EPA—Environmental Protection Agency

EPT—Expedited Partner Therapy

EUA—Emergency Use Authorization

EVD—Ebola Viral Disease

FBI—Federal Bureau of Investigation

FDA—Food & Drug Administration

FERPA—Family Educational Rights & Privacy Act

FOIA—Freedom of Information Act

FSPTCA—Family Smoking Prevention & Tobacco Control Act

FTC—Federal Trade Commission

GINA—Genetic Information Nondiscrimination Act

HAI—Health-care Associated Infection

HCW—Health Care Worker

HIA—Health Impact Assessment

HiAP—Health in all Policies

HIE—Health Information Exchange

HIPAA—Health Insurance Portability & Accountability Act

HIV/AIDS—Human Immunodeficiency Virus/Acquired Immunodeficiency Syndrome

HPV—Human Papillomavirus

IDU—Injecting Drug User

IOM—Institute of Medicine

IRB—Institutional Review Board

JAMA—Journal of the American Medical Association

MDR—Multidrug-resistant

MMWR—Morbidity & Mortality Weekly Report

MRSA—Methicillin-resistant Staphylococcus Aureus

MSEHPA—Model State Emergency Health Powers Act

MSPHPA—Model State Public Health Privacy Act

NDMS—National Disaster Medical System

NEP—Needle Exchange Program

NHLBI—National Heart, Lung & Blood Institute

NHTSA—National Highway Traffic Safety Administration

NINDS—National Institute of Neurological Disorders & Stroke

NLEA—Nutritional Labeling & Education Act

OHRP—Office for Human Research Protections

OSHA—Occupational Safety & Health Administration

PAHPA—Pandemic & All-Hazards Preparedness Act

PAHPRA—Pandemic & All-Hazards Preparedness Reauthorization Act

PCRS—Partner Counseling & Referral Services

PHA—Public Health Authority

PHE—Public Health Emergency

PHI—Protected Health Information

PHLR—Public Health Law Research

PHSA—Public Health Service Act

PI—Principal Investigator

PLCAA—Protection of Lawful Commerce in Arms Act

PREP—Public Readiness & Emergency Preparedness

PTSD—Post-traumatic Stress Disorder

RFRA—Religious Freedom Restoration Act

SNS—Strategic National Stockpile

SSB—Sugar Sweetened Beverage

STD—Sexually Transmitted Disease

STI—Sexually Transmitted Infection

TB—Tuberculosis

TFAH—Trust for America's Health

USDA—U.S. Department of Agriculture

USPSTF—U.S. Preventative Services Task Force

WHO—World Health Organization

XDR—Extreme Drug Resistant

PUBLIC HEALTH LAW

IN A NUTSHELL®

SECOND EDITION

PART 1

CORE STRUCTURE & BASES OF PUBLIC HEALTH LAW

Protecting and promoting the public's health are quintessential functions of government. Public health agencies and officials at the federal, tribal, state, and local levels are responsible (albeit in different ways) for accomplishing across societies what no person can secure individually: *assure the health of communities.* LAWRENCE O. GOSTIN, PUBLIC HEALTH LAW: POWER, DUTY, RESTRAINT 8–10 (2d ed. 2008).

Meeting this objective is not easy. It requires significant public and private sector partnerships, constant surveillance, access to accurate and reliable data, state-of-the-art research, enhanced practice methods, effective education and training, ethical guidance, respect for cultural norms and sensitivities, and sufficient financing. It also requires the law.

Law is pivotal to nearly every public or private effort to advance the public's health. Understanding the central role of law related to the public's health begins with an assessment of its core structure and bases. Chapter 1 examines prior and contemporary conceptions of public health law. It also introduces a modern definition of public health law as a guide for the remainder of the text. The source and scope of these laws at each level of government are explored in Chapter 2. This includes a brief overview of the structural foundations of public health law, namely constitutional principles of separation of powers, preemption, and federalism.

Consistent with an understanding of public health law that regularly balances communal and individual interests, Chapter 3 lays out primary rights-based limitations on the powers of government to protect the public's health. Examples of these rights include due process, equal protection, and freedom of speech. For additional reference, see also the U.S. Constitution Bill of Rights and 14th Amendment after the Preface/Introduction. Together with the structural principles noted in Chapter 2, these constitutional norms are revisited often throughout Parts 2 and 3 of the text.

CHAPTER 1

THE FIELD OF PUBLIC HEALTH LAW

Public health vigilance is essential because the threats to communal health are always changing. Just a century ago, outbreaks of infectious diseases like smallpox, polio, yellow fever, and malaria arose commonly in many U.S. localities. HANS ZINSSER, RATS, LICE AND HISTORY: A CHRONICLE OF PESTILENCE AND PLAGUES (1963). Today, natural occurrences of smallpox are globally eradicated. Many other communicable conditions like malaria and polio are controlled and largely forgotten in the U.S., though they continue to plague populations in developing countries. GEORGE ROSEN, A HISTORY OF PUBLIC HEALTH (1993).

Still, new communicable disease threats are always on the horizon. Some like HIV/AIDS in the early 1980s, H1N1 influenza in 2009, and Ebola viral disease (EVD) (most recently in 2014) emerge from distant locales. Others like the rapid spread of measles in 2015 are homegrown threats emanating from gaps in vaccination coverage. Jennifer Zipprich et. al., *Measles Outbreak—California, December 2014–February 2015*, 64 MMWR 153, 153 (2015).

Public health challenges in the U.S. have shifted to conditions such as cancers and other chronic illnesses, obesity, injuries, and environmental health risks. The future of public health invariably entails new risks that are either unknown currently or outside the public's view. The history of public health law evinces its constant evolution alongside these threats to support public and private approaches to address them.

A. PUBLIC HEALTH LAW: THEN & NOW

Protecting the public's health once centered largely on the control of infectious diseases and implementation of sanitary practices. FITZHUGH MULLAN, PLAGUES AND POLITICS: THE STORY OF THE U.S. PUBLIC HEALTH SERVICE 58 (1989). However, what it means to advance the public's health is always changing. In 1988, the Institute of Medicine (IOM) set forth a modern view of public health as ". . . what we, as a society, do collectively to assure the conditions for people to be healthy." IOM, THE FUTURE OF PUBLIC HEALTH 19 (1988). This definition reflects a considerable expansion of the mission and objectives of public health. As U.S. Surgeon General Vivek Murthy noted in 2015, "The truth is whenever large numbers of people are dying for preventable reasons, that's a public health issue." Lenny Bernstein, *Surgeon General Vivek Murthy Wants to Move U.S. Health Care Toward a "Prevention-based Society,"* WASH. POST (Apr. 23, 2015).

Consequently, nearly any public or private sector intervention that directly or indirectly affects communal health is within the gambit of modern public health practice, including environmental hazards, injury prevention, occupational safety, and housing. These interventions interplay with individuals' efforts to make healthy choices within a society committed to abating risks to the community's health.

The value of a broader vision for public health in the modern era is undeniable. It has contributed to more sophisticated and sweeping approaches on how to engineer improved public health outcomes, distribute health resources equitably, eliminate health disparities, and counter negative impacts on population health. Public health advocates have promoted, for example, the concept of "health in all policies" (HiAP) to encourage greater attention to health outcomes related to specific public or private decisions (e.g., the placement, design, and construction of modern housing). WORLD HEALTH ORG., HEALTH IN ALL POLICIES: TRAINING MANUAL (Vivien Stone ed., 2015). The Robert Wood Johnson Foundation frames its objectives around what it calls a "culture of health." Alonzo L. Plough, *Building a Culture of Health: Challenges for the Public Health Workforce*, 47 AM. J. PREV. MED. S388 (2014) (defining "culture of health" as what Americans are collectively doing to improve population-level well-being within a diverse society for long-term benefits to health and health systems).

Since health is fundamental to all economic sectors, policies that affect the social determinants of health (including schools, zoning, food, transportation, and workplaces) should be formulated in consideration of their potential positive and negative health impacts. IOM, FOR THE PUBLIC'S HEALTH: REVITALIZING LAW AND POLICY TO MEET NEW CHALLENGES (2011). In furtherance of this goal, governmental and private actors have developed innovative health impact assessments (HIAs) to better measure the public health ramifications of policies prior to their implementation. NAT'L ACADS., IMPROVING HEALTH IN THE U.S.: THE ROLE OF HIA (2011); JAMES G. HODGE, JR. ET AL., LEGAL REVIEW CONCERNING THE USE OF HIAS IN NON-HEALTH SECTORS (2012). WHO has defined HIA as "a combination of procedures, methods, and tools by which a policy, program, or project may be judged as to its potential effects on the health of a population, and the distribution of those effects within the population." European Centre for Health Policy, *HIA: Main Concepts and Suggested Approach*, Gothenburg consensus paper, Brussels, 1999. HIAs have been used to assess the health effects of:

- a bicycle lane proposal to connect 2 off-road bike trails in Washington, DC (2011);

- sugar-sweetened beverage (SSB) taxes on low income and communities of color in Los Angeles County (2013); and

- regulations for retail marijuana packaging in Colorado (2013).

See HIAs in the United States: HIA Project, PEW CHARITABLE TRUSTS (May 2, 2014).

Adopting an HiAP approach nationally that incorporates extensive use of HIAs to assess varied interventions consistent with a "culture of health" may invariably contribute to healthier societies. Yet, some suggest that this more expansive view of the field may dilute what it means to protect the public's health. By spreading thin available resources to address sometimes tangential issues, essential functions of public health (like infectious disease control) may be diminished or ignored. In an era in which public health agencies at all levels of government face chronic funding shortages (Kyle Kinner & Cindy Pellegrini, *Expenditures for Public Health: Assessing Historical and Prospective Trends,* 99 AM. J. PUB. HEALTH 1780 (2009)), instating a broader mission for public health may be aspirational, but largely beyond reach.

B.   DEFINING PUBLIC HEALTH LAW

Just as the practice of public health is not static, neither is public health law. The scope and range of public health law have expanded over decades. Historic conceptions focused largely on public health powers related to communicable disease control and sanitation. In 1926, Yale University lecturer and World War II veteran James Tobey set forth one of the earliest definitions of public health law: "Public health law is that branch of jurisprudence which [applies] common and statutory law to the principles of hygiene and sanitary science." JAMES A. TOBEY, PUBLIC HEALTH LAW: A MANUAL OF LAW FOR SANITARIANS 6–7 (1926). Tobey and other practitioners of this era mostly examined state and local laws authorizing traditional public health powers of vaccination, isolation, quarantine, testing, screening, treatment, inspection of commercial and residential premises, and abatement of unsanitary conditions or other health nuisances.

As the practice of public health shifted increasingly beyond infectious conditions over the next several decades, modern assessments of public health law emerged. In the 1st edition of his PUBLIC HEALTH LAW MANUAL in 1965, Columbia Law Professor Frank Grad reflected a broader view of public health law as including "provisions [that] have some considerable relationship to the maintenance of health and the prevention of disease."

No longer bound to historic notions of public health functions and core responsibilities, public health law continued to develop as a distinct field. In the 2nd edition of his MANUAL in 1990, Professor Grad noted: "[Public health law] seek[s] to enhance public health not only by prohibiting harmful activities or conditions but also by providing preventive and rehabilitative services to advance the health of the people . . . ." FRANK P. GRAD, THE PUBLIC HEALTH LAW MANUAL 9 (2d ed. 1990).

Among the most influential contemporary definitions of public health law is provided by Professor Lawrence O. Gostin at Georgetown University Law Center. In a series of articles, and later his seminal texts on public health law, Professor Gostin lays out a modern conception of the field that incorporates IOM's expansive view of public health:

> Public health law [is] the study of the legal powers and duties of the state, in collaboration with its partners (e.g., health care, business, the community, the media, and academe), to

ensure the conditions for people to be healthy, and of the limitations on the power of the state to constrain the autonomy, privacy, liberty, proprietary, and other legally protected interests of individuals.

LAWRENCE O. GOSTIN, PUBLIC HEALTH LAW: POWER, DUTY, RESTRAINT 4 (2d ed. 2008).

Professor Gostin's definition refers for the first time to the compelling balance at work in public health law between the powers of government to act "to ensure the conditions to be healthy" and the constraints on these powers to protect individual rights. Under this view, neither public health powers nor individual freedoms are absolute. Rather, they are consistently at play in determining the breadth and limit of the role of law in the interests of communal health. Professor Wendy Parmet at Northeastern School of Law recognizes this same dynamic when she notes "[p]ublic health law . . . focuses on the authority of government agencies charged with protecting public health as well as the rights of individuals subject to such regulations." WENDY E. PARMET, POPULATIONS, PUBLIC HEALTH, AND THE LAW 212–13 (2009).

These sophisticated themes not only raised the scholarly level of study of public health law, they also clarified its practice. Public health law is not solely about governments' inherent powers nor individuals' fundamental rights. It is about how these respective components merge to generate meaningful and defensible legal interventions to advance the population's health.

Based on these varied approaches, for the purposes of this text, I define *public health law* as those laws (e.g., constitutional, statutory, regulatory, judicial), legal processes, or policies at every level of government (e.g., federal, tribal, state, local) that:

(1) are *primarily* designed to assure the conditions for people to be healthy; or

(2) concern structural or rights-based limitations on the powers of government to act in the interests of communal health.

At the epicenter of this and other modern definitions of public health law is the dynamic interplay of legal powers and restraints central to the accomplishment of public health objectives through law. Like Professor Gostin, I incorporate IOM's conception of assuring conditions for people to be healthy. This view intimates a broad and active role for law beyond mere control of communicable diseases and improvement of sanitation. The extension of law in diverse areas like education, transportation, and housing to protect and promote health among populations is core to the modern field.

My definition also acknowledges significant limitations on the role of law. While laws can obligate public and private sectors to act in the interests of the public's health, they simultaneously curtail these powers. Unlike Professor Gostin's definition, which concentrates on rights-based limitations, my definition specifically recognizes rights-based *and* structural limitations on the public health powers of government. Discussed in more detail in Chapter 2, structural limits include principles of separation of powers (delineating responsibilities among the 3 branches of government) and federalism (distinguishing between federal and state governmental authorities). Rights-based limits embedded in constitutional norms and other laws include individual rights to free expression, freedom of religion, bodily integrity, privacy, equal protection, and due process.

Though still vast, public health law is corralled by my specification that any such law be ***primarily*** designed to assure healthy conditions. This qualification is meant to help rein in the field by excluding from its study those laws that may have only tertiary or unintended effects on the public's health. As noted in the Preface, many laws have some effect on communal health; not all of them fall squarely within the field of public health law for the purposes of its assessment and practice.

By way of an illustration, consider 2 types of local zoning laws. In 1 case, a city enacts a zoning ordinance directly to advance the public's health by limiting the numbers or locations of fast food restaurants near elementary or secondary schools. *See, e.g.,* Los Angeles, Cal., Ordinance 180103 (Sept. 14, 2008). This type of modern zoning law attempts to further the public's health by limiting kids' access to fast food to lower childhood obesity, a major national objective. As such, it fits neatly within the field. Like many public health laws, it also raises controversy as to whether (1) government can control private market choices to locate lawful businesses solely to address their potential impacts on child health; and (2) the legal approach itself is efficacious. *See, e.g.,* Alicia Chang, *Study: Limit on Fast-Food Outlets in South Los Angeles Failed to Reduce Obesity, Improve Diets*, U.S. NEWS & WORLD REP. (Mar. 19, 2015).

Contrast this 1st example with a 2nd local zoning law requiring private planners to limit the size and placement of commercial signage in suburban areas. *See e.g.,* Franklin County, Ohio Zoning Resol. § 541 (2014) (requires billboards to be smaller than 300 square feet, located at least 200 feet from a residential district, and at least 25 feet from a public street). The primary objective of these sort of zoning laws is to preserve or enhance community aesthetics or an area's natural beauty. A secondary effect of the law is to limit the commercial visibility of specific businesses (e.g., tobacco shops and liquor stores), which may result in some consumers failing to access these businesses. Ultimately, decreasing consumer access to tobacco and alcohol may have beneficial public health benefits. Yet, this type of zoning law falls outside my definition of "public health law" because its *primary* purpose is not "to assure the conditions for people to be healthy." For additional discussion of the potential public health uses of zoning regarding the built environment, see Chapter 9.

Distinguishing between these zoning laws may seem non-purposeful when both could positively impact the public's health. Some public health practitioners may strongly advocate for the implementation of aesthetic zoning laws largely because of their community health benefits regardless of whether city council members approve, or even know about, the public health implications of such laws. However, broadening the principal study of public health law to any statute, regulation, or other law having any tangential effect on the health of communities extends the field well beyond the scope of this text.

C. BUILDING EVIDENCE FOR PUBLIC HEALTH LAW

One of the dominant themes emanating from modern conceptions of the field is how law is an affirmative tool for public health improvements. *See, e.g.,* Anthony D. Moulton et al., *The Scientific Basis for Law as a Public Health Tool*, 99 AM. J. PUB. HEALTH 17, 24 (2009). Like other tools available to public health practitioners such as surveillance, epidemiologic investigations, or educational campaigns, law can be used effectively to accomplish communal health goals.

In some cases, law is the principal means to achieve a public health outcome. For years after the advent of effective and safe vaccines for childhood diseases, thousands of children nationally continued to develop preventable conditions. In response, many state legislatures enacted school vaccination

laws (conditioning attendance at school upon proof
of vaccination for specified conditions) in the early
1900s. As a direct result, childhood vaccination
rates climbed and related morbidity and mortality
plummeted, demonstrating the efficacy of school
vaccination laws. *See, e.g.,* James G. Hodge, Jr. &
Lawrence O. Gostin, *School Vaccination
Requirements: Historical, Social, and Legal
Perspectives*, 90 KY. L.J. 831 (2002). School (and
day-care) vaccination laws continue to be a core
component of child and adolescent health policy
(discussed initially in Chapter 3 and later in
Chapter 4).

While the efficacy of vaccination laws is firmly
established, many other public health laws lack a
sufficient nexus with public health improvements.
Reflecting a patchwork approach, many tribal,
state, and local jurisdictions have passed or
implemented public health laws over decades that
are merely thought to be functional, but not proven.
Though well-intended, these laws may be supported
more so by political guesswork or anecdotal cases
than efficacy. Initially, few researchers explored the
effectiveness of law as a public health tool even as
laws increasingly became a mode of choice to
address known public health threats. Scott Burris &
Evan D. Anderson, *Legal Regulation of Health-
Related Behavior: A Half-Century of Public Health
Law Research*, 9 ANN. REV. L. & SOC. SCI., July 16,
2013.

Mere belief that law is an effective tool for
improving public health outcomes is an insufficient

basis for legal intervention. Proof of efficacy may be needed to counteract politicized arguments against the use of law to address public health threats such as obesity, tobacco advertisements, and gun-related violence. Generating greater support on the effectiveness of public health laws is the focus of a modern research initiative launched in 2009 through the Public Health Law Research (PHLR) program funded by the Robert Wood Johnson Foundation. Program leaders, Professor Scott Burris and Professor Alexander Wagenaar, define "public health law research" as "the scientific study of the relation of law and legal practices to population health." ALEXANDER C. WAGENAAR & SCOTT BURRIS, PUBLIC HEALTH LAW RESEARCH: THEORY AND METHODS 4 (2013).

PHLR grantees have conducted independent research and examined existing evidence on the role of law in varied public health topics. For example, researchers have generated or found evidence to support the effectiveness of laws and policies in support of:

- fluoridating water to reduce tooth decay and improve oral health;

- raising taxes on alcohol to reduce overall consumption;

- requiring directed patrols to lower gun-related crime by uncovering and deterring illegal gun possession in high-risk areas;

- mandating use of child safety seats to substantially reduce injuries to children during vehicular crashes;

- implementing selective breath testing sobriety checkpoints to reduce the harms associated with alcohol impaired driving;

- using red light cameras to lower vehicle crash fatalities; and

- focusing on treatment and rehabilitation through drug courts to lower recidivism among individuals convicted of drug-related offenses.

PUB. HEALTH L. RES., http://publichealthlaw research.org.

D. THE ROLE OF PUBLIC HEALTH ETHICS

Acknowledging an expansive (and increasingly proven) role of law to protect the public's health may suggest that law- and policy-makers can use law at will to motivate or require choices or behaviors among individuals and groups. To be sure, law has been wielded in heavy-handed ways in the guise of promoting the community's health. Historic examples discussed later in the text include numerous instances in which state and local governments confined, vaccinated, tested, or imposed other measures on unwilling individuals without sufficient justification in the name of public health prevention and control.

The legality of public health interventions, however, cannot be divorced from their ethicality. Principles of ethics not only influence the development and enforcement of law, they often provide guidance where the law cannot. For example, public health law may allow for the confinement of persons with infectious diseases like tuberculosis (TB) when they present a threat to others. *See* SHEILA M. ROTHMAN, LIVING IN THE SHADOW OF DEATH: TB AND THE SOCIAL EXPERIENCE OF ILLNESS IN AMERICAN HISTORY (1994). An individual's liberties may be curtailed legally when that individual poses serious risks to others related to infectious diseases (*see* Chapter 4).

However, ethical norms limit the appropriate use of these legal authorities to those rare cases where individuals refuse either to voluntarily participate in treatment programs or defuse the risks of transmitting TB to others. Increasingly, modern TB control laws reflect this ethic of voluntarism to respect individual autonomy to the fullest extent possible even when others' health is at some slight risk.

The contributions of ethics in public health practice and policy are undeniable. As its own distinct field, public health ethics seeks to balance individual rights with the community's health needs. Built on the utilitarian goal of achieving the greatest health outcomes for the largest numbers possible, public health ethics reflect norms from other frameworks (such as the principles of autonomy, beneficence, non-maleficence, and justice at the heart of bioethics), but they are in fact distinct.

In 2002, the Public Health Leadership Society enunciated a series of 12 core public health ethics principles:

1. Public health should address principally the fundamental causes of disease and requirements for health, aiming to prevent adverse health outcomes.

2. Public health should achieve community health in a way that respects the rights of individuals in the community.

3. Public health policies, programs, and priorities should be developed and evaluated through processes that ensure an opportunity for input from community members.

4. Public health should advocate and work for the empowerment of disenfranchised community members, aiming to ensure that the basic resources and conditions necessary for health are accessible to all.

5. Public health should seek the information needed to implement effective policies and programs that protect and promote health.

6. Public health institutions should provide communities with the information they have that is needed for decisions on policies or programs and should obtain the

community's consent for their implementation.

7.   Public health institutions should act in a timely manner on the information they have within the resources and the mandate given to them by the public.

8.   Public health programs and policies should incorporate a variety of approaches that anticipate and respect diverse values, beliefs, and cultures in the community.

9.   Public health programs and policies should be implemented in a manner that most enhances the physical and social environment.

10. Public health institutions should protect the confidentiality of information that can bring harm to an individual or community if made public. Exceptions must be justified on the basis of the high likelihood of significant harm to the individual or others.

11. Public health institutions should ensure the professional competence of their employees.

12. Public health institutions and their employees should engage in collaborations and affiliations in ways that build the public's trust and the institution's effectiveness.

PUB. HEALTH LEADERSHIP SOC'Y, PRINCIPLES OF THE
ETHICAL PRACTICE OF PUBLIC HEALTH (2002).

These core principles of public health ethics
center on the inherent moral responsibilities of
providing for the public's health through
government and the private sector. James C.
Thomas et al., *A Code of Ethics for Public Health*, 92
AM. J. PUB. HEALTH 1057 (2002). They pertain not
merely to those who practice public health sciences
or deliver services (many of whom may also adhere
to ethics codes for their respective professions), but
also to how public health initiatives are applied.
Public health actors must assure their interventions
are effective, necessary, proportional, and
transparent. James Childress et al., *Public Health
Ethics: Mapping the Terrain*, 30 J.L. MED. & ETHICS
170 (2002). Consistent with modern social justice
theory, limited resources must be fairly allocated
and communal burdens adequately shared.
MADISON POWERS & RUTH FADEN, SOCIAL JUSTICE:
THE MORAL FOUNDATIONS OF PUBLIC HEALTH AND
HEALTH POLICY (2006).

Making decisions consistent with applied
principles of public health ethics can be complicated,
especially if government acts in paternal ways to
the detriment of individual choice. Though legally
sound and often democratically-driven,
programmatic decisions that dictate the terms in
which autonomous persons must behave or adhere
to specific protocols are ethically suspect. James
Childress et al., *Public Health Ethics: Mapping the
Terrain*, 30 J.L. MED. & ETHICS 170, 175–176 (2002).

Thus, while government can require children to be vaccinated as a condition of school attendance, legally mandating that adults (e.g., emergency room nurses) be vaccinated is ethically challenging. Alexandra M. Stewart et al., *Mandatory Vaccination of Health-Care Personnel: Good Policy, Law, and Outcomes*, 53 JURIMETRICS J. 431 (2013). Many health professionals view a government's or hospital's issuance of vaccine mandates as coercive even if the mandates reflect a duty among providers to protect patient safety and are empirically shown to reduce patient harms. *See* Richard K. Zimmerman et al., *Hospital Policies, State Laws, and Healthcare Worker Influenza Rates*, 34 INFECTION CONTROL & HOSP. EPIDEMIOLOGY 854 (2013).

Other measures, such as laws mandating seatbelt use in vehicles or helmets when operating motorcycles or bicycles, may be viewed as overly paternalistic. LAWRENCE O. GOSTIN, PUBLIC HEALTH LAW AND ETHICS: A READER 79–80 (2d ed. 2010). An alternative view is advanced by Richard Thaler and Cass Sunstein through their concept of *libertarian paternalism*. They posit how institutions can "self-consciously [attempt] to move people in directions that will make their lives better," without necessarily curbing individual choice. RICHARD H. THALER & CASS R. SUNSTEIN, NUDGE: IMPROVING DECISIONS ABOUT HEALTH, WEALTH, AND HAPPINESS 6 (2009). Thus, for example, instead of government making people purchase broccoli (which was famously argued in the health care reform debates in 2011–2012), it might consider requiring the placement of healthier foods at eye level in stores to encourage their consumption. *Id.*

Irrespective of one's approach to the role of ethics underlying legal interventions, public health ethics reflect as well a process approach to advancing communal health. Professor Nancy Kass at the Johns Hopkins Bloomberg School of Public Health lays out a series of ethical steps to consider before implementation of any public health program or intervention:

- Identify goals that aid in decreasing morbidity or mortality;

- Determine whether data exist to indicate that tactics will be effective;

- Consider potential burdens, particularly risks to privacy, liberty, and justice;

- Examine whether alternatives would mitigate these burdens while maintaining effectiveness;

- Distribute benefits and burdens fairly based on data rather than arbitrary or stereotypical reasons; and

- Analyze whether the benefits outweigh the burdens.

Nancy E. Kass, *An Ethics Framework for Public Health*, 91 AM. J. PUB. HEALTH 1776 (2001).

———————

Despite early views that limited the role of law to traditional public health areas of infectious disease control and sanitation, the field has matured to encompass a plethora of laws and policies. The fabric of public health law ties together public health practice, science, politics, and ethics to promote community health and safety. Relying on more than historic tradition and modern guesswork, new research reveals the efficacy of specific public health legal interventions. Law can be a tool for positive public health outcomes. Realizing its full potential, however, requires a strong understanding of the source and scope of public health laws at the federal, tribal, state, and local levels. This is the focus of Chapter 2.

CHAPTER 2

SOURCE & SCOPE OF PUBLIC HEALTH LEGAL POWERS

The source and scope of governmental powers to address communal health are core to the definition of public health law. Protecting the population's health is a fundamental responsibility of government. However, determining which level of government is empowered to implement and enforce public health laws is not always certain. Federal, tribal, state, and local governments often work together to address public health issues. Yet, sometimes they clash over who is in charge, or refuse to address public health initiatives even though they clearly have the legal power to act. The authority to act legally in the interest of the public's health hinges on the distribution of powers outlined in the U.S. Constitution.

Constitutional obligations of government to protect individuals and populations from communal health threats vary. Government's health responsibilities related to specific persons (e.g., prisoners, institutionalized persons with mental disabilities) are linked to these persons' non-autonomous status. Prisoners, for example, are wards of the state by virtue of their incarceration. Federal constitutional principles related to prohibitions against cruel and unusual punishments via the 8th Amendment necessitate the provision of basic health and public health services within correctional facilities. *Brown v. Plata*, 563 U.S. 493

(2011) (medical and mental health care provided in California's prisons fell below the standard of decency required by the 8th Amendment due in part to overcrowding).

Protecting the health of other vulnerable persons or the general public, however, is not guaranteed. In most cases, government is not required to assure the health of specific individuals, much less the public. In *DeShaney v. Winnebago Cnty. Dep't of Soc. Serv.*, 489 U.S. 189 (1989), for example, the U.S. Supreme Court considered a child's claim against Wisconsin county agencies. Joshua DeShaney was mercilessly abused by his father while supposedly under the watchful eye of local child welfare services. Eventually, the child suffered permanent physical and mental injuries. Joshua and his mother sued, alleging that Wisconsin officials deprived Joshua of his liberty under the Due Process Clause of the 14th Amendment. In dismissing the claim, Chief Justice Rehnquist, writing for the majority, famously concluded that absent a "special relationship" (e.g., related to prisoners or other wards), "a State's failure to protect an individual against private violence simply does not constitute a violation of [due process]." *Id.* at 197. "Poor Joshua," lamented Justice Blackmun in his dissent. *Id.* at 213.

In 2005, the Court clarified that due process rights also did not confer a property interest sufficient to assure government action concerning a woman seeking enforcement of a restraining order issued by a local court in Colorado. *See Castle Rock v. Gonzales*, 545 U.S. 748 (2005). Based on these and related decisions, the U.S. Constitution has not been interpreted to require federal or state governments to assure communal health. Contrast this position with constitutional "right to health" clauses in multiple other countries that are interpreted to include basic public health services and duties. *See, e.g.,* Benjamin M. Meier et al., *Bridging International Law and Rights-Based Litigation: Mapping Health-Related Rights Through the Development of the Global Health and Human Rights Law Database*, 14 HEALTH & HUM. RTS.: INT'L J. 1 (2012).

A. THE CONSTITUTIONAL FOUNTAIN OF PUBLIC HEALTH POWERS

While the Constitution does not require government to assure the conditions for people to be healthy, it does set the legal foundation for public and private health interventions. Principles of constitutional design (1) allocate power between the federal government and the states (a.k.a. federalism); (2) divide power among the 3 branches of government (a.k.a. separation of powers), and (3) limit government power (to protect individual freedoms, discussed in Chapter 3). In these ways, the Constitution acts like a fountain (originating the flow of power to protect the public's health) and a levee (curbing that power to protect individual interests).

1. FEDERALISM

Among the unique facets of American democracy is the Constitutional principle of federalism. Federalism distinguishes the powers among the levels of governments. As explained below, the powers of the national government are enumerated and limited. Through the 10th Amendment, states were reserved sovereign power over "all the objects, which, in the ordinary course of affairs, concern the lives, liberties and properties of the people; and the internal order, improvement, and prosperity of the State." U.S. CONST. amend. X. These residual powers authorize states to regulate matters affecting the health, safety, and general welfare of the public and its citizens.

Though ingenious in constitutional design, federalism as applied is not always predictable. There is no bright line separating federal and state authorities. In reality, governments' respective powers have historically overlapped, especially in areas like public health. In many cases, principles of cooperative federalism render agreeable outcomes. Yet, when federal and state powers collide, the application of federalism takes on many shades and near imperceptible gradations. James G. Hodge, Jr., *The Role of New Federalism and Public Health Law*, 12 J.L. & HEALTH 309, 316 (1998).

For example, states may (a) seek to invade areas set aside for exclusive federal interventions (e.g., enacting laws which interfere with Congress' regulation of interstate commerce) or (b) fail to recognize federal supremacy or authority (e.g., attempting to impose taxes on federal goods). These latter actions were more common in the nation's early history as states tested the limits of their sovereign powers. However, modern debates about the scope of Congress' powers to increase access to health services through the Affordable Care Act (ACA) reflect similar themes. *National Fed. of Ind. Bus. v. Sebelius,* 132 S. Ct. 2566 (2012) (discussed below); *see also* PATIENT CARE AND PROFESSIONALISM (Catherine D. DeAngelis ed., 2014).

Conversely, the federal government may intrude upon traditional state duties. Historically, federal exercises which interfered with traditional state powers were politically volatile. They were struck down routinely by courts that assigned considerable weight to sovereign state police powers under the 10th Amendment. *See Hammer v. Dagenhart,* 247 U.S. 251 (1918) (federal statute prohibiting the interstate commerce of child labor products infringed on the states' power to regulate child labor hours); later overruled in *United States v. Darby,* 312 U.S. 100 (1941).

In theory, federal laws which moved into areas traditionally left to the states were beyond Congress' jurisdiction and therefore unconstitutional. Federal expansion during the New Deal Era (1933–1938) relaxed traditional conceptions of federalism, ushering in numerous federal interventions in public health and other areas. These include establishment of the U.S. Public Health Service in 1939 and the Centers for

Disease Control in 1946. *See* James G. Hodge, Jr., *The Role of New Federalism*, 12 J.L. & HEALTH 309, 335 (1998). Supreme Court jurisprudence accommodated these changes in many ways. In 1941, the Court observed in *Darby*, 312 U.S. at 115 , that Congress' power may be "attended by the same incidents [as the] exercise of the police power of the states." Later years saw the introduction of sweeping federal health care reforms through the Social Security Act Amendments of 1965, 42 U.S.C. § 1395 (2010), establishing Medicare and Medicaid programs.

After decades of federal expansion into the public health sphere, political and judicial actors rediscovered core principles of federalism. Collectively labeled "new federalism" by constitutional scholars in the 1990s, a series of influential decisions by the U.S. Supreme Court resulted in its:

- adoption of a strong rule against federal invasion of "core state functions;"

- presumption against application of federal statutes to state and local political processes;

- disdain for federal action that "commandeers" state governments into the service of federal regulatory purposes;

- rejection of federal claims brought by private parties against states; and

- application of a plain statement rule that Congress must ". . . make its intention . . . unmistakably clear in the language of the statute" whenever it seeks to preempt state law so as to alter the balance of federalism. *Gregory v. Ashcroft*, 501 U.S. 452, 460 (1991).

Principles of new federalism re-opened state challenges of some federal public health laws on 10th Amendment grounds. ERWIN CHEMERINSKY, CONSTITUTIONAL LAW: PRINCIPLES AND POLICIES 269–74 (4th ed. 2011). The Supreme Court's decision in *United States v. Lopez*, 514 U.S. 549 (1995), is illustrative. The Court held that Congress exceeded its Commerce powers by statutorily making gun possession within a local school zone a federal criminal offense. Finding that possessing a gun within a school zone did not "substantially affect" interstate commerce, the Court declared the statute unconstitutional despite the laudable, underlying public health objective of preventing gun-related violence at or near schools. *Id.* at 567.

Federalism continues to dominate political and judicial processes. In 2012, the Supreme Court opined that Congress lacked the Commerce power to require individuals to purchase health insurance (a.k.a. "individual mandate") via the ACA. Writing for the Court, Chief Justice Roberts found instead that Congress' power to tax was sufficiently broad to justify the mandate. *Sebelius,* 132 S. Ct. at 2600. As a result, ACA's fundamental requirement that individuals purchase health insurance was upheld under federal tax authority, but not through Congress' power to regulate interstate commerce, thus preserving some traditional state-based authorities.

Later in 2015, the Supreme Court decided in *King v. Burwell*, 135 S. Ct. 2480 (2015), that the ACA's extension of tax credits (via the U.S. tax code, 26 U.S.C. § 36B) to individuals purchasing health insurance through state-established exchanges applies to insurance purchased through *any* state or federal exchange established under the ACA. To this end individuals residing in 34 states (as of June 2015) with federally-operated insurance exchanges may continue to receive federal subsidies for their health insurance purchases, which all states must recognize consistent with federal tax rules.

2.   SEPARATION OF POWERS

The federal Constitution (as well as states' constitutions) separate governmental powers into 3 branches: (a) the legislative branch (with the power to create laws); (b) the executive branch (with the power to enforce laws); and (c) the judicial branch (with the power to interpret laws). Constitutional separation of governmental powers not only provides a system of checks and balances, it also helps curb the potential for government oppression.

Pursuant to the separation of powers doctrine, each branch of government has unique constitutional authority to create, enforce, or interpret public health law and policy. Federal and state legislatures largely create health policy and allocate necessary resources to effectuate it. To accomplish this goal, legislators need reliable, accurate information on public health threats and interventions to make complex decisions that are also consistent with their constituents' interests, competing claims, and constitutional limits. *See* Chapter 7 for additional discussion.

The executive branch (primarily through public health departments or agencies) enforces health policy via delegated legislative authority. Such delegations can be extensive or narrow. For example, in creating a state public health agency, a state legislature may bestow it with broad powers to protect the public's health. Later, the legislature may then direct the agency to perform specific functions (e.g., conduct an HIA related to a transportation project). In either example, public health agencies take some direction from the legislature and must act accordingly within the scope of their delegated power. Federal and state executive agencies sometimes work in tandem with lawmakers to determine the extent and course of public health policies. In other cases, conflicts can arise such as when public health agencies attempt to create and administer complex health regulations which some legislators may not agree with in principle or policy.

Provided that legislatures articulate standards for issuance and enforcement of these regulations, the Supreme Court has approved such delegations consistent with principles of separation of powers. *See Chevron, U.S.A., Inc. v. NRDC, Inc.,* 467 U.S.

837 (1984). Sometimes executive agencies exceed the bounds of their legislative delegation. In *Boreali v. Axelrod,* 71 N.Y.2d 1 (Ct. App. N.Y. 1987), for example, New York's Public Health Council promulgated a comprehensive code to govern tobacco smoking in public areas. Although the New York state legislature authorized the Council to regulate generally in the interests of the public's health, the court found the Council overstepped its authority when it attempted to regulate tobacco far outside the bounds of its legislative delegation. In 2013, a New York appellate court used the same approach taken in *Boreali* to strike down a proposed ban on large portion sizes of sugar-sweetened beverages (SSBs). *N.Y. Statewide Coal. of Hispanic Chambers of Commerce v. N.Y. Dep't of Health and Mental Hygiene,* No. 653584/12 (N.Y. App. Div. July 30, 2013); *see* Chapter 8 for additional discussion.

Similarly, in 2013, the Kentucky Supreme Court admonished an effort of a local county board of health to curb indoor smoking. Bullitt County's Board of Health passed a regulation that prohibited tobacco smoke in all enclosed public places and places of employment. When challenged on appeal, the Supreme Court found that the regulation was unconstitutional because the Board exceeded its statutory authority (even though prior decisions affirmed that state law did not preempt local smoking ordinances). The problem with the Board's regulation stemmed from how it was enacted, and not what it pertained to. *Bullitt Fiscal Ct. et. al v. Bullitt Cnty. Bd. of Health,* 2012 WL 6062751 (Ky. June 19, 2013).

The judiciary is tasked with interpreting the law to resolve disputes. As per the prior examples above, courts exert substantial influence in public health law and policy. They decide whether public health statutes or regulations are constitutional, agency actions are legislatively authorized, public health officials have gathered sufficient evidence to support their interventions, and public or private actors are negligent. Deciding these types of issues is challenging.

Courts are bound by precedent (i.e., prior judicial decisions) and tend to defer to the policy decisions of state and local lawmakers under the separation of powers doctrine. As a result, judges often strive to decide cases consistent with the underlying intent of statutory or administrative laws. Still, judicial decisions on public health matters vary extensively for many reasons. Precedent extends only as far as a court's jurisdiction. Thus, while the U.S. Supreme Court's decisions on federal constitutional law have precedential value nationally, a state supreme court's decision on a matter of state law does not require another state's courts to decide a similar issue the same way.

Divergent judicial results also arise from the fact that some judges are politically elected (rather than appointed) or because of the unique facts of a particular case. Courts less familiar with public health issues or data may decide cases in reliance on different information. *See, e.g.,* N.Y. STATE PUBLIC HEALTH LEGAL MANUAL: A GUIDE FOR JUDGES, ATTORNEYS, AND PUBLIC HEALTH

PROFESSIONALS (Michael Colodner ed., 2011). Courts nationally struggle to distinguish valid scientific evidence (*see Daubert v. Merrell Dow Pharmaceuticals, Inc.*, 509 U.S. 579 (1993)) from "junk science" advanced by "denialists." *See* Leila Barraza et al., *Denialism and its Adverse Effect on Public Health*, 53 JURIMETRICS J. 307 (2013). In one publicized case in New Mexico, several courts weighed highly-suspect evidence of whether low frequency electromagnetic waves emanated from a neighbor's Wi-Fi and cell phones may have harmed the plaintiff's health. See George Johnson, *Science, Lost in a Legal Maze*, N.Y. TIMES, Mar. 24, 2015, at D3. For an illustration of divergent court decisions on the constitutionality of tobacco warning labels, *see* Chapter 8.D.

B.   FEDERAL PUBLIC HEALTH POWERS

In theory, the federal government has limited, defined powers. Consistent with principles of federalism, Congress draws its authority to act from specific, enumerated powers granted pursuant to Article II of the Constitution. These include the power to regulate interstate commerce, tax, and set conditions on federal spending. The aforementioned political and judicial expansion of these powers (through what is known as the doctrine of implied powers) allows the federal government considerable authority to act in the interests of public health and safety. The federal government may employ all means reasonably appropriate to achieve the objectives of its listed powers, including raising revenue for public health services and regulating private activities that endanger human health.

To preserve federal exercises of powers from intrusion or interference by state and local governments, the Supremacy Clause of the Constitution (art. VI, cl. 2) provides that federal constitutional, statutory, regulatory, and judicial laws preempt state and local laws. *See* CHEMERINSKY, CONSTITUTIONAL LAW, at 402–27. In the context of public health, federal preemption is a double-edged sword. Congressional passage of key pieces of legislation concerning vehicle safety, food policy, national security, environmental protection, transportation, and access to health services, among other areas, establish national, uniform standards essential to achieve public health objectives. Conflicting state laws are preempted. Depending on the extent of Congressional direction, state laws that provide less restrictive standards may also be preempted if meeting a lower standard defeats the purpose of federal law. *See, e.g., Shilling v. Moore*, 545 N.W.2d 442 (Neb. 1996) (to the extent the federal Health Care Quality Improvement Act affords greater protection for medical peer reviewers facing defamation actions than Nebraska's state law, Nebraska's law is preempted).

In some areas, such as environmental protection, federal law may "occupy the field" so completely as to negate any state or local regulations in the same area (even if federal law is insufficient to achieve essential public health outcomes). In this way, preemption can thwart public health legal interventions when federal law strips state or local governments of their ability to address public health issues. *See, e.g., United States v. City & Cnty. of Denver*, 100 F.3d 1509 (10th Cir. 1996) (Comprehensive Environmental Response, Compensation, and Liability Act preempted Denver's zoning ordinance prohibiting the maintenance of hazardous waste).

C. STATE PUBLIC HEALTH POWERS

Unlike the federal government's enumerated powers, states possess extensive authority to protect the public's health. Their public health powers derive largely from sovereign powers reserved to the states via the 10th Amendment and may extend to local governments through state delegations. The expansive and dominant role of state governments in public health is directly related to the breadth of their police and *parens patriae* powers, each of which is explained below.

1.   POLICE POWERS

Often thought of as the powers of government to conduct law enforcement activities, state "police powers" are much broader in scope. They represent the state's primary source of power to promote the general welfare of society. Historically, police powers have been defined as "the inherent authority of the state to enact laws and promulgate regulations to protect, preserve and promote the health, safety, morals, and general welfare of the people." ERNST FREUND, THE POLICE POWER: PUBLIC

POLICY AND CONSTITUTIONAL RIGHTS 3–4 (1904). In 2006, the Supreme Court noted how principles of federalism "allow the States great latitude under their police powers to legislate [to protect] the lives, limbs, health, comfort, and quiet of all persons." *Gonzales v. Oregon*, 546 U.S. 243, 270 (2006).

Police powers underlie most laws to prevent morbidity and mortality across populations. They are the source of public health powers to test, screen, vaccinate, treat, quarantine, and isolate individuals. They authorize as well the creation of state and local public health agencies, empowering them to conduct educational campaigns, surveillance, and epidemiological investigations. Many additional public health authorities discussed throughout the text are supported by state police powers. In furtherance of these powers, states may restrict (within federal and state constitutional limits) private interests in liberty, autonomy, and privacy, as well as economic interests in freedom to contract and use of property. *Allied Structural Steel Co. v. Spannaus,* 438 U.S. 234, 241 (1978).

2.   PARENS PATRIAE POWERS

In addition to their sovereign police powers, states also possess *parens patriae* powers. Translated literally as the "parent of the country," these powers authorize state government not only to act in the interests of the community's well-being, but also in relation to individuals' own best interests. LAWRENCE O. GOSTIN, PUBLIC HEALTH LAW: POWER, DUTY, RESTRAINT 95–96 (2d ed. 2008).

Parens patriae powers are invoked in 2 major ways. First, the state may seek legal standing in cases supporting the community's health and welfare (e.g., the state sues the federal government on behalf of the state's citizens to compel specific public health goals). *See, e.g., Massachusetts v. EPA*, 549 U.S. 497 (2007) (requesting Environmental Protection Agency (EPA) to regulate emissions of greenhouse gases). Second, the state may serve as guardian of, or provide protections for, persons who may otherwise lack capacity to look after their own interests or welfare. *Parens patriae* powers in this context allow the state to step in for the benefit of minors, persons with mental disabilities, the elderly, or prisoners or other "wards" of the state to avert or correct known physical or mental harms. For example, state government may rely on its *parens patriae* powers to protect a child from mental or physical abuse or neglect (*see Santosky v. Kramer*, 455 U.S. 745 (1982)); institutionalize a person with mental instabilities who poses a risk to him- or herself (*see Mezick v. State*, 920 S.W.2d 427 (Tex. App. 1996)); or prevent harms to incapacitated older persons from their caretakers (*see Congress Care Ctr. Assoc. v. Chicago Dep't of Health*, 632 N.E.2d 266 (Ill. App. Ct. 1994)).

Use of state-based *parens patriae* powers can be controversial when constitutional rights of the individual are at stake. In *Clark v. Cohen*, 794 F.2d 79 (3d Cir. 1986), Carolyn Clark was confined at a state-run mental institution for 28 years without notice or a hearing despite her repeated requests to receive training on how to live independently. After her release, she sued. The 3rd Circuit federal Court of Appeals affirmed that Clark's involuntary confinement violated her constitutional right to liberty and procedural due process. The court noted: "To deprive any citizen of his or her liberty upon the altruistic theory that the confinement is for humane therapeutic reasons and then fail to provide adequate treatment violates the very fundamentals of due process." *Id.* at 94 (citing *Wyatt v. Stickney*, 325 F. Supp. 781, 785 (M.D. Ala. 1971)).

D.   LOCAL PUBLIC HEALTH POWERS

County, city, or other local public health officials are on the front line of public health practice. They are directly responsible for conducting public health surveillance, implementing federal and state programs, operating public health clinics, and setting public health policies for their specific populations. The performance of local (and state) public health agencies may be evaluated consistent with national accreditation standards. Kim Krisberg, *Eleven Health Departments First to Attain Public Health Accreditation*, 43 THE NATION'S HEALTH 1 (2013).

Local governments' authority to act in the interests of the public's health extends largely from broad or narrow delegations of state police powers via state constitutional, legislative, or executive means. Such delegations provide local governments with a limited realm of authority, or "home rule," over public health matters of local concern within their jurisdiction. ANTIEAU ON LOCAL GOVERNMENT

LAW § 21.01 (2d ed. 2006); *see also City of Chicago v. Taylor*, 774 N.E.2d 22, 26–27 (Ill. App. Ct. 2002) (home rule is premised on the idea that local governments are best-positioned to assess their communities' needs and enact laws addressing local concerns). State legislatures may modify, clarify, preempt, or remove home rule at will, unless it is protected by state constitutions.

Exercises of local authority in the interests of public health can neither extend beyond limited jurisdictional boundaries nor conflict with or impair federal or state law. In 2001, for example, the city of Cleveland relied on its home rule powers to pass an ordinance prohibiting liquor advertising on billboards and other public signs. When an outdoor advertising firm sued to enjoin the city from enforcing the provisions, the court found that the ordinance was preempted by state law allowing alcohol advertising (and in violation of constitutional commercial speech protections, discussed in Chapter 8). *See Eller Media Co. v. City of Cleveland,* 161 F. Supp. 2d 796 (N.D. Ohio 2001).

Local governments' home rule authority may also be limited judicially. Through what is known as "Dillon's Rule," based on the holdings and scholarship of Iowa Supreme Court Justice John F. Dillon in the late 1800s, local governments are limited to those authorities expressly granted to them by state legislatures. Dillon's Rule suggests that local governments may exercise only those powers expressly granted or necessarily implied via statute, unless it is vested with broad home rule.

JOHN F. DILLON, THE LAW OF MUNICIPAL
CORPORATIONS 173 (2d ed. 1873).

Modern applications of Dillon's Rule are muted.
For example, the Tennessee Supreme Court opined
in 2001 that strict construction of the limits of local
power is only appropriate when there is a complete
lack of, or ambiguity in, state legislative intent.
Thus, Dillon's Rule may not apply whenever a state
legislature clearly grants comprehensive authority
to a local government, or the locality regulates in
the interests of the public's health. *Southern
Constructors, Inc. v. Loudon Cnty. Bd. of Educ.*, 58
S.W.3d 706 (Tenn. 2001).

E. TRIBAL PUBLIC HEALTH POWERS

Unlike state and local governments, tribal
governments owe their legal existence to the federal
government, from which many of their public health
powers flow. In the mid-1800s, the federal
government granted many American Indians
limited set-asides of land (reservations) on which
they formed sovereign tribal governments eligible
for direct federal assistance. As sovereigns, tribal
governments have public health powers similar to
states. In practice, however, protecting the health of
the tribal populations is a shared venture between
federal, state, and tribal governments.

Pursuant to the Snyder Act of 1921, 25 U.S.C.
§ 13, Congress directly assumed responsibility for
providing health care services to tribal
governments. Federal assistance continues through
long-term commitments for comprehensive health

services administered by the Indian Health Service, part of the Department of Health and Human Services (DHHS), and the Bureau of Indian Affairs. Over many years Congress has legislatively committed resources, facilities, and personnel to provide health care benefits to American Indians through collaborative efforts. The ACA has further strengthened the federal role through long-term financial and resource commitments. Indian Health Care Improvement Act, 25 U.S.C. §§ 1601–1683 (2010).

Management and supervision of Indian public health programs and facilities are left generally to tribal governments as part of a movement toward self-governance, furthered by Congress' enactment of the Tribal Self-Governance Act of 1994, 25 U.S.C. §§ 450–458hh (2012). Federally-recognized tribes may use Indian Health Service funds for specific health programs consistent with general conditions. This flexibility allows tribal governments to target and respond to differing health needs across their populations.

———————————

As discussed in this chapter, the powers of government to protect the public's health are extensive and overlapping. Inevitable conflicts between the levels (federal, tribal, state, local) and branches (legislative, executive, judicial) of governments evoke constitutional principles of federalism and separation of powers. These structural principles determine which level or branch is authorized to act in the interests of the public's health. Assessing the full constitutional limits of public health powers requires further exploration. Chapter 3 introduces how individual rights counter-balance governments' broad powers to protect the public's health, and then explains how structural and rights-based norms are inter-connected through one of the seminal cases in public health law, *Jacobson v. Massachusetts*, 197 U.S. 11 (1905).

CHAPTER 3

CONSTITUTIONAL RIGHTS & THE PUBLIC'S HEALTH

In addition to creating a structural foundation for the assignment and execution of governmental public health powers, the federal Constitution limits these powers through affirmative protections of individual rights and liberties. The Bill of Rights (the first 10 amendments to the Constitution), the 14th Amendment, and other constitutional provisions create a zone of individual rights that government may not invade absent justification. At the crux of public health in theory and practice is the need to balance tensions between population-based laws and individual rights.

A. FOUNDATIONS OF RIGHTS-BASED LIMITATIONS

An extensive array of constitutionally-protected individual rights affect how government regulates in the interests of the public's health. Unlike the private sector (which does not generally owe individuals respect for their constitutional rights), government cannot infringe on fundamental individual rights without sufficient justification. Constitutional rights are not absolute, but rather are subject to constant balancing under differing rules and tests. The U.S. Supreme Court has developed different levels of scrutiny (i.e., standards) that it and other courts apply in assessing potential infringements depending on multifarious factors. These levels include:

Strict scrutiny. When fundamental rights (e.g., bodily privacy) or "suspect classes" (e.g., race, ethnicity, alienage, national origin) are at stake, government's action must (1) be narrowly tailored to serve a compelling government interest and (2) often represent the least restrictive means for accomplishing the objective. *Adarand Constructors, Inc. v. Pena*, 515 U.S. 200 (1995) (federal program that incentivized hiring subcontractors based on racial classification was subject to strict scrutiny). Whenever strict scrutiny is invoked, it is exceedingly difficult for government interests to prevail, and as a result, they are typically struck down by courts.

Take, for example, a public health regulation or policy that discriminates openly (or what courts sometimes refer to as "on its face") against persons on the basis of race by denying them access to public health services. Following a devastating hurricane in Galveston, Texas in September, 1900, essential supplies were reportedly distributed first to the city's white citizens; whatever was left each day was later handed out to African-Americans. *See* PATRICIA B. BIXEL & ELIZABETH H. TURNER, GALVESTON AND THE 1900 STORM: CATASTROPHE AND CATALYST 80 (2000). Such a law or policy is contrary to equal protection principles (discussed below). Absent a compelling governmental interest (which is highly unlikely given patent discrimination), it is unconstitutional.

Intermediate (or heightened) scrutiny. In other instances in which government actions or laws implicate individuals on grounds of gender, legitimacy of birth, or other bases, courts will assess whether there is a substantial relationship with important government interests. *See United States v. Virginia*, 518 U.S. 515 (1996) (state-run military institute's policy of admitting only male students was unconstitutional). Meeting this intermediate standard is easier than under strict scrutiny, but is still difficult when government action lacks a close nexus with public health objectives. In some cases, such as implementation of maternal health interventions, public health agencies may have sufficient justification for discriminating on the basis of gender. *See, e.g., Geduldig v. Aiello*, 417 U.S. 484 (1974) (California disability insurance program which failed to cover pregnancy did not violate equal protection claims because men and women are not similarly situated; Congress later prohibited pregnancy discrimination in 1978).

In 2015, the Supreme Court extended the fundamental right to marry to same-sex couples in *Obergefell v. Hodges,* No. 14-556, 135 S. Ct. 2584 (2015). Some scholars thought the Court might reason that sexual orientation is classifiable as a "suspect class." Instead, it identified violations of substantive due process and equal protection principles to overturn state laws that denied same-sex couples marriage rights. Consequently, the Court declined to classify sexual orientation as a suspect class subject to strict scrutiny.

Rational basis scrutiny. In most other instances in which governments' actions infringe on individual rights or interests, a minimal level of scrutiny is applied. Government need only demonstrate that there is some rational basis for its expressed actions by showing a reasonable relationship to a legitimate government interest. *Vance v. Bradley*, 440 U.S. 93, 96–97 (1979) (government had a rational basis for implementing mandatory retirement age for Foreign Service employees which did not contravene principles of equal protection). Contrasted with strict scrutiny, whenever courts employ the rational basis test, they tend to defer to legislative or executive prerogatives consistent with separation of powers. So long as government can show some legitimate purpose, individual rights may be curtailed. As a result, public health laws measured under this standard usually survive scrutiny.

There are limited exceptions when the Supreme Court applies a more stringent form of rational basis review. In *City of Cleburne v. Cleburne Living Ctr., Inc.,* 473 U.S. 432 (1985), the Court invalidated a local zoning ordinance that attempted to restrict placement of a mental institution within a local community. It found there was no legitimate government interest underlying the ordinance that otherwise discriminated against persons with mental disabilities in violation of principles of equal protection.

B. BRIEF OVERVIEW OF SPECIFIC RIGHTS

The Constitution protects individuals and groups from unwarranted exercises of government, largely through the Bill of Rights and the 14th Amendment. These include fundamental rights to protect core freedoms (e.g., free speech), generalized rights to inhibit government oppression (e.g., due process), and rights designed to obviate government favoritism or discrimination (e.g., equal protection), as examined briefly below.

Public health practice may implicate 1st Amendment rights, specifically rights to free speech and expression, the right to assemble, and freedom of religion. These rights are held not only by individuals, but also corporations or other legally-recognized entities (e.g., associations, unions, and partnerships). The Supreme Court closely guards freedoms of speech and expression against government intrusion. *Tinker v. Des Moines Indep. Cmty. Sch. Dist.*, 393 U.S. 503 (1969); *Texas v. Johnson,* 491 U.S. 397 (1989). First Amendment protections for political, religious, and commercial speech range in their scope and application.

Political speech. Laws that directly impact political speech are subject to review under the Court's highest level of scrutiny. *Citizens United v. Federal Election Comm'n,* 558 U.S. 310 (2010). Political speech is "interactive communication concerning political change." *Buckley v. American Constitutional Law Found., Inc.*, 525 U.S. 182, 186 (1999) (citing *Meyer v. Grant*, 486 U.S. 414, 422 (1988)). This includes not only politics and candidates in general, but also "structures and forms of government, the manner in which government is operated . . . , and all such matters relating to political processes." *Mills v. Alabama*, 384 U.S. 214, 218–19 (1966). So long as such speech is covered (that is, it is not false, misleading, defamatory, implicating national security threats, or other limited contexts), the 1st Amendment assures individuals their right to speak publicly or privately.

Commercial speech. Government infringements on commercial speech, or "expressions related solely to the economic interests of the speaker and its audience," garner their own unique review. *Central Hudson Gas & Elec. Corp. v. Public Serv. Comm'n of N.Y.*, 447 U.S. 557 (1980). Infringements on commercial speech emanate typically from government attempts to (1) limit the time, place, and manner of advertising of specific, lawful products (e.g., tobacco) generally or to specific audiences (e.g., minors); or (2) require commercial entities to provide truthful information (e.g., warnings about known or potential product harms) or counter information (e.g., calorie labeling on menus). In such cases, the Supreme Court assesses each potential infringement typically under a 4-part test set forth in its *Central Hudson* decision, discussed later in Chapter 8.

Freedom of assembly. Pursuant to the 1st Amendment, individuals also have the right to gather, or assemble, for lawful purposes subject to reasonable restrictions. Freedom of assembly may not extend to group activities that negatively impact the community or the public's health. For example, political protesters who erected tents and accumulated garbage and human waste in New York City in 2011 were lawfully dispersed by the City and park owner to maintain hygiene and public safety. *In re Waller v. City of New York,* 933 N.Y.S.2d 541 (N.Y. Sup. Ct. 2011). Government may impose such measures provided restrictions are narrowly tailored, serve a compelling government interest, and provide alternative channels for individuals to communicate or associate. *Clark v. Community for Creative Non-Violence,* 468 U.S. 288 (1984).

Freedom of religion. The 1st Amendment Establishment Clause ["Congress shall make no law respecting an establishment of religion . . ."] and Free Exercise Clause ["or prohibiting the free exercise thereof . . ."] protect religious freedoms. They work in tandem to prohibit government from endorsing or "establishing" specific religious faiths and support individuals' freedom to practice their chosen religion. In many ways, these 2 facets of religious freedom are compatible to the extent they allow individuals to believe as they choose without governmental interference or influence through support for 1 religion over another. In the public health context, however, sometimes they are at odds, as explained further in relation to vaccination laws and policies in Chapter 4.

Due process. Additional rights often implicated through public health powers include principles of due process. Pursuant to the 5th Amendment (and later the 14th Amendment, which applies the Bill of Rights to the states) government shall not "deprive any person of life, liberty, or property, without due process of law." There are 2 major types of due process protections: procedural and substantive. Prior to or coextensive with deprivations of life, liberty, or property, government must provide individuals with some procedural steps or assurances (e.g., notice, right to counsel, right to an appeal). The level and extent of process due depend on the scope and extent of deprivation of rights involved. *Mathews v. Eldridge*, 424 U.S. 319 (1976).

Substantive due process requires government to have a sufficient justification for depriving individuals' life, liberty, or property interests. ERWIN CHEMERINSKY, CONSTITUTIONAL LAW: PRINCIPLES AND POLICIES 558 (4th ed. 2011). Any time government infringes on these basic interests in arbitrary, vague, or capricious ways, courts may find that such infringements violate substantive due process. *See, e.g., Foucha v. Louisiana*, 504 U.S. 71 (1992) (Louisiana law that commits a person acquitted from insanity charges violates substantive due process). Additional rights flow from court interpretations of the breadth of "life, liberty, or property," such as the right to travel, discussed below.

Right to travel. Although the Constitution does not expressly provide for a right to travel, it is firmly embedded in fundamental liberties (*see* CHEMERINSKY, CONSTITUTIONAL LAW, at 879), and the Privileges and Immunities Clause, which helps assure state citizens share similar benefits and protections in other states. U.S. CONST. art. IV, § 2, cl. 1. This Clause is a primary basis for protecting persons against (1) the erection of "actual barriers to interstate movement" and (2) disparate treatment for intrastate travelers. *Doe v. Miller,* 405 F.3d 700, 711 (8th Cir. 2005). Government cannot prevent individuals from entering or leaving a state (without strong justification), mistreat visitors to a state, and must extend similar benefits to persons who choose to reside in a state. *Saenz v. Roe,* 526 U.S. 489, 499 (1999).

While the right to travel is extensive, it can be restricted via government. A Florida law that required sex offenders to notify law enforcement when they permanently or temporarily change their address was approved against a right to travel challenge in *Doe v. Moore,* 410 F.3d 1337, 1348 (11th Cir. 2005). The 11th Circuit Court of Appeals found that there was a compelling state interest in "preventing future sexual offenses and alerting local law enforcement and citizens to the whereabouts of those that could reoffend." *Id.* In the same year, the 8th Circuit upheld an Iowa sex offender law that limited travel "to protect the health and safety of the citizens." *Miller,* 405 F.3d at 705. *See also Burman v. Streeval,* No. 4:11CV0569, 2011 WL 3562999 (N.D. Ohio Aug. 11, 2011) (prisoner's segregation for not consenting to TB test does not infringe his right to travel).

Equal protection. Principles of equal protection, derived from the 14th Amendment, require similar treatment for like individuals. They apply automatically to state and local governments via the language of the 14th Amendment, and to the federal government through the 5th Amendment. *See, e.g., Bolling v. Sharpe,* 347 U.S. 497 (1954) (federal government must adhere to same equal protection requirements as states, specifically concerning school desegregation, to avoid a denial of due process under the 5th Amendment).

Equal protection may be invoked by public health laws or policies that classify specific persons or groups. People with certain conditions or living in particular areas may be targeted for government public health interventions. Older adults may be entitled to special services not provided to younger persons. Children may benefit from public health programs for which adults are left out. Neither of these examples presents equal protection violations so long as government has some rational basis for distinguishing individuals in the interests of the public's health.

However, when classifications are based on "suspect classes" (e.g., race, ethnicity, nonmarital children) or other questionable grounds (gender), the level of scrutiny ramps up (as discussed above), and the intervention may be found contrary to principles of equal protection. CHEMERINSKY, CONSTITUTIONAL LAW, at 684–801. Some laws violate equal protection because they openly authorize discrimination on their face. For example,

a state quarantine order that applied solely to
persons of Asian descent, even though the
communicable disease targeted by the order was
transmissible among all races, is patently
unconstitutional. *Jew Ho v. Williamson*, 103 F. 10
(N.D. Cal. 1900).

Other laws are neutral as stated, but
discriminatory in their administration. Sometimes
"the impact of a law may be so clearly
discriminatory as to allow no other explanation than
that it was adopted for impermissible purposes."
CHEMERINSKY, CONSTITUTIONAL LAW, at 732.
Concerning laws which have a disparate impact,
discriminatory purposes (and likely effects) must be
proven for an equal protection violation to arise. *Id.*
at 713, 730. For example, in *Village of Arlington
Heights v. Metropolitan Hous. Dev. Corp.*, 429 U.S.
252 (1977), a city council in Illinois refused to rezone
an area of land to allow low and moderate income
housing construction. African Americans alleged the
zoning policy effectively denied them access to the
community. The Supreme Court agreed:
"[s]ometimes a clear pattern, unexplainable on
grounds other than race, emerges from the effect of
the state action even when the governing legislation
appears neutral on its face." *Id.* at 266.

Equal protection principles are reflected in
multiple federal, state, and local laws addressing
discrimination on many fronts. The federal Civil
Rights Act (CRA) of 1964 bans discrimination on the
grounds of race, ethnicity, and national or religious
origins (as well as sex in many, but not all, sectors).

Pub. L. No. 88–352, 78 Stat. 241 (codified as amended in scattered sections of 42 U.S.C. (2009)). Private membership clubs and public international organizations, for example, may discriminate on the basis of sex. EEOC COMPLIANCE MANUAL § 2–III(B)(4) (2009).

CRA's protections can advance some public health objectives. For example, in *EEOC v. Houston Funding*, 717 F.3d 425 (5th Cir. 2013), a woman who was fired for lactating was successful in her claim against her employer for sexual discrimination under CRA Title VII (as amended by the Pregnancy Discrimination Act of 1978, 42 U.S.C. § 2000e(k) (2008)). Additional protections for breastfeeding women are provided via the ACA, Pub. L. No. 111–148, § 4207 (amending 29 U.S.C. § 207), as well as state laws. In combination, these laws help promote maternal and child health by eliminating discrimination against women.

Rights to privacy. Rights to privacy extend from multiple parts of the Constitution and are constantly raised through public health policies and practices. There are 3 primary types of privacy: bodily, decisional, and informational. Anita L. Allen, *Taking Liberties: Privacy, Private Choice, and Social Contract Theory*, 56 U. CIN. L. REV. 461, 464–66 (1987). *Bodily* privacy extends principally from liberty principles inherent in due process as well as freedoms from unreasonable searches and seizures via the 4th Amendment. As discussed in Chapter 4, respect for bodily privacy prevents government from forcing an autonomous individual to receive specific treatment or undergo intrusive public health screening and testing without compelling justification.

Decisional privacy concerns individuals' interests in making core, personal decisions about their health or other status without unwarranted governmental interference. This facet of privacy supports persons' interests in making reproductive or other medical choices, determining the extent of medical or other care they desire, and deciding how best to parent their children. *See Prince v. Massachusetts*, 321 U.S. 158 (1944) (appealing child labor conviction on parental rights basis). This latter "right to parent" arises concerning public health programs that mitigate parental choices (*see* Chapter 4 for additional discussion).

Rights to *informational* privacy apply to persons' sensitive, private information, notably including health data. A bevy of privacy statutes and regulations govern the access, use, and disclosure of one's personally-identifiable medical information, but constitutional protections via due process are fairly lax. Provided government can demonstrate a rational basis for accessing or requesting identifiable data to promote or protect the public's health, as well as reasonable security measures, such uses are constitutionally permitted. *See Whalen v. Roe*, 429 U.S. 589 (1977) (discussed in Chapter 7).

Freedom from cruel and unusual punishment. The 8th Amendment prohibits government from inflicting "cruel and unusual punishment," based on evolving standards set in part by the Supreme Court. *Roper v. Simmons*, 543 U.S. 551 (2005). Though more often implicated in criminal cases related to the death penalty (*see Stanford v. Kentucky*, 492 U.S. 361 (1989)), and other punitive cases, the 8th Amendment also applies to some public health measures. In *Estelle v. Gamble*, 429 U.S. 97 (1976), the Court found that the prohibition of cruel and unusual punishment supports government's provision of medical care to prisoners. *Id.* at 103.

Respect for constitutional rights is often synergistic with advancing the public's health. However, some constitutionally-protected rights may deter or defeat interventions designed to prevent excess morbidity and mortality. These include constitutional protections favoring the right to bear arms and limiting government takings of private property discussed below.

Right to bear arms. The 2nd Amendment guarantees that the "right to keep and bear arms . . . shall not be infringed." This strongly-held right directly collides with public health interventions designed to curb gun-related violence and death in the U.S. Epic political and constitutional battles arise over the balance between efforts to prevent gun violence nationally and individuals' interests in owning and using firearms. IOM & NAT'L RESEARCH COUNCIL, PRIORITIES FOR RESEARCH TO REDUCE THE THREAT OF FIREARM-RELATED VIOLENCE (2013).

In *District of Columbia v. Heller*, 554 U.S. 570 (2008), the Supreme Court held that the District's attempt to prohibit the possession and use of handguns is unconstitutional, but allowed: (1) "prohibitions on possession of firearms by felons and the mentally ill;" (2) "laws forbidding the carrying of firearms in sensitive places such as schools and government buildings;" (3) "conditions and qualifications on the commercial sale of firearms;" and (4) prohibitions on the "carrying of 'dangerous and unusual weapons.' " *Id.* at 626–27. Two years later, the Court rejected a similar local hand gun law in Chicago, clarifying that the 2nd Amendment applies to the states through the 14th Amendment. *McDonald v. City of Chicago,* 561 U.S. 742 (2010).

Takings. Pursuant to its powers of eminent domain, government can take private property for public use. However, the 5th Amendment requires that any government taking be accompanied by "just compensation." Stated simply, government cannot take private property for public use without paying for it, subject to determinations of its economic value. As discussed in Chapter 9, compensating owners is not required when government legitimately exercises its power to abate public health nuisances.

Furthermore, what qualifies as a "public use" varies, but most definitely includes public health purposes. For example, a local government may justifiably take privately-held resources during a public health emergency so long as it pays for them later. The Supreme Court also recognizes a broader realm of qualifying uses. In *Kelo v. City of New London,* 545 U.S. 469 (2005), New London,

Connecticut addressed "economic distress" in its downtown and waterfront areas by taking private land for redevelopment. *Id.* at 472. The Court upheld the City's plan, acknowledging that economic development alone can actually constitute a "public purpose." *Id.* at 485.

C. VOLUNTARY, MANDATORY & COMPULSORY POWERS

Each of these individual rights or protections may be implicated and assessed under a different level of scrutiny as applied to specific public health powers, which may be classified as voluntary, mandatory, or compulsory in nature.

Voluntary interventions refer generally to measures that elicit the participation of individuals or groups acting on their own volition. Lawful efforts to address communicable diseases, for example, may include education campaigns. *See, e.g., Doe v. Irwin*, 615 F.2d 1162 (6th Cir. 1980) (family planning center offering voluntary sex education classes and contraceptives to minors); *see also* Chapter 8. They may also include vaccine drives, testing or screening programs, and treatment options. *See, e.g., Parents United for Better Sch., Inc. v. School Dist. of Phila. Bd. of Edu.*, 148 F.3d 260 (3rd Cir. 1998) (optional condom distribution program approved at a public school); *see also* Chapter 4. In each instance, individuals seek information or public health services based on their own choice, often reflected through their informed consent (such as prior to testing or treatment). Uses of voluntary public health powers are consistent with public health ethics (*see* Chapter 1) and highly favored in public health practice so long as they are efficacious.

Mandatory public health powers raise the stakes. When legally authorized, practitioners may implement public health interventions that no longer seek the voluntary actions of individuals. Rather, they set conditions on participation to encourage or require individuals or groups to protect the public's health to avoid penalties or loss of privileges. Requiring citizens to be vaccinated or else be fined, as described in section D, below, is an example. Others include testing, screening, and treatment programs that mandate individual compliance subject to varying conditions, such as receipt of treatment or other services. Participation in a treatment program may be conditioned on one's avoidance of more intrusive public health measures, such as isolation (*see* Chapter 4). In each of these and other instances, mandatory public health powers are often challenged based on infringements of individual freedoms and rights even though individuals ultimately retain the choice of participating.

With the exercise of *compulsory* public health powers, individual choice is no longer an option, nor is government offering the chance to participate to avoid penalties or receive valued services or benefits. One's participation will be garnered by force of varying magnitude as necessary. Compulsory interventions require individuals to participate or change their behaviors irrespective of their consent. In the early 1900s, New York City public health officials went door-to-door to forcibly vaccinate adults against smallpox or other infectious diseases. Implementation of the Chamberlain-Kahn Act of 1918, 42 U.S.C. §§ 24–25e, ch. 143, ch. XV, sec. 3–4e (1918), as amended in 1938, involved the forcible detention of known or suspected prostitutes for treatment and study. The Act was repealed in 1944. *Id.* at ch. 373 tit. XIII, § 1313.

A vestige of public health practice from bygone eras, compulsory public health powers are seldom used today because they run counter to public health ethics and significantly infringe on individual liberties. Exercises of compulsory powers may fail to survive constitutional scrutiny even if government has compelling interests (often because there are less restrictive alternatives available). Yet, examples of the use of compulsory powers in the control of infectious diseases remain. For example, forcible testing of persons charged with criminal transmission of HIV may be allowed to determine whether the individual has the condition and protect others who may have been exposed. *See In re Multimedia KSDK, Inc.*, 581 N.E.2d 911 (Ill. App. Ct. 1991).

Social distancing measures, including quarantine, isolation, and curfews (discussed in Chapter 4), may be implemented voluntarily, but when necessary, government can require affected persons to adhere to such measures, especially in public health emergencies. *See* TURNING POINT MODEL STATE PUB. HEALTH ACT § 5–101 (2003). Compulsory powers may also be used to protect the health of minors, prisoners, or others pursuant to *parens patriae* powers (discussed in Chapter 2).

D. BALANCING INDIVIDUAL & COMMUNITY INTERESTS

At the heart of public health law are struggles to determine the point at which government authority to promote the population's health must yield to individual constitutional rights. For much of this nation's history, this balance was firmly weighted in favor of public health interventions. Countless court decisions through the early 20th century found in favor of state or local governments seeking to protect the public's health, sometimes to the detriment of individual rights. James G. Hodge, Jr., *The Role of New Federalism and Public Health Law*, 12 J.L. & HEALTH 309 (1998). Courts justified these decisions in part by the strong need for public health measures to control infectious and chronic conditions for which there were no cures and scant, incomplete, or inaccurate epidemiologic data. Public health actors were granted significant deference to stymie significant threats to the health and economy of the community.

Yet other legal factors were also at play. In the early 1900s, Congress and the Supreme Court had yet to fully recognize the application of the Bill of Rights to state and local governments. CHEMERINSKY, CONSTITUTIONAL LAW, at 511–19.

Thus, for example, the protections of the 1st Amendment did not fully apply to state and local governments via the "incorporation doctrine" until 1925. *Gitlow v. N.Y.*, 268 U.S. 652, 666 (1925). Furthermore, courts' deference to public health legislation (through separation of powers principles) and respect for varying authorities among the levels of government (via federalism) were different.

Each of these issues is on display in one of the most famous and oft-cited public health cases in Supreme Court jurisprudence, *Jacobson v. Massachusetts*, 197 U.S. 11 (1905). The Commonwealth of Massachusetts legislature enacted a law empowering local boards of health to require the vaccination of residents if necessary for the public health or safety. Facing a potential outbreak of smallpox, the City of Cambridge Board of Health issued a vaccination requirement in 1902 that all persons be inoculated or face a $5 fine.

Henning Jacobson, a local reverend, refused the smallpox vaccination. He was convicted by a local court and ordered to pay the fine. On appeal, the Massachusetts Supreme Judicial Court upheld the conviction. Jacobson took his case to the U.S. Supreme Court, arguing that Cambridge's compulsory vaccination law was "unreasonable, arbitrary, and oppressive," and thus "hostile to the inherent right of every freeman to care for his own body and health." *Id.* at 26. His claim was grounded mainly in constitutional liberty interests which, he asserted, supported natural rights of persons to bodily integrity and decisional privacy (although he also argued on grounds of equal protection and other legal bases).

Rejecting Jacobson's appeal, the Supreme Court adopted a narrower view of individual liberty under substantive due process while taking a more community-oriented approach in which citizens owe duties to each other and society as a whole. Justice John M. Harlan, writing for the Court, stated:

> [T]he liberty secured by the Constitution . . . does not import an absolute right in each person to be, at all times and in all circumstances, wholly freed from restraint. There are manifold restraints to which every person is necessarily subject for the common good. On any other basis organized society could not exist with safety to its members. . . . *Id.*

Under the social contract theory advanced by the Court, a community has the right to implement public health requirements to protect itself against threatening diseases consistent with state police powers. The legacy of *Jacobson* is seen most clearly in the Court's defense of the breadth and necessity of public health authority under the police power (discussed in Chapter 2).

Yet the Court continued its analysis, offering a seminal change in the prior balance of police power authorities and individual rights. While acknowledging the extent of public health authority, Justice Harlan recognized specific limits to such exercises. As explained by Lawrence Gostin, utilizing state police powers in support of vaccination requirements or other compulsory public health initiatives is constitutionally permissible when exercised in conformity with the principles of:

(1) *public health necessity*—police powers used in the interests of communal health must be justified, and not exercised in arbitrary ways beyond what is reasonably required for the safety of the public;

(2) *reasonable means*—there must be some reasonable relationship between the public health intervention and the achievement of a legitimate public health objective that does not plainly invade individual rights;

(3) *proportionality*—public health powers that are arbitrary and oppressive in particular cases may require judicial intervention to prevent injustices or "absurd consequence[s]." *Id.* Even efficacious public health interventions may be unconstitutional if they are onerous or unfair; and

(4) *harm avoidance*—no compulsory public health measure should pose direct risks to specific persons with known adverse reactions. Thus, while persons may be required to be vaccinated for the common good, those who can demonstrate they are "unfit subjects" for vaccination because of the potential for adverse health consequences may not be subjected to the intervention. *Id.* at 12. Jacobson argued that he was not fit for vaccination, but the Court found he failed to present sufficient medical evidence in support of his claim. Requiring a person to be

immunized despite knowing harm, concluded the Court, would be "cruel and inhuman in the last degree." *Id.* at 39; *see* LAWRENCE O. GOSTIN, PUBLIC HEALTH LAW: POWER, DUTY, RESTRAINT 126–28 (2d ed. 2008).

Jacobson stands firmly for the proposition that police powers authorize states to require vaccination for the public good, but such powers must be exercised reasonably consistent with due process or other individual rights. Yet, there is another side to the case that reflects the Court's appreciation of structural constitutional constraints at the time.

Concerning Jacobson's rights-based claims, attorneys for the Commonwealth of Massachusetts argued in essence that the state and its legislative bodies have: (1) unquestionable powers and duties to protect the public's health (to which courts must defer); and (2) reasonably determined that smallpox vaccinations in affected communities further the public's health. In prior cases with similar facts, courts typically adjudicated in favor of government. However, the Commonwealth also recognized the nature and force of Jacobson's objections. The "antivaccination" movement during this period was vocal and strong (even if the minority). As well, the Cambridge Board of Health regulation failed to specify its lawful support. *See* Wendy E. Parmet et al., *Individual Rights versus the Public's Health— 100 Years after Jacobson v. Massachusetts*, 352 NEW ENG. J. MED. 652 (2005).

The Commonwealth attempted to counter Jacobson's liberty-based claim with arguments grounded in structural principles of constitutional law, including separation of powers, federalism, and social contract theory under Massachusetts' constitution. Concerning separation of powers, the Commonwealth argued that courts cannot contravene public health legislative judgments unless such were utterly arbitrary and unreasonable. Neither the Cambridge vaccination requirement nor the lower court's refusal to allow Jacobson's evidence of his fitness for vaccination was improper in light of the exercise of the state's overwhelming police powers.

Massachusetts' attorneys intimated that courts should not question the rational judgments of a local legislative body acting under a proper delegation of police power from the Commonwealth, which the Supreme Court acknowledged. "[The] [C]ourt would usurp the functions of another branch of government if it adjudged, as a matter of law, that the mode adopted under the sanction of the state, to protect the people at large was arbitrary and not justified by the necessities of the case." *Jacobson*, 197 U.S. at 28. Both the Court and the Commonwealth agreed in principle that when the legislature has spoken, it is entitled to significant judicial deference (even if constitutional rights are implicated). As Justice Harlan noted, "no court . . . is justified in disregarding the action of the legislature simply because in its . . . opinion [a] particular method was—perhaps or possibly—not the best." *Id*. at 35.

Principles of federalism also come into play. Though these principles undulate over time between state sovereignty and federal supremacy, in 1905 they were pointed firmly in the direction of the states. The Court acceded. "The safety and health of the people of Massachusetts are, in the first instance, for that Commonwealth to guard and protect. They are matters that do not ordinarily concern the national government." *Id.* at 38. It, however, also recognized its own judicial role. "While this [C]ourt should guard with firmness every right appertaining to life, liberty, or property . . . , it is of the last importance that it should not invade the domain of local authority except when it is plainly necessary to do so . . . ." *Id.* Clearly the Court respected principles of federalism in support of states' public health powers, but retained its authority to arbitrate potential constitutional violations of individual freedoms.

Finally, the Supreme Court acknowledged the Commonwealth's presentation of principles of communal responsibility inherent in social contract theory. The Massachusetts constitution sets forth "as a fundamental principle of the social compact that the whole people covenants with each other and that all should be governed by certain laws for the common good," *id.* at 27, notably including public health laws.

These structural principles (separation of powers, federalism, and social contract theory) shed greater light on how and why *Jacobson* was decided. Sovereign states are instituted to, among other things, protect the public's health for the benefit of their citizens. The Commonwealth used its broad police powers in the pursuit of protecting the community. The federal judicial branch must respect that exercise consistent with separation of powers and federalism. To the extent the Commonwealth's actions furthered the public's health, they counter-balance potential infringements of individual constitutional rights.

As constitutional norms change, these observations may no longer govern review of modern public health cases involving the juxtaposition of state police powers and individual rights. Yet, *Jacobson* must be read more broadly than it is oft-cited in support of (1) government regulation of persons in the interests of public health and safety, (2) limitations on individual liberty interests as needed to protect communal health, and (3) various school vaccination requirements, isolation, quarantine, fluoridation, and other public health measures.

The true legacy of *Jacobson* is its historical and modern guidance on when and how to balance the states' use of public health powers with individual rights and interests. The case remains good law because of the Court's essential recognition that protecting the public's health is synergistic with respecting individual liberties. *See* James G. Hodge, Jr., *Jacobson v. Massachusetts: Alternate Perspectives*, 33 J.L. MED. & ETHICS 26 (Supp. 2005).

Understanding the breadth of the field of public health law coupled with the source, scope, and limits of government's public health powers provides an appropriate backdrop for further study. In Part 2, specific legal authority to prevent and control public health conditions, including communicable and chronic diseases as well as avoidable injuries and corresponding deaths, is examined. At all levels of government, these conditions not only justify the use of significant public health powers, but also raise some of the most difficult tradeoffs with respect to individual rights and structural norms.

PART 2

LEGAL AUTHORITY TO PREVENT & CONTROL PUBLIC HEALTH CONDITIONS

Threats to the public's health are numerous and diverse. Long-standing (e.g., TB) and emerging (e.g., EVD) communicable diseases remain a scourge of populations. Chronic conditions, including heart disease, cancers, and diabetes, afflict millions of Americans. Preventable injuries and concomitant deaths negatively impact or cut short the lives of children and adults across the globe. Core to the mission of public health is the mitigation of the effects of these and other threats to individual and community health.

American government at all levels has available numerous, traditional, and long-standing powers to address public health risks. It may exercise these public health powers directly, or defer to partners in the private sector for their execution or assistance. So long as these powers are properly grounded in constitutional authorities and limits, the legal options are extensive. When wielded in the interests of community wellness, public health legal powers can be an effective tool for improving outcomes. However, if exercised (1) with impunity for individual liberties or other constitutionally-protected rights, (2) counter to core principles of public health ethics, or (3) in politically insensitive ways, public health authorities may lack legal and practical justifications for their actions.

This Part discusses the legal bases for interventions to address major challenges to communal health stemming from communicable diseases (Chapter 4), chronic conditions (Chapter 5), and injuries and deaths (Chapter 6). Public health powers used to address some communicable conditions, such as testing, screening, vaccination, or treatment, may equally apply to chronic illnesses, such as cancers. However, some of these powers are used almost exclusively in response to a particular type of threat (e.g., use of expedited partner therapy to address sexually-transmitted diseases).

Execution of public health powers to address any condition implicates careful tradeoffs and constant balancing between individual freedoms and community needs. As in Part 1, these themes are revisited in many contexts throughout the illustration of public health powers and their related impacts on individual rights.

CHAPTER 4

PREVENTING & TREATING COMMUNICABLE CONDITIONS

The global history of public health practice is intrinsically tied to the prevention and control of communicable diseases. From the founding of the U.S. to modern times, curbing the threat of illnesses spread between and among individuals has been a constant objective. Even as the mission of public health has expanded to assuring the conditions for people to be healthy (discussed in Chapter 1), controlling the spread of communicable diseases remains a focal point for federal, tribal, state, and local public health agencies. In pursuit of this objective they are equipped with preventive tools, techniques, and data stemming from considerable advances in public health surveillance and control practices. Key to the prevention and control of communicable diseases, however, is the law.

The legal interventions to respond to communicable disease threats are multifarious. Intermixed with some of the most ancient of communal health authorities (e.g., isolation and quarantine) are relatively new public health powers (e.g., directly-observed therapy) that together comprise the bastion of public health abilities to address communicable conditions. Exploration of these powers and associated trade-offs begins with an assessment of the scope and impact of communicable conditions on human health in the U.S. and abroad.

A. COMMUNICABLE CONDITIONS— DEFINED

A communicable condition is defined broadly as "an illness caused by an infectious agent or its toxins that occurs through the direct or indirect transmission of the infectious agent or its products" from different sources. N.Y.C., N.Y., HEALTH CODE tit. 24, § 11.01 (2010). Defining communicable diseases is easy. Predicting their spread (a main thrust of epidemiology) and controlling their impacts on populations are not.

Many communicable diseases are transmitted between humans through air-borne agents (e.g., influenza), casual contact (e.g., chicken pox), from mother to child (e.g., HIV), or via the transfer of blood or other bodily fluids from unprotected sexual contact (e.g., gonorrhea). Some infectious diseases are contracted through other living vectors such as animals (e.g., rabies), insects (e.g., Lyme disease), or plants/fungi (e.g., Valley Fever). Environmental sources such as water (e.g., cryptosporidium) and food (e.g., salmonella) also serve as dominant modes of transmission of infectious diseases.

Communicable conditions present enormous public health challenges. Some infectious agents may be primary bioterrorism threats (e.g., smallpox, anthrax, tularemia, plague, and botulism). NAT'L ACADS. & DHS, BIOLOGICAL ATTACK: HUMAN PATHOGENS, BIOTOXINS, AND AGRICULTURAL THREATS (2004). As discussed further in Chapter 10, their appearance in any individual or group in the U.S. garners immediate and substantial public health investigation and control efforts because of the likelihood of bioterrorist activity.

Other diseases that transmit easily between humans can also wreak havoc on populations. The 1918–1919 "Spanish flu" pandemic killed upwards of 100 million people globally. JOHN M. BARRY, THE GREAT INFLUENZA: THE STORY OF THE DEADLIEST PANDEMIC IN HISTORY 397 (2005). According to the World Health Organization (WHO), the 2009–2010 H1N1 pandemic flu infected millions and killed tens of thousands worldwide. WHO, EVOLUTION OF A PANDEMIC: A(H1N1) 2009 (2013). Even annual flu outbreaks can be lethal, lending to preventable mortality ranging from 3,000–49,000 deaths per year in the U.S. alone. CDC, *Estimates of Deaths Associated with Seasonal Influenza—U.S., 1976–2007,* 59 MMWR 1057 (Aug. 27, 2010) (statistics based on 30 years of CDC surveillance data).

Many infectious conditions are less easily transmitted, but still necessitate public health attention. In 2013 alone, approximately 9 million people globally contracted TB, multidrug resistant (MDR-) TB, or extreme drug resistant (XDR-) TB, and nearly 1.5 million people died from TB-related causes. WHO, GLOBAL TB REPORT 7 (2014). Dwindling resources and continued global migration suggest more persons may perish from this centuries-old disease (once known as consumption) in the years ahead. Localized outbreaks of TB still occur in the U.S., mostly in urban environments. Kiren Mitruka et al., *TB Outbreak Investigations in the U.S., 2002–2008,* 17 EMERGING INFECTIOUS

DISEASES 425 (2011). In 2015, over 2 dozen persons
in a Kansas town were diagnosed with TB largely
through exposure to a single source. Liz Szabo, *27
Kansas Students Test Positive for TB*, USA TODAY
(Mar. 19, 2015).

Sexually-transmitted infections (STIs) present
significant, often undetected risks internationally
and in the U.S. Since its emergence in the early
1980s, HIV/AIDS has claimed over 39 million lives
globally. WHO, HIV/AIDS: FACT SHEET NO. 360
(2014). CDC estimates over 1.2 million Americans
are living with HIV infection, including 168,300
(14.0%) whose infections have not been diagnosed.
CDC, *Monitoring Selected National HIV Prevention
and Care Objectives by Using HIV Surveillance
Data*, 19 HIV SURVEILLANCE SUPPLEMENTAL REP. 3
(2014). Almost 50,000 persons in the U.S. contracted
the disease in 2013 alone. CDC, FACT SHEET: NEW
HIV INFECTIONS IN THE U.S. (2012).

The most common STI is genital human
papillomavirus (HPV). Nearly 79 million Americans
are infected with HPV according to CDC estimates.
CDC, GENITAL HPV INFECTION—FACT SHEET (2014).
Nearly all sexually-active men and women will get
at least 1 type of HPV at some point in their lives.
Though the condition is largely asymptomatic in
most persons, some strains can lead to genital
warts, and more significantly, cervical and other
cancers. CDC, *STD Treatment Guidelines, 2010*, 59
MMWR 1, 69–70 (Dec. 17, 2010).

Hundreds of thousands of individuals are infected
with 2 other prominent STIs, gonorrhea or

Chlamydia. Nearly 17,400 new infections of syphilis were also reported in 2013. CDC, FACT SHEET: STD TRENDS IN THE U.S.: 2011 NATIONAL DATA FOR CHLAMYDIA, GONORRHEA, AND SYPHILIS (2014). Left untreated, each of these STIs can lead to significant long-term disabilities, including cancers and infertility, or death.

Improper food handling practices and questionable sanitation from farms to factories also contribute significantly to the spread of infectious diseases. Over 19,000 lab-confirmed cases of food-related illness were reported to CDC in 2013. The actual number of cases is likely many times higher. Salmonella poisonings alone led to 2,003 hospitalizations and 27 deaths that same year. Stacy M. Crim et. al., *Incidence and Trends of Infection with Pathogens Transmitted Commonly Through Food,* 63 MMWR 15, 329 (2014).

Water-borne infectious agents, including the sometimes deadly cryptosporidium, cause hundreds of infections annually. They arise predominantly through exposure to microorganisms in recreational water or through contaminants in public or private water supplies. CDC, *Surveillance for Waterborne Disease Outbreaks and Other Health Events*, 60 MMWR 1 (Sept. 23, 2011). In 1993, undetected cryptosporidium contaminations in the city water supply of Milwaukee, Wisconsin led to 69 deaths. Phaedra S. Corso et al., *Cost of Illness in the 1993 Waterborne Cryptosporidium Outbreak, Milwaukee, Wisconsin,* 9 EMERGING INFECTIOUS DISEASES 426, 430 (2003); *Markweise v. Peck Foods Corp.,* 556

N.W.2d 326 (Wis. Ct. App. 1996) (resulting litigation against the city and others was dismissed due to failure to provide advance notice of claim).

Whether spread via air-borne, casual or sexual contact, or other vectors, communicable conditions remain a challenge despite public health victories over many diseases that once plagued populations (e.g., polio, measles, mumps, and rubella). U.S. public health authorities rely on their legal authority to engage in a series of voluntary, mandatory, or compulsory measures (discussed in Chapter 3) to prevent or control infectious diseases, as described in the sections below.

B.   TESTING & SCREENING

Public health powers to test and screen for communicable conditions are authorized generally or in relation to varied conditions via statute or regulation in all states and many localities. Though often conflated, testing and screening are different public health powers. Diagnostic tests (or procedures) are used to ascertain the presence or absence of a particular condition in an individual. Screening involves the application of specific tests to the population. Ronald Bayer et al., *HIV Antibody Screening: An Ethical Framework for Evaluating Proposed Programs*, 256 JAMA 1768, 1768 (1986).

Thus a person who is a member of a high-risk population for a specific infectious condition may be subjected to *screening* that may lead to administration of a diagnostic *test* to confirm infection. During the 2014 global Ebola pandemic, for example, U.S. authorities screened over 17,000 air travelers arriving from West African "hot zones" for symptoms; those with initial symptoms (e.g., high fever) may have been requested to submit to further testing. Sabrina Tavernise & Anemona Hartocollis, *Monitoring System Is Criticized as Rare Virus Causes a Death in New Jersey*, N.Y. TIMES, May 27, 2015, at A15.

Multiple practical factors militate whether public health authorities may engage testing or screening programs or initiatives, including their affordability, accuracy, efficacy, ethicality, and potential for positive interventions based on results. *See, e.g.,* Bob Ortega, *FDA to Scrutinize HPV Test Linked to False Readings*, ARIZ. REPUBLIC, July 31, 2013, at A1 (FDA to review laboratory use of specific HPV test based on reported high rates of false positive results).

Testing and screening programs that (1) include pre- and post-counseling, (2) seek voluntary compliance expressed through advance informed consent, (3) avoid coercive tactics, and (4) elude unwarranted classification of protected groups are legally acceptable. Each year the U.S. Preventative Services Task Force (USPSTF) issues a series of national guidelines determining whom should be tested for varied communicable conditions which may be followed at the discretion of health care workers and their patients. USPSTF, THE GUIDE TO CLINICAL PREVENTIVE SERVICES v (2012).

Even voluntary testing and screening programs can still raise legal concerns over privacy. In 2006,

CDC adjusted its national recommendation for the administration of HIV/AIDS tests to include all persons ages 13–64 seeking routine physicals or other treatment. Bernard M. Branson. et. al., *Revised Recommendations for HIV Testing of Adults, Adolescents, and Pregnant Women in Health-Care Settings*, 55 MMWR 1, 7 (Sept. 22, 2006). CDC's recommendation included an "opt-out" feature, meaning testing would be done automatically unless rejected by the patient. In 2013, President Obama expressed continued support for the voluntary testing of Americans to facilitate advance detection and treatment of HIV. Elise Viebeck, *Obama Urges Widespread Testing for HIV*, HILL, June 27, 2013; OFFICE OF NATIONAL AIDS POLICY, NATIONAL HIV/AIDS STRATEGY: UPDATE OF 2014 FEDERAL ACTIONS TO ACHIEVE NATIONAL GOALS AND IMPROVE OUTCOMES ALONG THE HIV CONTINUUM 3, 7 (2014).

While some have raised privacy concerns related to this opt-out mode of implementation, CDC's recommendation reflects a watershed shift in national HIV/AIDS strategy following nearly 2 decades of various testing and screening programs focused on high-risk groups (e.g., homosexual men, pregnant women, injecting drug users (IDUs), sex offenders). IOM, HIV SCREENING AND ACCESS TO CARE: EXPLORING BARRIERS AND FACILITATORS TO EXPANDED HIV TESTING (2010). These types of screening efforts were challenged legally based on their potential to infringe the bodily and informational privacy of at-risk individuals. *See In re Juveniles A, B, C, D, E*, 847 P.2d 455 (Wash.

1993) (HIV screening of juvenile and adult sex offenders is not a violation of constitutional right to privacy). Additional challenges arose over the use of named-based reporting of test results to local, state, and federal public health authorities. *See Middlebrooks v. State Bd. of Health*, 710 So. 2d 891 (Ala. 1998) (state statute requiring name-based reporting of HIV/AIDS patients by physicians does not violate informational privacy rights) (discussed further in Chapter 7).

Other legal issues stem from testing or screening programs. Like most states, Minnesota public health authorities oversee a screening program to search for initial, potential genetic or other conditions among newborns. Charlotte Tucker, *Fifty Years of Screening: Testing Newborns Can Prevent Lifelong Illness*, 43 NATION'S HEALTH 9 (2013). In *Bearder v. State*, 806 N.W.2d 766 (Minn. 2011), parents of 25 children sued Minnesota's Department of Health and its Commissioner for "collecting, using, storing, and disseminating the children's blood samples and test results without obtaining written informed consent in violation of the Genetic Privacy Act." *Id.* at 766. To the extent that Minnesota authorities used blood samples for unrelated research, the court held that they exceeded their authority under the state's screening statutes. *Id.* at 776.

Government requirements that persons be tested or screened without consent for public health purposes can implicate 4th Amendment prohibitions of "unreasonable searches and seizures." The U.S.

Supreme Court has clarified that the 4th Amendment applies to physical searches of one's person, effects, or property as well as bodily searches (e.g., blood or DNA tests). *See Skinner v. Railway Labor Execs. Ass'n,* 489 U.S. 602 (1989) (alcohol and drug testing of railway employees is reasonable and consistent with need for public safety); *Maryland v. King*, 133 S. Ct. 1 (2013) (DNA testing of arrestees via cheek swabs presents only a minimal intrusion on defendants' expectation of privacy).

Under the 4th Amendment government must generally issue a warrant based on probable cause prior to initiating a search. *Contra In re Application of the U.S.A. for Historical Cell Site Data*, 724 F.3d 600 (5th Cir. 2013) (allowing the warrantless search of cellular device location records for law enforcement purposes). This warrant requirement may also apply to "searches" such as intrusive blood or other diagnostic tests. However, pursuant to what is known as the "special needs doctrine," government may conduct searches without a warrant (outside the context of law enforcement) when requiring a warrant would be impractical or impossible. *See also* discussion of searches of premises in Chapter 9.

In *Ferguson v. City of Charleston*, 532 U.S. 67 (2001), a local policy requiring the non-consensual testing of pregnant women or new mothers for drug-related conditions (notably cocaine) at the state-supported Medical University of South Carolina was challenged as an unlawful search. Initially implemented in the 1990s during what some called an epidemic of "crack babies," the public health purpose underlying the screening program was to identify women who exposed their fetuses or infants to illicit drugs through maternal-child transmission. Yet, test results were also reported to local law enforcement for potential prosecution of the mothers. The end result was pernicious, noted the Supreme Court, in linking unsuspecting, often African-American women seeking publicly-funded maternal care with criminal charges. As a result, the testing policy did not comport with the special needs doctrine, and was declared unconstitutional. *Id.* at 84. *See also Glover v. Eastern Neb. Cmty. Office of Retardation*, 867 F.2d 461 (8th Cir. 1989) (public agency employees serving mentally disabled persons cannot be required to be tested for Hepatitis B and HIV where the risk to patients was insufficient to justify the intrusion on privacy).

C. TREATMENT & RELATED THERAPIES

One of the primary benefits of public health testing and screening programs is the potential to match positive cases with available treatments. Treatment services are provided typically through private sector health practitioners, although many states continue to fund government-run public health clinics that deliver basic health services often to the most needy in the community. Funding crises threaten the future existence of public health clinics in some jurisdictions. *See, e.g.,* Bobby Kerlik, *Pennsylvania Supreme Court Halts Corbett Plan to Close Health Centers,* PITTSBURGH TRIB.-REV., July

18, 2013 (temporary injunction of Governor's plan to shut down 26 of the state's public health centers).

When effective treatments exist, failing to make them available for persons who are tested or screened via public health programs is unethical. STEPHEN HOLLAND, PUBLIC HEALTH ETHICS 162 (2007). Otherwise, there are few legal hurdles to implementing voluntary treatment programs so long as options are explained to individuals and they are given meaningful opportunities for informed consent. *See Canterbury v. Spence*, 464 F.2d 772 (D.C. Cir. 1972). Legal issues related to consent concerning treatment of minors may arise. In *Anspach ex rel. Anspach v. City of Phila.*, 503 F.3d 256 (3rd Cir. 2007), parents objected to the provision of contraceptives to their 16-year-old daughter at a local public health clinic. The court rejected their claim that the clinic's services were coercive and contrary to their constitutional parental rights. The court deemed the services as voluntary in nature.

Significant constitutional questions can arise when treatment for communicable diseases is no longer optional either because government sets significant conditions for its receipt (e.g., release from isolation) or attempts to force a person to be treated. Concerning conditional treatment, public health powers are sufficiently broad to require individuals to complete treatment as a condition of participation in specific activities or release from confinement where:

- absent treatment, the individual's communicable condition and behaviors present significant health risks to others;

- treatment options do not place the individual at greater risk of harm;

- requirements for completion of treatment are reasonable, appropriate, and consistent with the current standard of care; and

- adequate procedural due process protections are followed (as discussed in Chapter 3).

1.   DIRECTLY-OBSERVED THERAPY

One prominent example of conditional treatment predominately used in treating persons with TB (and potentially other communicable diseases requiring long treatment regimens) is directly-observed therapy (DOT). DOT is designed to assure an infected individual is fully treated by requiring a public health worker, health care practitioner, or a family member to administer or observe the individual receiving regular treatments (e.g., ingesting pills or receiving injections).

DOT has proven efficacious in assuring execution of TB treatment, limiting the development of drug resistant strains of TB (which may stem from incompletions of drug regimens), and lowering the potential for further transmission. It is legally authorized in many states (*see, e.g.,* N.M. STAT. ANN. § 24–1–15.1 (2009)), particularly for persons with TB who voluntarily comply. Sometimes, participation in DOT is mandated particularly concerning (1) recalcitrant patients (*see City of Newark v. J.S.*, 652 A.2d 265 (N.J. Super. 1993); *City of Milwaukee v. Washington*, 735 N.W.2d 111 (Wis. 2007)), or (2) prisoners (*see De Gidio v. Pung*, 704 F. Supp. 922 (D. Minn. 1989)).

2.   EXPEDITED PARTNER THERAPY

Another type of conditional treatment is known as expedited partner therapy (EPT). CDC endorsed the use of EPT first in 2006 for national implementation. CDC, *STD Treatment Guidelines,* 55 MMWR 5, 5–6 (Aug. 4, 2006). The public health concept underlying EPT is straight-forward: when treating patients with STIs like Chlamydia or gonorrhea, sufficient doses of safe, prescribed antibiotics should be provided not just for the patient, but also their close sexual partner. Providing treatment for both the patient and partner expedites treatment to the partner, resulting in reduced infections and lowering the spread of STIs by breaking the circle of transmission. CDC has conducted or funded significant research demonstrating the efficacy of EPT related to specific STIs. *See* Matthew Golden et. al., *Uptake and Population-Level Impact of EPT on Chlamydia Trachomatis and Neisseria Gonorrhoeae: The Washington State Community-Level Randomized Trial of EPT,* 12 PLOS MED. (2015).

Legal dilemmas related to EPT principally concern the provision or dispensing of a drug to the partner who has not been diagnosed by a health care practitioner or received a prescription in the normal course of health or pharmaceutical care. The potential for adverse events for the partner (though nearly non-existent), misuse of the antibiotics (leading to potential drug resistance), and liability for issuing prescriptions without examining an individual all pose potential legal obstacles to its wider practice across states. James G. Hodge, Jr. et al., *EPT: Assessing the Legal Environment,* 98 AM. J. PUB. HEALTH 23, 23–28 (2008).

Multiple states have overcome these issues by directly authorizing the practice of EPT through legislative or regulatory routes. In other states, EPT is incorporated by reference to existing CDC STI guidance. *See* MONT. ADMIN. R. §§ 37.114.515, 37.114.530 (2013). Elsewhere, purported legal concerns may not actually prohibit its practice. An extensive assessment of state public health laws in 2008 found that most states' laws already support, or at least do not prevent, EPT in practice. Hodge, Jr. et al., *supra,* 98 AM. J. PUB. HEALTH at 23–28. As of 2015, EPT is legally permissible in 37 states and potentially allowable in 9 states. Only 4 states legally prohibit EPT in practice. CDC, *Legal Status of EPT.*

3.   FORCED TREATMENT

Courts are highly reticent to allow the confinement of autonomous individuals to administer forced treatment or medication (notwithstanding potential exercises of DOT discussed above). The U.S. Supreme Court has espoused that individual liberty interests via substantive due process include rights to refuse treatment and sustenance. *See Cruzan v. Director, Mo. Dep't of Health*, 497 U.S. 261 (1990). Whether the Court would counter-balance of these liberty interests with a compelling public health need to forcibly treat autonomous adults in specific instances is uncertain.

In 1 case, a local homeless woman with TB who failed to adhere to DOT was placed in a county jail because she posed a threat to the public's health. The Wisconsin Supreme Court upheld her confinement because the jail was "a place where proper care and treatment [would] be provided [and] the spread of disease [would] be prevented," with no less restrictive options available. *In re Washington*, 735 N.W.2d 111, 114 (Wis. 2007); *see also City of New York v. Antoinette*, 630 N.Y.S.2d 1008 (S. Queens Cty. 1995) (allowing forcible detention of person with active TB in hospital based on clear and convincing evidence that detention was necessary).

The U.S. Supreme Court has clarified that compelled medication of prisoners or other wards related to communicable diseases is permissible provided it is appropriate and essential for the health or safety of the individual or others in the absence of less intrusive alternatives. *See Riggins v. Nevada*, 504 U.S. 127 (1992). If the safety of the individual or others is not at stake, however, medication may not be forced generally even among legal wards of the state. *See Sell v. United States*, 539 U.S. 166 (2003) (requiring stricter assessment for forced medication of prisoner with antipsychotic drugs solely to render him fit to stand trial).

D. PARTNER NOTIFICATION

Testing, screening, and treatment are essential tools to find and address "index cases" (i.e., persons that have specific communicable conditions). An additional practice often coupled with these interventions, especially with conditions like HIV/AIDS, TB, or bioterrorism agents, is what is known traditionally as "contact tracing," and modernly as "partner notification" or "partner counseling and referral services" (PCRS). E. Foust et. al., *Partner Counseling and Referral Services to Identify Persons with Undiagnosed HIV—North Carolina, 2001,* 52 MMWR 1181 (2014) (PCRS helps HIV-infected persons notify partners of their need for HIV testing, care, and counseling).

The basic, public health premise of PCRS is to seek the assistance of infected persons to help locate and notify their contacts or partners of potential exposure. Partner notification generally entails infected individuals working with their health providers or public health officials to identify prospective partners. For example, following confirmation of a positive HIV test, a doctor or practitioner at a local public health clinic may ask an individual if she has had any recent, unprotected sexual contact with others. Based on this information, she may be encouraged to (1) notify her partners of their potential exposure, (2) seek the doctor's assistance in notifying them, or (3) permit the local public health department to provide this information.

In the latter 2 instances, notification of the partners is combined typically with testing, counseling, and treatment referrals. In each case, notice is intended to be non-identifiable (i.e., a practitioner does not directly identify the index case who exposed a partner to HIV). In reality, some partners can inevitably identify the source of their exposure. For example, a person who is in a long-term monogamous sexual relationship may clearly know who exposed her to HIV through partner notification. Although unintended, the potential for identification of index cases via partner notification raises significant health information privacy issues (discussed further in Chapter 7). Some index cases may face physical or mental abuse from their partners once notified of their exposure. Richard L. North & Karen H. Rothenberg, *Partner Notification and the Threat of Domestic Violence Against Women with HIV Infection,* 329 NEW ENG. J. MED. 1194 (1993); Andrea Gielen et. al., *Women Living with HIV: Disclosure, Violence, and Social Support,* 77 J. URB. HEALTH 480 (2000).

When conducted via government, PCRS participation may also implicate rights against self-incrimination protected by the 5th Amendment. A local public health official may ask an adult with HIV to identify potential sexual contacts including minors. The adult's participation in unprotected sexual acts with a minor may be criminal under multiple state laws in several jurisdictions. *See* Zita Lazzarini et al., *Criminalization of HIV Transmission and Exposure: Research and Policy Agenda*, 103 AM. J. PUB. HEALTH 1350 (2013); *People v. Dempsey*, 610 N.E.2d 208 (Ill. Ct. App. 1993) (HIV+ man convicted of criminal transmission and aggravated sexual assault when he forced his 9-year-old brother to perform oral sex on him); THOMAS SHEVORY, NOTORIOUS H.I.V.: THE MEDIA SPECTACLE OF NUSHAWN WILLIAMS (2004) (documenting prosecution of Williams for allegedly having unprotected sex with multiple minors after having received HIV+ test results); Jay Tokaz, *Jury Rules Nushawn Williams Has Condition Making Him Likely to Commit More Sex Crimes,* BUFFALO NEWS (June 28, 2013) (Williams completed his 12-year prison sentence in 2010 but remains imprisoned under a N.Y. law allowing confinement of dangerous sex offenders indefinitely).

For these reasons, partner notification practices almost always involve the voluntary assent of the index cases. Still, access to specific information about others' exposure might be deemed essential to thwart major threats to the public's health such as an outbreak of smallpox caused by bioterrorists.

E.   VACCINATION

Widespread vaccination of the population is one of the premier public health achievements of the 20th century due in part to legal support at all levels of government. The federal Food and Drug Administration (FDA) is authorized to approve vaccines for use in the population. 42 U.S.C. § 262 (2012). CDC's Advisory Committee on Immunization Practices (ACIP) annually sets vaccination requirements and recommendations, which most states follow in part as a condition of the receipt of federal vaccine funds. DHHS uses these recommendations and other data to provide incentives for the manufacture of vaccines and set expectations for public or private insurance coverage. Steven H. Woolf & Doug Campos-Outcalt, *Severing the Link Between Coverage Policy and the USPSTF*, 309 JAMA 1899 (2013).

All states require vaccination of children and adolescents for a host of communicable diseases as a condition of attendance at elementary, secondary, and occasionally higher education schools. Local and state departments of education and health collaborate to monitor the administration of school vaccination requirements. Increasingly states also tie attendance at day-care or other operations to completion of vaccination regimens. *See* CDC, SCHOOL AND CHILDCARE VACCINATION SURVEYS 1 (2007–2008).

Public health authorities routinely operate vaccine information campaigns in response to annual influenza, help set policies for vaccinating public and private HCWs, and encourage or require vaccination in real-time during outbreaks or emergency events. In most cases, vaccines are administered with consent of the individual or a minor's parent or guardian, although the scope of consent varies. In *Boyd v. Louisiana Med. Mut. Ins. Co.*, 593 So. 2d 427 (La. Ct. App. 1991), for example, the court held that informed consent did not have to include notice of the 1 in 8 million risk of contracting polio from a vaccine because a reasonable person with knowledge of this risk would still take it.

The U.S. Supreme Court approved government's imposition of vaccines to control epidemic diseases in 1905 in *Jacobson* (discussed in Chapter 3), and separately endorsed school vaccination programs in 1922. *Zucht v. King*, 260 U.S. 174 (1922). Still, vaccination implementation across jurisdictions is inconsistent in part because of legal exceptions. Based on respect of 1st Amendment freedom of religion principles (discussed initially in Chapter 3), nearly all states (except Mississippi and West Virginia) allow for religious exemptions from school vaccination requirements. More than 20 states also recognize philosophically-based exceptions. Saad B. Omer et al., *Vaccination Policies and Rates of Exemption from Immunizations: 2005–2011*, 367 NEW ENG. J. MED. 1170 (Sept. 2012).

State standards for administering these exceptions vary. In some states, parents seeking exemptions for their children must (1) provide significant, notarized documentation of their sincere religious beliefs and proof of their denomination's rejection of vaccine; (2) participate in an education session on childhood vaccines; or (3) seek state health department or court approval. In many states, however, receiving an exception to vaccination mandates is as easy as completing and filing a form through school administration.

In an era where misinformation widely circulated through social media leads some parents to believe childhood vaccinations are the cause of autism or other childhood conditions, lax requirements for religious or philosophical exemptions can lower vaccination compliance rates in some jurisdictions. Resulting outbreaks of preventable conditions, such as measles and whooping cough, among unvaccinated children and others across the U.S. have increasingly become routine. Fuyuen Y. Yip et al. *Measles Outbreak Epidemiology in the U.S.*, 1993–2001, 189 J. INFECTIOUS DISEASES S54, S59 (2004).

In December 2014, a measles outbreak that began from a single infected person at Disneyland, California led to the infection of 117 people in 7 states. Most of these infected persons were unvaccinated due to religious or philosophical exemptions or were too young to be vaccinated for measles. Nakia S. Clemmons et al., *Measles—U.S., January 4–April 2, 2015*, 64 MMWR 373, 373–376 (2015); *Measles Cases and Outbreaks*, CDC (May 8, 2015). In response, California passed legislation signed by Governor Jerry Brown on June 30, 2015 to eliminate most religious or philosophical exemptions to childhood vaccine requirements by 2016. *See* Charlotte Alter, *California Governor Jerry Brown Signs Mandatory Vaccine Law*, TIME (June 30, 2015); Adam Nagourney, *California Mandates*

Vaccines for Schoolchildren, N.Y. TIMES (June 30, 2015) (California becomes the largest U.S. state to require school children to receive vaccinations absent medical exemption). Additional states also introduced a variety of bills designed to curb exemptions with varying rates of success. *See* Y. Tony Yang, Leila Barraza & Kim Weidenaar, *Commentary, Measles Outbreak as a Catalyst for Stricter Vaccine Exemption Legislation*, JAMA doi:10.1001/jama.2015.9579 (2015).

While most state or federal courts approve statutory vaccination exceptions, constitutional conundrums under the 1st and 14th Amendments lead to divergent decisions. In *Brown v. Stone*, 378 So. 2d 218 (Miss. 1979), the Mississippi Supreme Court invalidated the state's religious exemption on equal protection grounds because most parents would not qualify for it. In *Boone v. Boozman*, 217 F. Supp. 2d 938 (E.D. Ark. 2002), a federal district court demonstrated how the companion portions of the 1st Amendment to protect religious freedom can be interpreted inappositely. The court struck down Arkansas' religious-belief exemption as a violation of the Establishment Clause (because it had the purpose or effect of advancing religion) as well as the Free Exercise Clause (because it supported the religious rights of those within a "recognized church or religious denomination" but not others). Overriding the court's decision, the Arkansas legislature later reformed its statutory exceptions language. ARK. CODE ANN. § 6–18–702(d) (2005) (vaccination is not required "if the parents or legal guardian[s] of [a] child object thereto on the grounds that immunization conflicts with [their] religious or philosophical beliefs." *Id.* at § 6–18–702(d)(4)(A)).

Both of these cases diverge from most courts' permissive view of the constitutionality of religious or philosophical vaccine exemptions. Yet, they reflect the considerable legal tensions at stake in the implementation of vaccines against the backdrop of religious beliefs and public misperceptions about vaccines' risks. *See, e.g.,* James G. Hodge, Jr. & Lawrence O. Gostin, *School Vaccination Requirements: Historical, Social, and Legal Perspectives,* 90 KY. L.J. 831 (2002).

The Religious Freedom Restoration Act (RFRA), 42 U.S.C. § 2000cc et seq (2015), passed first by Congress in 1993 and later by 22 states, provides additional protection for individuals' religious beliefs beyond the 1st Amendment. RFRA may be used to expand already permissive religious-based vaccine exemptions, but it may also undermine immunization requirements. Broad definitions of who constitutes a "person" under the Act and how one may "exercise" religion may allow additional religious-based objections to vaccine requirements. Even if one can demonstrate a particular vaccine mandate substantially burdened the exercise of religion, as required by RFRA, government may still prevail by demonstrating a compelling governmental interest that is furthered through the least restrictive means. *See e.g.,* James G. Hodge Jr., *Protecting Religious Freedoms and Protecting the Public's Health,* 130 PUB. HEALTH REP. 1, 8–11 (2015); NAT'L WOMEN'S LAW CTR., THE HOBBY LOBBY

"MINEFIELD": THE HARM, MISUSE, AND EXPANSION OF THE SUPREME COURT DECISION (2015). State-based school vaccination or other requirements may survive this sort of judicial scrutiny.

Vaccines are extremely safe when used consistent with FDA approvals for specific populations. However, the potential for adverse reactions to vaccines among select patients may arise. When negative outcomes related to the administration of vaccines occur, the National Vaccine Injury Compensation Program, created in 1986, provides no-fault relief for affected persons provided they can show their injuries or deaths are related to the administration of a vaccine listed by the Program. National Childhood Vaccine Injury Act of 1986, 42 U.S.C. §§ 300aa-1 to 300aa-34 (2012). To date, nearly 14,000 claims have been adjudicated through appointed Special Masters. HEALTH RES. SERVS. ADMIN., NATIONAL VACCINE INJURY COMPENSATION PROGRAM, STATISTIC REPORTS: ADJUDICATIONS (May 4, 2015). Primary recourse through the Program is necessitated in part by the Act's limitation on state-based claims for damages related to design defects (discussed in Chapter 6) of vaccines. *See Brusewitz v. Wyeth*, 562 U.S. 223 (2011). Additional vaccine-related liability protections stemming from preparedness and response efforts in declared emergencies are discussed in Chapter 10.

F.   SOCIAL DISTANCING MEASURES

The legal powers to prevent and control communicable diseases through testing, screening, treatment, and vaccination are core facets of public health practice. Sometimes public health authorities must respond through powers designed not only to detect and deter infectious diseases, but also to separate individuals and populations who pose risks to others. Through social distancing measures, public health agents create space among individuals and groups to thwart the spread of communicable conditions.

1.   STATE & LOCAL QUARANTINE & ISOLATION

Quarantine, isolation, curfew, and closure are among the oldest public health powers. Although wielded historically in ways that occasionally castigated affected persons, the purpose of these measures is not punitive. Rather, they are designed solely to limit the spread of air-borne or other easily-transmitted conditions, particularly when other interventions are ineffective. Still, application and enforcement of these measures can affect constitutional rights to freedom of movement, bodily integrity, and privacy. For these reasons, social distancing techniques may be administered or enforced sparingly despite sometimes broad legal authorization at the state or local levels.

While all social distancing measures share the same basic goal of separating healthy and infectious individuals to limit further transmission, these powers are distinct. *Isolation* refers to the separation of a person or group of persons known or suspected to be infected with a communicable disease to prevent the spread of infection. *Quarantine* refers to the separation of a person or group presumed or known to have been exposed to a communicable disease to obviate infections with those not exposed. Simply stated, isolation involves separating infected persons while quarantine is used to separate persons merely exposed to infectious conditions. All states' public health laws authorize the isolation or quarantine of individuals for varied communicable diseases. TFAH, READY OR NOT? PROTECTING THE PUBLIC'S HEALTH IN THE AGE OF BIOTERRORISM (2004).

The powers to quarantine or isolate are used routinely across the U.S., often without significant legal or political controversy. There are, of course, exceptions, including the quarantine of nurse Kaci Hickox in New Jersey and Maine during the Ebola outbreak in 2014. Hickox initially tested positive with an elevated fever via screening at the Newark (N.J.) airport where she returned from multiple weeks abroad treating EVD patients in Sierra Leone. On October 24, 2014, New Jersey Governor Chris Christie and state public health authorities determined that she must be quarantined. Hickox was housed in a tent adjacent to a local hospital in Newark. For over 60 hours, Hickox was physically separated from family, friends, and others while monitored regularly for additional signs of EVD infection. Anemona Hartocollis & Emma G. Fitzsimmons, *Tested Negative for Ebola, Nurse Criticizes Her Quarantine*, N.Y. TIMES (Oct. 25, 2014).

On October 27, 2014, Hickox was allowed to return to her residence in Maine after objecting to her situation in New Jersey. Soon upon her return, Maine Governor Paul LePage and Health Commissioner Mary Mayhew promptly attempted to impose a mandatory 21-day "home quarantine" court order on Hickox after she and her boyfriend left their house to ride bikes. Jennifer Levitz, *Nurse Defies Ebola Quarantine in Maine*, WALL ST. J. (Oct. 30, 2014). After another HCW, Dr. Craig Spencer, was determined to be EVD+ just 24 hours after visiting varied public destinations in New York City, Maine's limited quarantine against Hickox was framed as a public health necessity. Faith Karimi, *From Guinea to the U.S.: Timeline of First Ebola Patient in New York City*, CNN (Oct. 25, 2014). Hickox challenged the quarantine order in court.

On October 31, a federal district court judge found that the State lacked "clear and convincing evidence" that Hickox posed sufficient risks to the community to support her mandatory home quarantine. *Mayhew v. Hickox*, No. FORDC-CV-2014-36, 2014 U.S. Dist. (D. Maine Oct. 31, 2014). Her initial high temperature reading at the Newark airport proved to be an anomaly. She evinced no further EVD symptoms thereafter. Lacking any additional proof of harm, Hickox's quarantine order was deemed unnecessary and unlawful. Still, Hickox was required by the court to complete a self-monitoring program for signs of Ebola infection until mid-November 2014, which she complied without incident.

2. FEDERAL QUARANTINE & ISOLATION

CDC is empowered to quarantine or isolate individuals with specific infectious diseases, as well as operate several quarantine stations in major transportation hubs across the U.S. James J. Misrahi et al., *DHHS/CDC Legal Response to SARS Outbreak*, 10 EMERGING INFECTIOUS DISEASES 353 (2004). CDC's limited quarantine authority was thoroughly tested in a well-publicized case in 2007. David P. Fidler et al., *Through the Quarantine Looking Glass: Drug-Resistant TB and Public Health Governance, Law and Ethics,* 35 J.L. MED. & ETHICS 526, 526–33 (2007).

Andrew Speaker, an attorney practicing in Atlanta (CDC's home base), contracted TB during his prior travels. Although local health authorities in Georgia asked him to limit his future travel, Speaker left Atlanta's airport for an extensive European trip. While away, CDC determined from lab samples that he may have developed XDR-TB. They notified Speaker and asked him to report to health authorities in Italy where he was located at the time. He refused. Following an international media storm, Speaker eventually returned to the U.S. days later by flying into Canada and driving across the border into New York State.

Upon his return, CDC issued its 1st federal quarantine order since the early 1960s. Speaker surrendered to public health authorities and received treatment at a Denver hospital that regularly treats TB patients. Multiple persons close to Speaker during his extensive travel were briefly placed under limited quarantine to ascertain whether they had contracted TB. Eventually CDC determined that Speaker never had XDR-TB, but rather had contracted a more common and less severe type of the disease. A subsequent lawsuit brought by Speaker against CDC alleging privacy and other violations was summarily dismissed on September 14, 2012. *Speaker v. CDC*, 489 F. App'x 425 (11th Cir. 2012).

3. CURFEWS & CLOSURES

Curfews and *closures* are typically used in response to epidemics, mass disasters, or following particular outbreaks of food-borne illnesses from commercial or other sources. They are designed to set limits on the time or place regarding the assembly of individuals so as to mitigate the spread of disease. State or local public health officers may, for example, issue orders to set curfew for communities affected by disease to disassociate individuals temporarily from gathering in large groups.

Provided orders for curfews are necessary, temporary infringements on individuals' liberty, notably their right to travel, are allowed. *See In re Juan C.*, 33 Cal. Rptr. 2d 919, 922 (Cal. Ct. App. 1994) ("Though the right to travel ... is constitutionally protected, [it] may be legitimately curtailed [via curfew] when a community has been ravaged by flood, fire or disease, and its safety and welfare are threatened." (citing *Zemel v. Rusk,* 381 U.S. 1, 15–16 (1965)). Closure orders may be implemented by public health agencies (in concert with law enforcement) to shut down places that either are the source of an outbreak (e.g., a restaurant responsible for serving contaminated food) or through which disease may be spread (e.g., a school where student gatherings may further spread influenza).

4.   PERSONAL LIBERTIES

Intrusions on personal liberties of these or other social distancing measures vary. Isolation or quarantine orders, for example, can significantly restrict individual movement by authorizing the forcible removal of persons from their homes for the duration of their infectivity. In reality, these orders typically seek voluntary compliance. Public health officials encourage affected individuals to remain at home and utilize universal precautions to prevent the spread of disease, unless they need particular medical care for which placement in a health care setting is more appropriate.

To support uses of coercive public health powers against judicial challenges, public health authorities must be prepared to show that:

- the subject of social distancing measures is actually, or is reasonably suspected of, being infectious or exposed to infectious conditions;

- the subject poses a specific threat to the public's health. For example, quarantine of a group of persons concerning their exposure to an infectious condition, such as smallpox, is warranted to prevent the transmission of a deadly pathogen spread via bioterrorism. Quarantine of a group of persons exposed to annual influenza, which does not substantially threaten most persons' health, is likely unlawful;

- the terms of placement are safe and habitable. In 1909, the South Carolina Supreme Court struck down a quarantine order served on an older woman with leprosy in part because she was removed from her "cottage" home to a "pesthouse, coarse and comfortless." *Kirk v. Wyman*, 65 S.E. 387 (S.C. 1909);

- the terms of confinement are warranted. In 1892, about 1,200 Russian Jews were quarantined unjustifiably outside New York City. Most (about 1,150) were healthy people who unfortunately lived in proximity to 50 ship passengers who had developed typhus. HOWARD MARKEL, QUARANTINE! 59 (1997). In *Jew Ho v. Williamson*, 103 F. 10 (N.D. Cal. 1900), a federal district court outlawed a plague-related quarantine order over several blocks of modern-day Chinatown in San Francisco as "unreasonable, unjust, . . . oppressive," and discriminatory. *Id*. at 26; and

- procedural due process is provided (as noted in Chapter 3). In *Greene v. Edwards*,

263 S.E.2d 661 (W. Va. 1980), the West
Virginia Supreme Court required public
health authorities to apply the same
procedural protections concerning the
involuntary commitment of persons with
mental illness to those confined because of
their infection with TB. This includes
adequate notice, right to a hearing, right to
counsel, right to present and confront
witnesses, right to a verbatim transcript,
and implementation of a clear and
convincing standard to justify isolation. *Id.*
at 663.

In summary, modern courts tend to strictly
scrutinize impositions of social distancing measures
that affect individual liberties and bodily privacy.
Public health authorities must demonstrate a
compelling governmental interest in support of a
well-targeted intervention for which there is no less
restrictive alternative. LAWRENCE O. GOSTIN,
PUBLIC HEALTH LAW: POWER, DUTY, RESTRAINT 444–
45 (2d ed. 2008). Even as courts tend to defer to the
judgments of legislators or health officials as to the
need for specific public health interventions
(consistent with separation of powers),
constitutional requirements can limit the use of
significant public health powers to control infectious
diseases.

————————————

Communicable diseases will always be a primary
part of the public health agenda, but additional

legal challenges arise from the emergence of chronic conditions. Collectively, these conditions comprise major new foci for public health improvement. Some traditional legal powers, such as testing and screening, are aptly applied to non-communicable conditions. Other powers, like quarantine and isolation, have little use related to chronic conditions. As a result, new legal routes to counter varying threats to community health must be considered. Exploration of these paths begins in Chapter 5.

CHAPTER 5
ADDRESSING CHRONIC CONDITIONS

While communicable diseases discussed in Chapter 4 comprise considerable public health efforts, greater impacts on population health in the 21st century have emanated from chronic conditions. Sensational diseases like EVD, avian flu or HIV/AIDS grab the public's attention as to how public health authorities intervene, but heart disease, cancers, diabetes, and other conditions are the real killers across society. These 2 types of conditions, communicable and chronic, are often intertwined. The heavy focus on controlling EVD in West Africa over multiple months, for example, strips resources away from other public health measures to address chronic (and other communicable) conditions, leading to deleterious impacts on populations. As Harvard professor Dr. Paul Farmer noted in June 2015, "There are more people who are going to die from Ebola, but not have Ebola." Betsy McKay, *Ebola Casts A Long Shadow*, WALL ST. J., June 5, 2015, at A1.

Though defying precise definition, chronic conditions are at the source of millions of deaths in the U.S. and contribute to massive disability among the living. Chronic conditions may be caused by multiple factors, but they share a common facet: they are often preventable. Assessing how law can be a tool in the fight against avoidable morbidity and mortality stemming from chronic illnesses requires a close examination of the scope and limits of public health efforts to alter individual and population-based behaviors.

A.   CHRONIC CONDITIONS—DEFINED

Unlike communicable conditions, most chronic conditions are not transferred directly between humans or from other vectors to humans. Beyond this, defining chronic conditions is subject to interpretation. Richard A. Goodman et al., *Defining and Measuring Chronic Conditions: Imperatives for Research, Policy, Program, and Practice*, 10 PREVENTING CHRONIC DISEASE E66 (2013).

Chronic conditions are generally characterized by their "uncertain etiology, multiple risk factors, . . . long latency period, . . . prolonged course of illness, noncontagious origin, functional impairment or disability, and incurability." Matthew McKenna & Janet L. Collins, *Current Issues and Challenges in Chronic Disease Control, in* PATRICK L. REMINGTON ET AL., CHRONIC DISEASE EPIDEMIOLOGY AND CONTROL   1–24   (2d   ed.   2010).   These characterizations, however, do not necessarily clarify what conditions are included and those that are not.

DHHS defines chronic illnesses generally as those "conditions that last a year or more and require ongoing medical attention and/or limit activities of daily living." DHHS, MULTIPLE CHRONIC CONDITIONS: A STRATEGIC FRAMEWORK 2 (2010). The National Center for Health Statistic defines chronic illnesses as including conditions that are not cured once acquired or present for 3 months or longer. Concerning infants, any condition present since birth is categorized as chronic. NAT'L CTR. FOR HEALTH STATISTICS; *Definition of "Condition,"* 486–7 app. (2011). Under these conceptions, chronic conditions include heart disease, many cancers, diabetes, and clinical depression, but not the common cold or temporary injuries.

No matter how defined, the health care costs and public health impacts of physical or mental chronic conditions in the U.S. are staggering. Chronic illnesses are the nation's leading contributor to death and disability. According to CDC, 50% of all adults have at least 1 such condition (and nearly ½ of them have multiple conditions); 26% of the American population is limited in their daily activities by these conditions; and 70% of all deaths annually are attributable to chronic conditions. Nearly 75% of health care costs each year are devoted to their treatment. CDC, CHRONIC DISEASES AND HEALTH PROMOTION (2013). Worse yet, "[t]he number and proportion of Americans living with chronic conditions [are] increasing" as the population ages. By 2030 Johns Hopkins professor Gerry Anderson predicts that over 170 million Americans will have multiple chronic conditions. GERARD ANDERSON, CHRONIC CARE: MAKING THE CASE FOR ONGOING CARE 9 (2010).

While the types and impacts of chronic conditions vary by population (e.g., children, adults, elderly), major examples include:

- *Heart disease*—Nearly ¼ of U.S. deaths annually (610,000) are caused by heart disease. CDC, *Heart Disease Fact Sheet* (Feb., 19, 2015). Costs of health care services, medications, and lost productivity related to coronary heart disease alone exceeded $108 billion in 2011. Paul A. Heidenreich et al., *Forecasting the Future of Cardiovascular Disease in the U.S.*, 123 CIRCULATION 933 (2011).

- *Cancers*—Even though the definition of cancer is constantly evolving as scientists learn more about its properties, its collective impact on human health is incredible. *See* Tara Parker-Pope, *Scientists Urge Narrower Rules to Define Cancer*, N.Y. TIMES, July 30, 2013, at A1. In general, "cancer" refers to a wide array of illnesses involving the development of abnormal cells that can divide rapidly and infiltrate and destroy bodily tissues. Mayo Clinic Staff, *Cancer*, MAYO CLINIC (May 23, 2015). In 2013, over 1.66 million new cases of cancer arose in the U.S., with projected deaths of 580,350, many by lung cancers caused by smoking (228,190). Rebecca Siegel et al., *Cancer Statistics 2013*, 63 CA: CANCER J. FOR CLINICIANS 1, 11–30 (2013).

- *Diabetes*—Type 1 and 2 diabetes affect 29.1 million people (9.3% of Americans). Over 1.7 million people age 20 years or over were newly diagnosed with diabetes in 2012. In addition to requiring daily monitoring and management for many patients, diabetes is also the leading cause of kidney failure, non-traumatic lower limb amputations, and new cases of blindness among adults. CDC, NATIONAL DIABETES STATISTIC REPORT (2014).

• *Alzheimer Disease*—Up to 5 million Americans are living with Alzheimer disease and face an average of 3–9 years between diagnosis and death. At least 1 study estimated that over 500,000 deaths in 2010 were attributable to this spectrum of diseases (which is over 5 times greater than numbers reported via official death certificates). If this study is accurate, Alzheimer disease was actually the 3rd leading cause of death in the U.S. in 2010. Bryan D. James, et al., *Contribution of Alzheimer Disease to Mortality in the U.S.*, 82 NEUROLOGY 1045 (2014).

Additional chronic conditions with catastrophic effects on the population's health include arthritis, asthma, chronic obstructive pulmonary disease (COPD), depression, epilepsy, glaucoma, hemophilia, hypertension, osteoporosis, post-traumatic stress disorder (PTSD), and stroke.

B.   CAUSES OF CHRONIC CONDITIONS

The causes of chronic conditions are as diverse as the conditions themselves. Contributing factors include genetics, stress, occupation, socioeconomic status, environmental exposures, adverse medical events, and lack of access to public health or health care services.

Dietary factors are also at play in relation to the proliferation of these conditions. Three of the 4 primary modifiable health risk behaviors at the source of most chronic conditions relate to what Americans consume. These 3 behaviors are poor nutrition, tobacco use, and excessive alcohol consumption (physical inactivity is the 4th). Regular ingestion and use of what I like to call "consumable vices," including tobacco, alcohol, sugar, salt, caffeine, nicotine, and high-fat foods, contribute significantly to the development of chronic diseases. *See* James G. Hodge, Jr. et al., *The Consumable Vice: Caffeine, Public Health, and the Law*, 27 J. CONTEMP. HEALTH L. & POL'Y 76 (2010); DAVID A. KESSLER, THE END OF OVEREATING: TAKING CONTROL OF THE INSATIABLE AMERICAN APPETITE (2009).

CDC suggests that poor dietary choices coupled with low levels of physical activity are the leading causes of death annually in the U.S. This finding comports with major increases in rates of obesity among children, adolescents, and adults over the past 3 decades. When CDC first began to measure national obesity rates in 1966, approximately 13% of adults were considered obese and 4% of kids were considered overweight. By 2010, using similar criteria, nearly 35% of American adults are obese, and 33% of children and adolescents are obese or overweight. James G. Hodge, Jr. et al., *New*

Frontiers in Obesity Control: Innovative Public Health Legal Interventions, 5 DUKE FORUM FOR L. & SOC. CHANGE 1 (2013); Cynthia L. Ogden et al., *Prevalence of Childhood and Adult Obesity in the U.S., 2011–2012,* 311 JAMA 806 (2014).

Absent changes, the future of Americans' battle with obesity is bleak. The Trust for America's Health (TFAH) projected in 2012 that adult obesity rates would climb to 44% by 2030, costing up to $66 billion in direct health care costs and $580 billion in lost economic productivity per year. TFAH, F AS IN FAT: HOW OBESITY THREATENS AMERICA'S FUTURE 28 (2012). Only recently have public health officials recognized small declines in obesity prevalence. In August 2013, CDC reported that obesity rates among preschool-age children from poor families fell based on 2008–2011 data from nearly 20 jurisdictions — "the first time a major government report has shown a consistent pattern of decline for low-income children after decades of rising rates." Sabrina Tavernise, *Poor Children Show a Decline in Obesity Rate,* N.Y. TIMES, Aug. 7, 2013, at A1. Still, obesity data consistently reveal that American's battle with obesity is getting worse. *See, e.g.,* Ariana Eunjung Cha, *America's Getting Even Fatter: Startling Growth in Obesity Over Past 20 Years.* WASH. POST. (June 22, 2015). Researchers Lin Yang and Graham Colditz found that 75% of men and 67% of women ages 25 and older are now overweight or obese, reflecting double-digit increases for both sexes based on data 20 years ago. Lin Yang & Graham A. Colditz, *Prevalence of Overweight and*

Obesity in the United States, 2007–2012. JAMA INTERNAL MED. (June 22, 2015).

Tobacco products used regularly by nearly 20% of Americans are a major contributing factor to over 480,000 annual deaths in the U.S. Ahmed Jamal et. al., *Current Cigarette Smoking Among Adults— U.S., 2005–2013,* 63 MMWR 1108 (2014). Even though fewer young persons may be turning to tobacco products, expanding use of e-cigarettes raises additional and new risks of chronic conditions. Over 13% of teens reportedly tried e-cigarettes in 2014, a ten-fold increase from similar figures in 2011. Liz Szabo, *CDC Report: More Teens Toke From E-cigarettes,* USA TODAY, April 17, 2015, at 2A. Communities like Tempe, Arizona have passed ordinances to prohibit the use of e-cigarettes in public places. TEMPE, AZ., CODE ch. 22, art. II § 2–43 (2015).

Other consumable vices besides tobacco present significant health risks as well. Excessive alcohol consumption contributes to over 50 different diseases and injuries that in sum constitute the 3rd leading preventable cause of death. CDC, ALCOHOL USE AND HEALTH (2013). Many Americans' high salt diets raise substantially the risk of coronary heart disease, stroke, heart attack, and kidney damage. Theodore A. Kotchen, *Salt in Health and Disease—a Delicate Balance,* 368 NEW ENG. J. MED. 1229 (2013).

Recent studies concerning the impacts of over-consumption of sugar in American's diets led 1 observer to conclude that "[s]ugar is indeed toxic."

Mark Bittman, Editorial, *It's The Sugar, Folks*, N.Y. TIMES, Feb. 28, 2013, at A23. Researchers have conservatively linked ingestion of sugar, largely through beverages, to 25,000 deaths in the U.S. in 2010 (and 180,000 deaths globally). Gitanjali M. Singh et al., *Mortality Due to SSB Consumption: A Global, Regional, and National Comparative Risk Assessment,* 127 CIRCULATION AMP22 (2013). In another global study, researchers conclusively tie increased ingestion of sugar with higher rates of diabetes, independent of obesity rates. Sanjay Basu et al., *The Relationship of Sugar to Population-Level Diabetes Prevalence: An Econometric Analysis of Repeated Cross-Sectional Data,* 8 PLoS ONE e57873 (2013).

In 2014, researchers compared thousands of adults who consumed 17–21% of their daily intake from added sugars to those who consumed about 8% over 2 decades. They found that the group consuming more sugar had a 38% higher risk of cardiovascular disease mortality even after controlling for overall diet quality. This suggests that the risks of added sugar intake are independent from the effects of a generally unhealthy diet. Quanhe Yang, PhD, et al., *Added Sugar Intake and Cardiovascular Disease Mortality Among U.S. Adults,* 174 JAMA INTERNAL MED. 516 (2014).

C.   LEGAL AUTHORITIES

Chronic conditions differ from communicable ones in many ways, but similar public health powers can be used to address their incidence. *See, e.g.,* Wendy C. Perdue et al., *A Legal Framework for Preventing Cardiovascular Disease*, 29 AM. J. PREVENTIVE MED. 139 (2005). Public health laws authorizing counseling, testing, screening, and treatment are used extensively to counteract chronic conditions. Federal and state recommendations for testing and screening of various cancers, often based on guidance from medical and public health organizations, are routinely followed by health care practitioners and patients.

Even vaccinations may help stymie the rate of some chronic conditions. For example, to the extent that HPV vaccine deters infection, individuals can avoid the onset of related cancers of the reproductive organs and other parts of the body. As a result, CDC recommends HPV vaccines for boys and girls beginning at ages 11–12. Mark H. Sawyer et al., *Recommendations on the Use of Quadrivalent HPV in Males—ACIP, 2011*, 60 MMWR 1705, 1707 (Dec. 23, 2011). Though safe and efficacious, uptake of HPV vaccinations nationally has been curtailed by political and other views focused on the proper age in which an STI-related threat should be curtailed via vaccine. *See* James Colgrove et al., *HPV Vaccination Mandates—Lawmaking amid Political and Scientific Controversy*, 363 NEW ENG. J. MED. 785, 787 (2010); Shannon Stokely et al., *HPV Coverage Among Adolescent Girls, 2007–2012, and Postlicensure Vaccine Safety Monitoring, 2006–2013—U.S.*, 62 MMWR 591, 594 (July 26, 2013).

Education campaigns alert the public to risks (sometimes through graphic illustrations) of chronic conditions related to tobacco, alcohol, or drug use. A New York City health department education campaign in 2009 targeted the ingestion of SSBs through advertisements depicting consumers gulping down thick globs of fat. Sewell Chan, *New Targets in the Fat Fight: Soda and Juice*, N.Y. TIMES, Sept. 1, 2009, at A22. Additional discussion of public health education is provided in Chapter 8.

Of course, not all public health powers used to prevent communicable diseases apply to chronic conditions. Social distancing measures (e.g., isolation, quarantine, curfews) often lack utility (and constitutionality) when applied to most chronic conditions. Other public health powers are relied on to: (1) alter individual and group behaviors contributing to the onset of chronic illness; (2) change environmental impacts that lend to their proliferation; or (3) prevent factors in which such illnesses may arise or result in significant harms to individuals or the public. Core among these legal strategies are the powers to tax and spend; regulatory laws directly governing the environment and private sector; and anti-discrimination protections. Each of these legal areas is discussed below.

1.   THE POWER TO TAX

Governments' powers to tax involve more than raising revenue. These powers are used strategically and lawfully to change or alter behaviors, often in the interests of preventing or treating chronic conditions. The power to tax necessarily includes the power to spend, including setting significant conditions on how governmental resources may be used when doled out to public or private entities (discussed below). At its core, governments' "power over the purse" allows it considerable discretion in collecting and disbursing individual and corporate resources for the betterment of society. ERWIN CHEMERINSKY, CONSTITUTIONAL LAW: PRINCIPLES AND POLICIES 279–80 (4th ed. 2011).

While each level of government has some authority to tax, the federal government's taxing prowess (pursuant to U.S. CONST. art. I, § 8) is considerable. Particularly since the institution of national income taxes in 1913, Congress has used its taxing authority extensively. ROY G. BLAKEY & GLADYS C. BLAKEY, THE FEDERAL INCOME TAX 71 (2006). As Chief Justice Roberts noted in 2012 in the Supreme Court's decision on the constitutionality of the ACA, the power to tax includes the power to "affect individual conduct." *National Fed. of Ind. Bus. v. Sebelius,* 132 S. Ct. 2566, 2596 (2012).

So long as it acts consistent with principles of federalism and individual rights, Congress can (and regularly does) use its taxing power in the interests of the public's health. Related to the prevention and control of chronic illnesses, for example, the federal government (and many states) tax products like tobacco to help discourage their consumption. DHHS & CDC, REDUCING TOBACCO USE: A REPORT

OF THE SURGEON GENERAL 337 (2000). They do so based on the proven economic theory that to the extent taxes substantially raise the price of cigarettes, people will smoke less, and their overall health and risk of developing chronic conditions will improve. *Id.* at 359. On this same basis, some states and localities have considered taxing junk foods or high-calorie beverages to limit consumption. Michael F. Jacobson & Kelly D. Brownell, *Small Taxes on Soft Drinks and Snack Foods to Promote Health,* 90 AM. J. PUB. HEALTH 854 (2000).

In 2015, the Navajo Nation (population ~175,000) approved implementation of a 2% tax on all junk food sold on its reservation spanning across Arizona, New Mexico, and Utah. Revenues are to be devoted to healthy eating and other public health programs. Implementation of the Healthy Diné Nation Act, NAVAJO NATION CODE ANN. tit. 24 (2014), also eliminates a 5% sales tax on healthy foods. Sabrina Toppa, *This Place Just Became the First Part of the U.S. to Impose a Tax on Junk Food,* TIME (Mar. 30, 2015).

In 2014, Berkeley, California passed a tax on SSBs, including a 1¢ per ounce tax on soda. Laura Mandaro, *Nation's First Soda Tax is Passed,* USA TODAY (Nov. 2014). Berkeley's ordinance assimilates some of the same provisions of Mexico's SSB tax which some assert has helped to lower national consumption. *See* Eliza Barclay, *Mexico's Sugary Drink Tax Makes a Dent in Consumption, Study Claims,* NPR (June 19, 2015). Some evidence suggests that increasing taxes on SSBs will directly lower children's BMIs, saving billions on health care costs nationally while also generating considerable state and local tax revenues. *See* Jane E. Brody, *Prudent Ways to Fight Childhood Obesity*, N.Y. TIMES, June 23, 2015, at D7.

The flip-side of direct taxation to change consumer behaviors is the use of tax subsidies or credits to encourage product purchases or other market factors in the interests of the public's health. Congress, for example, created positive tax incentives for individuals to purchase individual health insurance through the ACA. By encouraging employees to obtain insurance, access to preventive and other health services may be expanded with direct public health benefits.

Raucous political debates over the passage and implementation of the ACA, and many other tax-related measures in Congress and across the states, reflect political realities in creating new tax schemes to positively change consumer behaviors. The public and its legislative representatives often disdain new tax proposals, especially when government attempts to change behaviors of autonomous individuals in paternalistic ways. Yet, when politically satiable, government's use of its direct power to tax to address chronic conditions is virtually without limit.

2.   THE POWER TO SPEND

Collecting revenues through taxes also allows governments to disburse resources in ways that promote the "general welfare," including communal health. And whenever government, particularly at the federal level, has money to spend, it may set conditions on its receipt. Through its constitutional powers to spend, Congress may lawfully impose a myriad of conditions on the disbursement of federal funds to which tribal, state, or local governments (or private entities) must adhere. CHEMERINSKY, CONSTITUTIONAL LAW at 285–86. Of course, any public or private entity can always reject specific conditions attached to funding streams, but they will lose access to sometimes significant public health resources.

Examples of Congress' use of its spending power to address chronic (or other) conditions are broad. They range from the setting of conditions on the receipt of basic health care resources (e.g., Medicaid) to specific allotments for public health surveillance (e.g., HIV/AIDS reporting, discussed in Chapter 7) and research on chronic conditions like obesity and Alzheimer disease. Though Congress' power is extensive, the Supreme Court has set some limits on the use of conditional spending, particularly between federal and state governments.

In *South Dakota v. Dole*, 483 U.S. 203 (1987), the Court approved Congress' condition that states seeking select highway transportation funds upgrade their drinking age to 21 (largely to reduce alcohol-related crashes and fatalities on federal highways). Rejecting a federalism-based challenge, Chief Justice Rehnquist clarified that Congress' exercise of its conditional spending power is constitutional as applied to the states so long as:

(a) it serves some general purpose (for which the Court is typically deferential to Congress' stated purposes consistent with principles of separation of powers);

(b) the choices and conditions are clear and unambiguous;

(c) the conditions are related to some national project or program;

(d) states are not induced to engage in unconstitutional acts (e.g., use of federal funds to discriminate against persons on the basis of race). In *Agency for Int'l Dev. v. Alliance for Open Soc'y Int'l,* 133 S. Ct. 2321 (2013), the Court struck down an "anti-prostitution pledge," which prohibited the issuance of HIV-related grants to recipients who did not affirmatively state their opposition to prostitution and sex trafficking. Such conditions violated the free speech rights of recipients under the 1st Amendment; and

(e) states are not compelled to accept the funds. *Dole,* 483 U.S. at 207–11.

For years following the Supreme Court's decision in *Dole,* virtually no Congressional exercise of its conditional spending power was adjudged by courts to "compel" states to accept federal funds. States always have the option of rejecting federal dollars if they do not like the terms underlying a conditional spending proposal. However, in the Court's decision on the constitutionality of the ACA, Congress' plan to add millions of new beneficiaries to the Medicaid program (which provides health services to largely low-income families) was rejected. *Sebelius*, 132 S. Ct. at 2604–05.

The ACA provided each state the option of expanding its Medicaid population to include a larger proportion of low-income adults by 2014, or else face the loss of all its federal Medicaid funds. In response to states' federalism-based challenges, Chief Justice Roberts opined that this choice unconstitutionally compelled states to comply due in large part to (a) the enormous sums at stake if states chose not to expand their programs; and (b) a significant "shift in kind, not merely degree" of the original purposes of the Medicaid program via expansion. *Id.* at 2604–06. Though the Court rejected the ACA's compelled conditions, it crafted a constitutional compromise. The ACA's Medicaid deal would survive if the Centers for Medicare and Medicaid Services (CMS), part of DHHS, conditions only the states' receipt of expansion funds (instead of their entire Medicaid budget) on their willingness to extend their Medicaid populations.

By setting greater limits on Congress' use of its spending power to condition receipt of federal funds, the *Sebelius* case dampened Congress' ability to extend access to basic health insurance to more Americans, a primary public health objective of the ACA. *See, e.g.,* Nicole Huberfeld et al., *Plunging Into Endless Difficulties: Medicaid and Coercion in [NFIB v. Sebelius]*, 93 Bos. L. Rev. 1 (2013).

Without the threat of losing their entire Medicaid budget, 22 states have expressed unwillingness to expand their programs (even though the federal government pays the bulk of the costs for new Medicaid enrollees over several years). *22 States Are Refusing to Expand Medicaid. Here's What That Means for Their Residents*, WHITE HOUSE (Jan. 27, 2015). As a result, millions of Americans may continue to be denied access to publicly-funded, basic health services, including preventive care. The Court's decision, however, also creates new possibilities for state and local governments to challenge other federal public health spending programs, including long-standing environmental laws, on similar grounds that the terms of receipt of federal funds are onerous and unconstitutional.

3.   THE POWER TO REGULATE

The potential to influence individual and governmental choices through the powers to tax and spend is commanding. Yet, government also has the power to directly regulate private entities and individuals consistent with prevention and control strategies related to chronic conditions. As noted in Chapter 3, so long as legislative bodies provide articulable standards for executive agencies to regulate, federal, tribal, state, and local public health officials can administer and enforce laws to further the public's health.

Through public health regulation, for example, government can:

- Ban or limit the sale of products deemed harmful to the public's health (among other purposes). James G. Hodge, Jr. & Megan A. Scanlon, *The Legal Anatomy of Product Bans to Protect the Public's Health*, 23 ANNALS OF HEALTH LAW 20 (2014). Following discovery of the harmful effects of lead largely on child development, its removal from paint, gasoline, and other products is now mandated. Shana R. Cappell, *Lead Paint Poisoning and the Resource Conservation and Recovery Act*, 35 COLUM. J.L. & SOC. PROBS. 175, 178 (2002). In 2015 multiple states considered regulatory bans of "palcohol," a new powdered form of alcohol proposed for market release following federal review and approval. Rachel Abrams, *Powdered Alcohol Meets Resistance in the U.S. Before it Ever Comes to Market*, N.Y. TIMES (Apr. 3, 2015).

- Limit possession of products that may harm specific populations. Federal and all state governments prohibit persons under the age of 18 from purchasing tobacco products. In 2015, Hawaii raised the minimum age to purchase tobacco products to 21. S.B. 1030, 28th Leg., 2015 (Haw. 2015). Researchers found that 75% of adults favored increasing the legal minimum age to purchase all tobacco products from 18 to 21 years old. Tanya Basu, *Majority of Americans Agree You*

Should be 21 to Buy Tobacco, TIME, July 7, 2015. Consequently, other states besides Hawaii and localities are also considering raising the age for lawful tobacco purchases to 21. Joseph Netto, *Raise the Smoking Age? Report Predicts Big Health Benefits if We Do*, CNN (Mar. 13, 2015);

• Control how products are manufactured or sold. In some places, for example, the sale of alcohol is restricted to certain locations during set days and hours. *See, e.g.*, S.C. CODE ANN. § 61-6-1500(A)(1)(a). Many states that legalize the sale of marijuana for medicinal uses set narrow manufacturing and licensing requirements to help assure the product does not find its way to unlawful purchasers or users (in violation of the federal Controlled Substances Act, 21 U.S.C. §§ 801–971 (2012)). MARIJUANA POLICY PROJECT, KEY ASPECTS OF STATE AND D.C. MEDICAL MARIJUANA LAWS (2014).

• Require entities to create or sell products in conformity with public health mandates. As discussed in Chapter 8, the ACA requires chain restaurants across the U.S. to post calorie counts for their menu items similar to practices implemented already in several jurisdictions. With ready access to calorie data at the point of sale, consumers can make healthier choices and

> potentially lower their overall calorie consumption;

- Set meaningful restrictions on consumer uses of products in public places. Federal, state, and local smoke-free laws over the past several decades have targeted public environments from cars to planes to public squares to eradicate public exposures to second-hand smoke (*see, e.g.,* Amy R. Confair et al., *Factors Affecting Successful Enactment of Legislation Prohibiting Smoking in Cars with Children,* 53 JURIMETRICS J. 375 (2013)); and

- Create safer workplaces that reduce exposures to harmful elements or practices. Federal and state regulations governing coal mines have significantly reduced the incidence of "black lung" deaths. Federal workplace standards issued via the Occupational Safety and Health Administration (OSHA) have not only helped reduce injuries (discussed in Chapter 6), but also lowered chronic conditions through workplace safety initiatives.

These notable examples are merely illustrative. Governmental regulatory powers to address chronic (and other) conditions extend into multiple facets of public and private life. Though capable of heavy-handed enforcement, public health agencies typically seek cooperative and contributive efforts among public and private actors to conceive, draft, and implement regulatory controls. In general, public health regulations are lawful so long as executive agencies act within the scope of their delegated powers, adhere to procedural requirements in creating and enforcing regulatory provisions, have legitimate public health support for the need to regulate, and do not otherwise offend constitutional or other principles of law. Particularly at the local level, complying with this latter requirement can be dubious.

In April 2011, for example, the Cleveland City Council enacted an anti-obesity ordinance to ban trans fats in foods served in restaurants and other food shops. A few months later, the Ohio legislature amended state law to prohibit municipalities from regulating the ingredients used by food servers. The net effect of the Ohio legislature's amendment of state statute was to preempt Cleveland's trans fats ordinance. The City sued the State claiming that the amendment unconstitutionally stripped the City of its home rule (discussed in Chapter 2). After the trial court decided in favor of the City, the Ohio Court of Appeals affirmed that the legislature's amendment unlawfully overrode Cleveland's home rule. Consequently, it reinstated the City's trans-fat ordinance. *City of Cleveland v. State*, 989 N.E.2d 1072 (Ohio Ct. App. 2013).

4.   ADDRESSING DISABILITY BIAS

Many chronic conditions are by definition disabling. Persons who are impaired in their major life activities due to their chronic illness may be entitled to special protections from discrimination under the federal Americans with Disabilities Act (ADA), 42 U.S.C. §§ 12101–12213 (2012), and additional laws at the federal, state, and local levels. Implemented pursuant to Congress' interstate commerce powers, the ADA protects persons with actual disabilities as well as those who are simply regarded by others as having a disability. *Id.* at § 12102(1). Collectively, disability laws help to eliminate discrimination against some persons with chronic conditions in the workplace and many other settings.

While the dimensions of individual disability protections via the ADA are beyond the scope of this text, disability laws can contribute to the reduction of chronic illness in key ways. ADA requirements to support reasonable accommodations in many settings directly benefit persons with disabilities, but also have reciprocal benefits for others. Building redesigns (e.g., to include elevators or lifts) and retrofitting of community plans (e.g., to include ramps or paved trails) consistent with the ADA have transformed the built environment across the country, leading to safer communities that help reduce injuries and diminish chronic conditions.

Universal precautions in health care settings, ushered in part via the ADA's requirements to accommodate patients and HCWs with disabilities, have lowered infectious disease transmission, improved care for chronic conditions, and improved the efficiency of care in some instances. In 1 survey, over 42% of U.S. businesses report enhanced workplace safety based in part on ADA-influenced improvements. Helen A. Schartz et al., *Workplace Accommodations: Evidence Based Outcomes*, 27 WORK 345, 349 (2006).

Protecting disabled workers buttresses support for indoor smoking bans to accommodate persons with asthma or other conditions, as well as improve air quality for all workers. Lainie Rutkow et al., *Banning Second-hand Smoke in Indoor Public Places Under the ADA: A Legal and Public Health Imperative*, 40 CONN. L. REV. 409, 409 (2007). Telecommuting options to assist disabled workers under the ADA help reduce commute times, lower accident rates, decrease the spread of infectious diseases, and minimize work-related stress. Brianne M. Sullenger, *Telecommuting: A Reasonable Accommodation under the ADA as Technology Advances*, 19 REGENT U. L. REV. 537, 542–43 (2006).

Disability protections addressing unwarranted discrimination, however, may be contravened by other public health laws that directly or indirectly reflect bias related to the causes of chronic conditions, or persons who suffer from them. For example, anti-tobacco policies at the federal and state levels authorize discrimination against smokers and other tobacco consumers in the interest of protecting the public's health. Smokers may not light up in many public places, can be denied life insurance outright or charged more for health insurance, or be restricted in their employment options (or not hired at all for that matter). Each of these policies have underlying legal support grounded in protecting the public's health directly or indirectly (by discouraging smoking). Yet persons with chronic illnesses, including many smokers, are largely disadvantaged.

Persons who use illicit drugs may be addicted to these substances and, consequently, are greatly limited in their major life activities. However, the ADA expressly excludes illicit drug use among those items classifiable as disabilities. 42 U.S.C. § 12114 (2013). Few may agree that users of heroin, cocaine, crystal meth, or other dangerous drugs are entitled to disability rights, but policies related to their treatment are beginning to change. Once castigated and charged via criminal courts, users of addictive drugs are now provided options to avoid full prosecution so long as they participate in drug treatment programs. In Connecticut, courts are statutorily authorized to order offenders who are drug- or alcohol-dependent into treatment in lieu of prosecution or incarceration. CONN. GEN. STAT. §§ 17a-692 to 17a-701 (2013).

In June 2013, the American Medical Association (AMA) called for a reclassification of obesity as a disease. Andrew Pollack, *A.M.A. Recognizes Obesity as a Disease,* N.Y. TIMES, June 18, 2013. If broadly adopted, this might help qualify all forms of obesity, like its associated condition, Type II diabetes, for disability protections and related health insurance coverage. Currently only "severe obesity" (when body weight is more than 100% over norm) may qualify as a disability under the ADA. EEOC COMPLIANCE MANUAL § 902.2(c)(5)(ii) (2009).

For now, obesity remains a major public health target with some policies having potentially deleterious impacts on obese or overweight persons. Consider proposals in some states or localities to (a) authorize charging obese persons more for their health insurance premiums (*see, e.g.,* TENN. CODE ANN. § 56–7–3013 (2013) (insurers can establish premium schedules based on obesity); or (b) set workplace wellness bonuses based on levels of physical activity (*see, e.g.,* MASS. GEN. LAWS ANN. tit. IX, ch. 62 § 6N (2013) (establishing a $10,000 tax credit for employers seeking to create a wellness program); MISS. CODE ANN. § 41–97–9 (2012) (creating model program for employee wellness including incentives).

Each of these incentive-driven policies may negatively impact persons who are overweight or obese to the extent they are charged more for similar services, cannot participate fully to garner benefits, or simply lose opportunities because of their weight. Disability protections may prevent some of these impacts (e.g., ADA employment protections apply to persons simply "regarded as" having a disability). Conversely, some public health laws and policies represent an affront to equality of persons with conditions that are, or will soon be, chronic.

Addressing chronic conditions through law requires creative options and resulting trade-offs. Implementing public health laws to deter individual behaviors that lead to chronic illnesses seems overly paternalistic to some. For others, application of such laws is unfair related to their own conditions, the onset of which may not be of their own doing. Still, at the source of government regulatory approaches related to chronic conditions is the laudatory goal of preventing excess morbidity and mortality. Carrying out this same objective concerning injury prevention necessitates the extensive use of additional legal tools, namely civil litigation and criminal enforcement, as discussed in Chapter 6.

CHAPTER 6

MITIGATING THE INCIDENCE & SEVERITY OF INJURIES & OTHER HARMS

In addition to addressing communicable and chronic conditions, a 3rd major prong of the underlying mission of public health agencies, advocacy organizations, and other partners concerns preventing injuries and related harms or deaths. Public health practitioners define injuries broadly as "any unintentional or intentional [bodily] damage ... resulting from acute exposure to thermal, mechanical, electrical, or chemical energy or from the absence of such essentials as heat or oxygen." NAT'L COMM. FOR INJURY PREVENTION & CONTROL, INJURY PREVENTION: MEETING THE CHALLENGE 4 (1989).

Coupled with these acute harms are long-term, chronic injuries related to repeated exposures to products like tobacco, alcohol, or drugs. Injuries arise from multiple, additional sources, some of which are unintentional (e.g., vehicle crashes) and others which are not (e.g., homicides). The collective impact of injuries on the population each year is significant, as explained in section A, below.

The public health tragedy underlying most injuries, harms, and related deaths is that they are nearly all preventable through changes in behaviors, products, and the environment via public health education (*see* Chapter 8), engineering, and the law. Many types of laws, including themes discussed already in Part 2 (e.g., screening, treatment, powers to tax and spend, regulations) are used to prevent injuries and deaths. Two additional areas of law to prevent and control injuries and harms in the U.S. include tort and criminal law.

Deleterious practices leading to unintentional injuries are intrinsically tied to "tort" laws (addressing civil wrongs). Through actual or threatened tort litigation, the design, manufacture, sale, and use of an array of products including food, drugs, guns, tobacco, toys, and vehicles have changed to prevent injuries. How tort actions lead to product changes over time in the interests of consumer safety and the public's health are discussed further in section B.

Criminal law presents a different and controversial approach to address injuries and related deaths. By penalizing individual or corporate behaviors that contribute to injuries, the underlying public health premise of criminal law (and tort law for that matter) is that they can deter injurious acts. This premise may be suspect. Take, for example, strict laws prohibiting illicit drug possession to protect individuals from potentially fatal drug overdoses. Persons prosecuted under these laws may receive what some deem as just punishments, namely criminal fines and incarceration. Yet, without additional interventions (e.g., drug rehabilitation and treatment programs), these punishments may (1) negatively impact their health and their families' well-being, particularly among lower socio-economic groups, and (2) fail to treat the underlying addiction. The extent to which such laws deter others from similar behaviors is often presumed, but not always well-known. As discussed in section C, the traditional use of criminal law to punish behaviors that cause or contribute injuries to oneself or others is evolving consistent with new understandings of the public health consequences of these laws.

A.   PRIMARY SOURCES OF INJURIES, HARMS & DEATHS

Sources and impacts of preventable injuries, harms, and deaths in the U.S. are classifiable in 3 major areas: (1) occupational or environmental hazards, (2) products, and (3) risky behaviors. In 2013, occupational hazards (e.g., fires, falls, harmful substances, equipment) across a swath of industries led to more than 3 million nonfatal injuries and 4,585 deaths. BLS, EMPLOYER REPORTED WORKPLACE INJURIES AND ILLNESSES: 2013 (2014); BLS, REVISIONS TO THE 2013 CENSUS OF FATAL OCCUPATIONAL INJURIES COUNTS (2015).

Vehicular crashes are a leading cause of preventable injuries and deaths outside the workplace. CDC estimates 2.5 million adults required emergency treatment following such crashes in 2012 alone. Gwen Bergen, et. al., *Vital Signs: Health Burden and Medical Costs of Nonfatal Injuries to Motor Vehicle Occupants—U.S., 2012,* 63 MMWR 894 (2014). Transportation-related incidents (including vehicles, buses, trains, subways) caused 37,938 deaths in 2013. DHHS, *Deaths: Final Data for 2013*, 64 NAT'L VITAL STAT. REP. 2 (2015).

Many factors traditionally contribute to vehicular crashes, including alcohol and drug use, highway design, and weather-related hazards. An emerging risk in the 21st century is "distracted driving," related mostly to use of cellular or navigation devices, but also including eating, drinking, grooming, and reading while operating vehicles or other machinery. Various studies show that the risk of being in a vehicle crash while using a cellular device (even hands-free devices) approximates the same risk as driving drunk. David L. Strayer et al., *A Comparison of the Cell Phone Driver and the Drunk Driver,* 48 HUMAN FACTORS 381, 390 (2006). The National Safety Council estimated that 24% of vehicle crashes in 2010 involved text messaging or talking on a cell phone. NAT'L SAFETY COUNCIL, ANNUAL ESTIMATE OF CELL PHONE CRASHES 2010 (2012). A 2015 study of over 1,200 drivers in Texas found that persons under the age 25 are 4 times more likely to use a cellular device while driving than other people. The study authors also report that female drivers are 63% more likely to speak on their phones than males. Michelle L. Wilkinson, et al., *Prevalence and Correlates of Cell Phone Use Among Texas Drivers,* 2 PREVENTATIVE MED. REP. 149, 150 (2015). In 2013, 3,154 people were killed in crashes involving distracted driving (10% of all fatal crashes); 445 died while the driver was using a cell phone at the time of the crash. U.S. DEP'T OF

TRANSP., TRAFFIC SAFETY FACTS RESEARCH NOTE: DISTRACTED DRIVING 2013 1 (2015).

Products used or consumed regularly also pose substantial risks of injury to human health. In 2011 alone, for example, an estimated 262,300 toy-related injuries were treated in emergency departments nationally. YONGLING TU & CSPC, TOY-RELATED DEATHS AND INJURIES CALENDAR YEAR 2011 3 (2012). In addition to the risks of food-borne illnesses (discussed in Chapter 4) and "consumable vices" like alcohol, caffeine, drugs, sugar, salt, and high-fat foods (discussed in Chapter 5), foreign objects (e.g., bones, glass, plastics, shells, stones) found in packaged and served foods injure thousands per year. Frederick N. Hyman et al., *FDA Surveillance of the Role of Foreign Objects in Foodborne Injuries*, 108 PUB. HEALTH REP. 54, 55 (1993).

Poisons are also a primary threat. In 2013, there were 2,188,013 human exposures reported nationally in the U.S. and 2,113 exposure-related fatalities. James B. Mowry et al., *2013 Annual Report of the American Association of Poison Control Centers' National Poison Data System*, 52 CLINICAL TOXICOLOGY 1032, 1038 (2014). Deaths related to poison exposures, especially among children, were considerably higher in past decades. Reduced death rates may be attributed in large part to the national organization and creation of poison control centers offering rapid emergency information and guidance to callers online and via call centers. THE LEWIN

GROUP, INC., FINAL REPORT ON THE VALUE OF THE POISON CENTER SYSTEM (2012).

Use of illicit and prescription drugs leads to hundreds of thousands of injuries or harms and thousands of deaths each year. In 2011, the number of drug-induced deaths (40,239) exceeded deaths by vehicle crashes nationally. Donna L. Hoyert & Jiaquan Xu, *Deaths: Preliminary Data for 2011,* 61 NAT'L VITAL STAT. REP. 1, 19 (Oct. 2012). Misuse of prescription opioids, such as oxycodone and methadone, have killed more Americans since 2008 than heroin and cocaine combined. Leonard J. Paulozzi et al., *Vital Signs: Overdoses of Prescription Opioid Pain Relievers-U.S., 1999–2008,* 60 MMWR 1487 (Nov. 4, 2011).

The drug, naloxone, temporarily blocks opioid receptors in the brain to restore breathing in overdose patients until emergency medical assistance can be provided. States like Massachusetts have reported reduced death rates due to opioid overdose in communities that have implemented community-based naloxone distribution programs. DRUG POLICY ALLIANCE, EXPANDING ACCESS TO NALOXONE: REDUCING FATAL OVERDOSE, SAVING LIVES 2 (2011); NETWORK FOR PUBLIC HEALTH LAW, LEGAL INTERVENTIONS TO REDUCE OVERDOSE MORTALITY: NALOXONE ACCESS AND GOOD SAMARITAN LAWS 2 (2015).

Injuries and deaths tied to horrific acts of violence are highly-publicized (e.g., shooting rampages at Columbine High School, CO (1999); Virginia Tech University (2007); Aurora, CO (2011); Tucson, AZ

(2011), Newtown, CT (2012), and Charleston, SC (2015)). Behind the headlines, however, are thousands of preventable deaths each year due to individual risky or violent acts, most of which receive little media attention. *See, e.g.*, Wendy E. Parmet, *Valuing the Unidentified: The Potential of Public Health Law*, 53 JURIMETRICS J. 225 (2013). In 2013, over 33,500 deaths resulted from gunshot wounds in the U.S. (far exceeding rates per capita in other industrialized countries). *U.S. Firearm Deaths and Rates per 100,000,* NAT'L CTR. FOR INJURY PREVENTION & CONTROL, CDC (2013). Over 84,000 individuals were treated in emergency departments for nonfatal gunshot wounds that same year. *Overall Firearm Gunshot Nonfatal Injuries and Rates per 100,000,* NAT'L CTR. FOR INJURY PREVENTION & CONTROL, CDC (2013).

Domestic and interpersonal violence, including abuse, stalking, rape, bullying, and suicide, impose additional threats of injury or deaths. One in every 4 women will experience domestic violence and 1.3 million women are victims of physical assault by an intimate partner each year. NAT'L COAL. AGAINST DOMESTIC VIOLENCE, DOMESTIC VIOLENCE FACTS (2007). More than 33% of women and 25% of men in the U.S. experience rape, physical violence, and/or stalking by an intimate partner at some point in their lives. CDC, NATIONAL INTIMATE PARTNER & SEXUAL VIOLENCE SURVEY: 2010 SUMMARY REPORT 2 (Nov. 2011).

Across the U.S., 41,149 persons committed suicide in 2013. DHHS, *Deaths: Final Data for 2013,* 64

NAT'L VITAL STAT. REP. 2 (2015). Public health research shows that suicide rates are higher in states where gun ownership is more prevalent. *See, e.g.,* Matthew Miller et al., *Firearms and Violent Death in the U.S.*, *in* REDUCING GUN VIOLENCE IN AMERICA, at 11; Sabrina Tavernise, *With Guns, Killer and Victim Are Usually Same*, N.Y. TIMES, Feb. 14, 2013, at A1.

In 2013, over 678,000 cases of child abuse and neglect were reported, including 1,484 fatalities of children ages of 0–17 years old. DHHS et al., CHILD MALTREATMENT 2013 21, 54 (2015). Youth violence is the second leading cause of death for people ages 15–24. In 2011, 20% of high school students reported being bullied on school grounds; 16% reported cyber bullying. CDC, UNDERSTANDING YOUTH VIOLENCE: FACT SHEET (2012). That same year, over 700,000 persons between the ages of 10–24 years old received emergency treatment for injuries sustained from physical assaults. CDC, YOUTH VIOLENCE: FACTS AT A GLANCE (2012). According to CDC, nearly 8% of students nationally attempted suicide in 2011. CDC, *Youth Risk Behavior Surveillance—U.S. 2011*, 61 MMWR 1 (June 8, 2012).

Measuring these and other injuries and deaths across the country illustrates the tragic nature of preventable threats to the public's health. Multiple public health legal interventions are used or designed to help mitigate these impacts. As discussed in Chapters 4 and 8, for example, many injuries related to products are prevented through federal and state statutory and regulatory laws that directly intervene to alter the environment (e.g., building safer highways) or limit products or their uses (e.g., through consumer product safety agencies). When these or other legal interventions fail to sufficiently address the threats, or perhaps do not present a viable policy option, 2 additional legal areas may be used to prevent and control injuries, namely tort and criminal law.

B.   ADDRESSING HARMS THROUGH TORT LAW

Tort law encompasses various causes of action for civil wrongs (or "torts") that harm individuals or groups in some compensable way. Tort litigation includes actions brought by individuals or classes of persons for various physical, mental, and psychological harms caused by another's negligent or intentional acts. In most cases, the end result of successful claims in tort is monetary damages that are either *compensatory* (e.g., designed to pay an injured individual for actual costs plus pain and suffering) or *punitive* (e.g., designed to punish specific behaviors that led to individual harm).

Occasionally, damages may also include a court ordering a defendant to (1) pay additional costs for the injured person's litigation expenses, or (2) adjust its practices going forward through the court's power to enjoin, or stop, one's actions. For example, a court may enjoin a governmental agency from selling residences that contain lead-based paint. *See City-Wide Coal. Against Childhood Lead Paint*

Poisoning v. Philadelphia Hous. Auth., 356 F. Supp. 123 (E.D. Pa. 1973).

In many ways, tort law is all about injury prevention. Tort cases constitute a substantial tool for preventing accidental or intentional acts that injure others. *See* Stephen P. Teret, *Litigating for the Public's Health*, 76 AM. J. PUB. HEALTH 1027 (1986). By providing recourse for individuals injured through risky behaviors or dangerous products, tort actions can discourage others from engaging in such behaviors, as well as encourage or require reform in entire industries (e.g., toys, vehicles) in the design, manufacture, or sale of products that may harm consumers. *See* Jon S. Vernick et al., *Role of Litigation in Preventing Product-related Injuries,* 25 EPIDEMIOLOGIC REVS. 90 (2003). These themes are illustrated through tort causes of action grounded in negligence, intentional acts, and strict liability.

1.   NEGLIGENCE

Negligence refers generally to one's failure to conform to a standard of conduct, the consequences of which may result in injury to others. Proving a case of negligence sufficient to recover damages is not as easy. It is not enough to suggest one acted carelessly or without regard for others' safety or health. Rather, a plaintiff must show via a preponderance (> than 50%) of the evidence that (a) there exists a duty of care; (b) which is breached by another; (c) causally resulting in harm; (d) leading to actual damages. Successful claims in negligence thus include a duty, breach, causation, and damages.

Individuals engage in all sorts of careless or flippant behaviors, many of which are not negligent because the law recognizes no underlying duty of care. A legal duty of care requires one to conform to a standard of behavior or conduct so as to protect others from unreasonable risks of injury or other harms. *See, e.g., Randi W. v. Muroc Joint Unified Sch. Dist.*, 929 P.2d 582 (Cal. 1997) (school must provide information of sexual misconduct of prior teacher in recommending the teacher for employment at another school).

Legal duties typically emanate from positive actions (i.e., what one does) but sometimes as well from omissions (i.e., what one fails to do). Thus, an individual may owe another the duty to avoid driving erratically, but not to lend assistance to a stranger who succumbs to cardiac arrest on the street. However, in specific cases involving special relationships, one's duty to another may be heightened. Thus, a doctor may owe a legal duty to assist a patient if she suffers an injury in his office because of a special legal relationship between physicians and their patients.

Once a duty is established, a plaintiff must show the defendant failed to conform to it. Breaches of duties may be shown in several ways. A defendant may act contrary to what a "reasonable person" would do under the circumstances. This is a question of fact, the outcome of which varies. A breach may also be shown through a failure to follow customary practices or existing laws. Through what is known as *negligence per se*, a defendant may be adjudged to have breached a duty when he is shown to have acted inconsistently with statutory or regulatory laws. *See Martin v. Herzog,* 126 N.E. 814 (N.Y. 1920) (violation of a statute mandating the use of headlights for vehicles constitutes *negligence per se* as to the duty one owes other travelers).

An action in negligence may only be warranted if it can also be shown that the defendant's breach reasonably caused one's injury. Courts tend to assess evidence based on whether the plaintiff's damages (a) would not have arisen "but for" the defendant's breach ("causation in fact") or (b) were a foreseeable consequence of the defendant's actions, or failures to act ("proximate cause"). This element can be difficult to prove in many cases, especially when injuries occur or are discovered some time after an incident. *See Fisher v. United States,* 705 F. Supp. 2d 57 (D. Mass. 2010) (finding in favor of a refrigerator repairman who developed epilepsy about a year after experiencing an electric shock from exposed wires in an uncovered junction box); *Izell v. Union Carbide Corp.,* 180 Cal.Rptr.3d 382 (Cal. Ct. App. 2014) (allowing claim of a construction business owner who developed mesothelioma 33 years after exposure to asbestos).

Unless courts allow for the tolling of the statute of limitations (which bars tort claims after a set period of time) to the point of discovery of one's illness (instead the actual date in which the injury may have occurred), such claims may be rejected. *See, e.g., Field v. Gazette Pub. Co.*, 59 S.W.2d 19 (Ark. 1993) (dismissing claim based on lead exposure allegedly from unsafe work conditions due to statute of limitations that began from the date of exposure, not ascertainment); *contra Boldt v. Jostens, Inc.*, 261 N.W.2d 92 (Minn. 1977) (causal relationship between employee's disability and her prior exposure to glue at her workplace was allowed based on medical expert testimony).

Finally, a plaintiff must show actual damages or losses. In other words, the plaintiff must actually have been harmed by the breach of duty such that damages can be assessed. Courts do not require defendants to pay for plaintiffs' fictional damages (e.g., undocumented allegations of psychological trauma). "Real damages" in the form of calculable losses due to physical or mental injuries or death must arise. These might include, for example, medical costs of treatment for physical or mental injuries, loss of wages, or temporary or permanent disabilities. When acts of negligence cause the death of others (e.g., vehicular crashes), "wrongful death" claims may entail more extensive damages for the benefit of close family members.

2.   INTENTIONAL ACTS

Some torts are not based on mere negligence, but rather involve intentional acts. Striking one intentionally in a fight may assuredly result in tort liability stemming from an assault even if the victim is injured only nominally. Unlike cases of negligence there is no need to show the defendant failed to conform to set standards. If the defendant intentionally commits an assault or other act causing another harm, he may be liable unless he has a sufficient defense.

In the controversial Florida case in 2013, George Zimmerman, a volunteer neighborhood patrol who shot and killed an unarmed minor, Trayvon Martin, claimed to be acting in self-defense. Zimmerman was acquitted of criminal charges, but later faced tort actions based in wrongful death. This same defense may be raised again to escape potential civil liability. *See* Lizette Alvarez, *Settlement is Reached in Slaying*, N.Y. TIMES, April 5, 2013; Jay Weaver et al., *Trayvon Martin Case: Civil-Rights Leaders Call on Justice Department to Act*, MIAMI HERALD, July 14, 2013.

Additional intentional torts include false imprisonment (unjustifiably holding someone against their will), infliction of emotional distress (causing mental harm to another), and invasion of privacy (infringing on an individuals' bodily privacy interests), among others. W. PAGE KEETON ET AL., PROSSER AND KEETON ON TORTS 33–107 (5th ed. 1984). To deter such harmful conduct, courts may enter judgments including minimal compensatory payments as well as injunctions against further contact between the defendant and the person bringing the action.

3.   STRICT LIABILITY

Strict liability refers to the legal principles by which some defendants are held responsible regardless of whether they conform to standards of negligence or intend a specific harm. Sometimes the nature of one's activities or behaviors incur liability automatically when others are injured or killed. Typically defendants conducting abnormally-dangerous activities may be strictly liable if (a) they knowingly engage in the activity; (b) resulting harms to foreseeable persons are proximately caused; and (c) the defendants are not otherwise insulated or immune from liability via statute or common law.

For example, a defendant engaged in transporting hazardous materials on public thoroughfares may be held strictly liable if some harm related to its movement occurs to others. It does not matter whether the defendant was negligent in transporting the materials. Strict liability is assessed as a sort of "cost of doing business" in abnormally-dangerous activities. *See Siegler v. Kuhlman*, 502 P.2d 1181 (Wash. 1972) (gas truck driver strictly liable for wrongful death of motorist from explosion of gas spill).

4.   PRODUCTS LIABILITY

In the area of injury prevention, strict liability theories have their greatest application through product liability. Some products may be negligently manufactured or designed. Others may fail to meet manufacturers' own warranties. In either instance, resulting harms to users may lead to liability for the manufacturer. However, proving cases of negligence or breach of warranty is historically problematic and sometimes cost-prohibitive for some injured parties.

Recognizing the limitations of claims in negligence or contract related to the manufacture or sale of products, state legislatures and courts apply strict liability principles to products (but not services) that are capable of injuring or killing individuals. This includes most defective products, such as vehicles or toys, that threaten the public's health through their potential to injure users. However, some inherently dangerous products, like alcohol, guns, and tobacco, are held to a higher standard of proof before courts may assess liability related to their sale or use due in part to historic acceptance of these products and their dangers in the marketplace.

Determining whether a product is defective varies. Some courts assess whether a product is safe when used in an intended or reasonably foreseeable manner. Others balance whether predictable uses of a product outweigh its utility. While any product may conceivably be made safer, courts applying this standard balance the costs of safer construction or design against the product's hazards as currently manufactured. Some products, like prescription drugs, carry known risks, but also substantial benefits. They may be deemed "unavoidably unsafe" and thus protected from liability because they cannot be manufactured without some risk to users.

Grundberg v. Upjohn Co., 813 P.2d 89 (Utah 1991) (FDA-approved prescription drug for insomnia is deemed unavoidably unsafe).

Product liability applies under 4 predominant themes (*see* LAWRENCE O. GOSTIN, PUBLIC HEALTH LAW: POWER, DUTY, RESTRAINT 191–96 (2d ed. 2008)):

a. *Manufacturing Defects.* Some defects relate to non-conformances in manufacturing based on the maker's design. A product may not conform to the manufacturer's plans for its production and as a result be dangerous to its end user or others. Persons seeking recourse do not have to explain how the manufacturing defect occurred or why, only that it led to injury. *See, e.g., Magnuson by Mabe v. Kelsey-Hayes Co.*, 844 S.W.2d 448 (Mo. Ct. App. 1992) (strict liability claim was allowed without proof of negligence when truck tire came loose and struck a child in passing car, causing extensive injuries and permanent disability).

b. *Design Defects.* When negligent designs of products proximately cause harms to consumers or others, manufacturer liability may result if (i) the foreseeable risks of the product could have been mitigated through an alternative design, and (ii) failing to use an alternative design results in an unsafe product. Unlike with manufacturing defects, a prevailing claimant has to illustrate how a safer, affordable design could have made the product less risky.

On a late night in the summer of 1988 outside
Carrollton, Kentucky, a drunk driver collided with a
school bus transporting mostly children back from a
church field trip. The bus exploded, contributing to
the deaths of 27 people (24 of which were children).
Parents sued the Ford Motor Company and a
vehicle body manufacturer which supplied bus
frames to Ford. The parents alleged that a design
defect regarding the placement of an unprotected
gas tank near the front of the bus contributed to
their children's' injuries and deaths when the tank
ignited on impact with the other driver's vehicle.
JAMES S. KUNEN, RECKLESS DISREGARD: CORPORATE
GREED, GOVERNMENT INDIFFERENCE, AND THE
KENTUCKY SCHOOL BUS CRASH (1994). The parents
settled reportedly for over $50 million. Chris
Kenning, *25 Years Later, Carrollton Bus Crash
Survivors Still Struggle*, RETRO CINCINNATI, May
13, 2013.

Tragically, the bus involved in the crash was built
just days before implementation of the Federal
Motor Vehicle Safety Standards, 49 C.F.R. § 571.301
(1977). These standards required repositioning of
gas tanks toward the middle of bus frames and
encasing tanks in steel mesh to prevent punctures
during crashes. James S. Kunen, *Two Families
Fight to Make Ford Pay for the Kentucky School-Bus
Disaster That Killed Their Daughters*, PEOPLE, Oct.
31, 1988. These measures may have prevented the
deaths of many on board the vehicle in 1988.

Not all manufacturers of defectively designed
products are tagged with liability. In June 2013, the

U.S. Supreme Court ruled against Karen Bartlett in favor of a generic drug manufacturer. Bartlett lost two-thirds of her skin, was placed in a medically-induced coma, and was left legally blind after taking a generic medication to reduce her shoulder pain. The cause of harm related to the original design of the patented drug, and not its generic equivalent. The Court rule that generic drug manufacturers are not liable for defective drug designs that originated with their original developers. *Mutual Pharm. Co., Inc. v. Bartlett*, 133 S. Ct. 2466 (2013); *see also Brusewitz v. Wyeth*, 131 S. Ct. 1068 (2011) (limiting state torts claims for design defects against vaccine manufacturers) (noted also in Chapter 4).

c. *Failures to Instruct or Warn.* Sometimes manufacturers fail to provide sufficient instructions on how to use a product safely or warnings of its known risks. A failure to instruct or warn may arise where a manufacturer does not provide sufficient guidance on a product's proper and safe use. In *Technical Chem. Co. v. Jacobs*, 480 S.W.2d 602, 605 (Tex. 1972), the Texas Supreme Court defined a product as unreasonably dangerous or defective when an ordinary person would not have marketed the product without "supplying warning as to risk and dangers involved in using the product as well as instructions as to how to avoid those risks and dangers." *Id.* at 605.

A consummate example of a product requiring instructions or warnings is lawn mowers. Failing to warn consumers about the dangers of placing hands or other appendages under the mower while its blade is operating contributed to thousands of injuries and related lawsuits. *See e.g., Ames v. Sears, Roebuck & Co.*, 514 A.2d 352 (Conn. App. Ct. 1986) (lawn mower manufacturer/seller liable for failing to warn consumer of absence of "stop dead" control). As a result of tort litigation, manufacturers now provide ample warnings of these dangers. As well, most mowers are manufactured with safety switches or handles to help limit the possibility of injuries by cutting the motor instantly if the switch or handle is released. 16 C.F.R. § 1205.5 (2012) (requiring manufacturers to install controls on any walk-behind rotary power mower).

Additional products have been modified following tort litigation to reduce consumers' risks of injury. *See, e.g., McCormack v. Hankscraft Co.*, 154 N.W.2d 488 (Minn. 1967) (faulty tip-proof vaporizer was redesigned to add stability); *Howard v. Ford Motor Co.*, No. 763785–2 (Cal. Sup. Ct. Oct. 11, 2000) (court ordered recall of Ford ignition system that stalled vehicles leading to deadly crashes). *See generally* Jon S. Vernick et al., *Role of Litigation in Preventing   Product-related   Injuries*,   25 EPIDEMIOLOGIC REVS. 90 (2003).

d. *Misrepresentation.* A product may also be deemed defective where a manufacturer labels or advertises it so as to give a false impression. Failing to disclose known risks of prescription drugs may constitute a claim for misrepresentation, as would advertisements or product packages that make false claims or intentionally conceal known facts about the product's dangers. In 2013, PepsiCo, Inc. paid $9 million and agreed to remove the words "all natural" from the labels of its Naked® juice products to settle a lawsuit claiming the product contained synthetic ingredients. Candice Choi, *Pepsi to No Longer Call Naked Juices 'Natural,'* WALL ST. J., July 26, 2013.

There are considerable limits to liability for misrepresentation. Take, for example, the case of 2 obese teenagers and their parents who sued McDonald's® Corporation. *Pelman v. McDonald's Corp.*, 396 F.3d 508 (2d Cir. 2005). They alleged McDonald's® advertisements and representations constituted a deceptive scheme to encourage consumers to purchase its products through false, misleading, or incomplete information in violation of New York state law regulating deceptive business practices. Though the teens' claims initially survived on appeal, they were later rejected on their request to certify a class (which would have allowed them to expand the number of affected claimants). Their claims were ultimately dismissed in 2011. Many states' legislatures now prohibit the bringing of similar claims against fast food or other restaurants through what are sometimes known as "cheeseburger" bills. Bonnie Hershberger, *Supersized America: Are Lawsuits the Right Remedy?*, 4 J. FOOD L. & POL'Y 71, 82 (2008).

Product liability actions can be used not only to compensate injured persons, but also to reform entire product lines. Once any court determines that a particular product is defective pursuant to an individual or class action, manufacturers have a strong incentive to immediately correct the defect to avoid future litigation. Sometimes this entails the complete removal of the product from the marketplace because a product cannot be made safer (e.g., lawn darts). Other times, the product is redesigned (e.g., vehicles), repackaged (e.g., cigarettes), or re-purposed (e.g., prescription drugs, like Viagra®, created for one condition (blood pressure), but marketed for another (erectile dysfunction) to correct or address the defect. Federal and state consumer product safety commissions also regularly monitor products that pose risks to users and issue recalls or recommendations for their removal or redesign based on similar bases. *See* Eileen Flaherty, *Safety First: The Consumer Product Safety Act of 2008*, 21 LOY. CONSUMER L. REV. 372, 377–78 (2009); *see also* Chapter 8 for more information.

Finally, in some cases (e.g., tobacco, alcohol, guns), products that have known dangerous effects even when used by consumers as intended are allowed to remain on the marketplace based on legislative or other historic protections from liability. Tort litigation surrounding the manufacture, sale, and trade of guns provides a consummate example. For years, gun-related suits grounded in tort law percolated among state and local governments based on multiple theories. It was argued that guns were improperly designed because they (a) were easy to use, even for small children; (b) lacked clear indicators whether they were loaded; and (c) failed to use available technology to prevent unauthorized uses. *See, e.g.,* Stephen P. Teret et al.,

Makings Guns Safer, 14 ISSUES IN SCI. & TECH. 37 (1998).

While many of these cases failed, new theories emerged. Some sued gun manufacturers on the premise that their mass production of guns precipitated known sales to persons (e.g., felons, mentally-disabled) who cannot lawfully purchase them. If so, the manufacturers may have breached a duty of entrustment, suggesting personal property owners owe a duty not to allow others to possess property if it is foreseeable they may use it in harmful ways. Handing a stick of dynamite to a known pyromaniac with a match might surely implicate the tort of negligent entrustment. As applied to gun makers, however, the theory largely fell flat. *See, e.g., Hamilton v. Beretta U.S.A. Corp.*, 750 N.E.2d 1055 (N.Y. 2001); *contra Ileto v. Glock*, 349 F.3d 1191 (9th Cir. 2003). Additional cases grounded in public nuisance law also arose (see Chapter 9.C.1).

In partial response to this litigation in 2005, Congress passed the Protection of Lawful Commerce in Arms Act (PLCAA), 15 U.S.C. §§ 7901–7903 (2012). It forbids civil or administrative actions or proceedings against a gun manufacturer, seller, or trade association for damages, injunctions, abatement, or other relief resulting from the criminal or unlawful misuse of guns or other products, subject to several narrow exceptions. *Id.* at § 7903(5). The PLCAA brought to an end virtually all litigation against gun manufacturers for harms to the public's health related to the criminal use of non-defective firearms protected by the 2nd Amendment. Jon S. Vernick et al., *Availability of Litigation as a Tool for Firearm Injury Prevention: Comparing Guns, Vaccines, and Motor Vehicles*, 97 AM. J. PUB. HEALTH 1991 (2007).

C.   CRIMINAL LAW & PUBLIC HEALTH

Tortious behavior can also be criminal in nature, allowing for dual causes of action (as per the George Zimmerman case in Florida noted previously above). One who drives negligently and causes a crash might only face a civil suit for injuries to the other driver or related property damages. One who engages in the same negligent acts under the influence of drugs or alcohol may face tort and criminal actions. This is because the person's behavior constitutes a civil wrong (harm to another driver and property damage) and an offense against the state (driving under the influence (DUI) of alcohol on public thoroughfares).

Criminal laws are typically set forth in statute at the federal, tribal, or state levels, although local governments with sufficient home rule may also address criminal acts via ordinances. The nature and extent of government's ability to define and declare unlawful criminal acts exceed the scope of this text. However, at least part of the authority for criminal laws is the protection of the safety, health, and welfare of communities under government's "police powers," discussed in Chapter 2. *See, e.g., United States v. Skinner*, 973 F. Supp. 975 (W.D. Wash. 1997) (Washington law criminalizing a blood-alcohol level of .10% or higher within 2 hours of driving is consistent with state's police powers); *see also* Rachelle Blidner, *'They're going where they belong:' Tenn. pair sentenced for killing daughter by forcing her to drink 2 liters of grape soda*, N. Y. DAILY NEWS (Dec. 9, 2014) (woman plead guilty to 2nd degree murder and aggravated child abuse after forcing her 5-year-old stepdaughter to drink 2.4 liters of grape soda as punishment, leading to her death from hyponatremic encephalopathy).

At one time public health laws were tied to extensive criminal enforcement of acts deemed contrary to the public's health. LAWRENCE O. GOSTIN, PUBLIC HEALTH LAW: POWER, DUTY, RESTRAINT 151–53 (2d ed. 2008). Not long ago, for example, attempted suicide was a criminal offense in most states. *See* 83 C.J.S. *Suicide* § 6 (2013). Charging individuals with a crime or attempted suicide can be pointless when their behaviors warrant public health or medical interventions, instead of criminal sanctions. Consequently, most states have repealed these laws. *See* Catherine D. Shaffer, *Criminal Liability for Assisting Suicide*, 86 COLUM. L. REV. 348, 350 (1986) (noting that no state statutorily criminalizes attempted suicide although some punish assisted suicide).

Modern public health officials disdain associating positive legal interventions to protect the public's health with criminal penalties. This is due in part to prior abuses and adherence to the pervasive ethic of voluntarism throughout public health practice. Yet in the context of injury prevention and control, criminal law may still be used to prosecute and punish those who commit domestic violence; abuse or abandon children; create dangerous or unsafe workplaces; engage in bullying in schools or workplaces; commit homicides, assaults, or batteries; fire guns in unsafe ways (e.g., in a heavily-populated environment); allow children access to loaded guns or dangerous weapons; sell or serve adulterated products, tobacco, alcohol, or drugs to minors; or intentionally attempt to transmit HIV or other communicable conditions.

This litany represents only a few of the many ways that government criminalizes behaviors in the interests of injury prevention. Provided it acts consistently with strong constitutional protections against unwarranted prosecutions, governments' powers to punish acts resulting in injuries to others are extensive. Whether criminal prosecution of these or other behaviors actually carries significant public health benefits is less certain. *See, e.g.*, Julia F. Costich and Dana J. Patton, *Enforcement: Linking Policy and Impact in Public Health*, 53 JURIMETRICS J. 293 (2013).

In some cases, criminal laws may arguably deter behaviors sufficiently to the improvement of the public's health. DUI laws were significantly upgraded across states in the latter part of the 20th century in response to mounting evidence of the extensive role of excessive alcohol and drug use in driving violations and resulting crashes. Coupled with aggressive advertising and educational campaigns as well as enforcement efforts, public incidence of DUI declined, along with related injuries and deaths. Thomas H. Nochajski & Paul R. Stasiewicz, *Relapse to Driving Under the Influence (DUI): A Review*, 26 CLINICAL PSYCHOL. REV. 179 (2006). Many credit the passage of DUI laws with lower rates of related crashes, but coextensive public health education campaigns also contributed substantially to reshaping societal views and behaviors concerning drinking and driving.

In other cases, criminal laws may not only fail to improve public health outcomes, they may actually worsen them. Aforementioned laws that rely on criminal prosecutions and incarceration to deter illicit drug use lack efficacy. Prior and recent studies have shown recidivism rates among those prosecuted for drug possession are reduced through drug treatment and rehabilitation programs in lieu of incarceration. *See* David B. Wilson et al., *A Systematic Review of Drug Court Effects on Recidivism,* 2 J. EXPERIMENTAL CRIM. 459 (2006).

Criminal laws designed to deter individuals' actions are sometimes offensive (even if they work) or drive some behaviors underground. As to the former, motorcycle helmet laws passed in most states in the 1970s to address significant injuries and deaths among cyclists have been repealed in many states. Even though these laws are shown to reduce motorcycle-related deaths (in some cases by ½ in a given year), they have been criticized politically as paternalistic. *See Simon v. Sargent,* 346 F. Supp. 277 (D. Mass. 1972), *aff'd,* 409 U.S. 1020 (1972) (Massachusetts' motorcycle helmet law did not violate substantive due process); *see also Benning v. State*, 641 A.2d 757 (Vt. 1994) (Vermont's motorcycle helmet law upheld against a challenge that it infringed individuals' right to liberty). As a result, motorcycle helmet laws have been statutorily repealed in many states (but not Massachusetts, 540 MASS. CODE. REGS. § 22.08 (2013), or Vermont, 23 VT. STAT. ANN. § 1256 (2013)). Motorcycle-related deaths in jurisdictions turning back helmet laws have predictably risen. See, e.g., Kristen J. Mertz & Harold B. Weiss, *Changes in Motorcycle-Related Head Injury Deaths, Hospitalizations, and Hospital Charges Following Repeal of Pennsylvania's Mandatory Motorcycle Helmet Law*, 98 AM. J. PUB. HEALTH 1464, 1466 (2008) (number of Pennsylvanians dying from motorcycle-related injuries increased 40% after the state's helmet law was repealed).

Laws criminalizing women and medical practitioners engaged in receiving or providing abortions led to "back alley" practices that disabled or killed thousands of women prior to the U.S. Supreme Court's decision in *Roe v. Wade*, 410 U.S. 113 (1973). One lesson of the Prohibition era was that criminalizing the possession and sale of alcoholic beverages across the nation did not necessarily temper its use. Instead, it (1) shifted the venues for its consumption from public to private places, and (2) transformed sellers from known distributors to unknown "moonshiners" and "bootleggers." DWIGHT VICK & ELIZABETH RHOADES, DRUGS AND ALCOHOL IN THE 21ST CENTURY: THEORY, BEHAVIOR, AND POLICY 131–32 (2010). Countless

Americans drank adulterated or unsanitary liquor as a result; others lost their lives trying to police those engaged in unlawful use and sales.

Criminal laws that are finely crafted, reflective of social norms, fairly enforced, and shown to be effective in lessening injuries or deaths without violating constitutional guarantees can help reduce injuries and deaths in furtherance of the public's health. Conversely, some criminal laws are bluntly constructed, impinge autonomy for purely paternalistic reasons, are improperly enforced largely against minority groups or other protected classes, or unnecessarily impact individual rights (*see Ferguson v. City of Charleston*, 532 U.S. 67 (2001), discussed in Chapter 4). These sort of criminal laws are poor substitutes for efficacious public health laws and policies better designed to address the harms of injuries and resulting deaths.

Mitigating injuries and deaths, whether intentional or otherwise, involves applications of tort and criminal laws, among other tools. As illustrated in this chapter and all of Part 2, public health agents possess many powers to address varied public health conditions with accompanying trade-offs inherent in balancing individual and communal interests. Use of tort and criminal law against select parties may seem contrary promoting the public's health. Yet, these actions impact society, alter behaviors, and allay clear (and sometimes latent) risks.

PART 3

LAW & THE PROMOTION OF THE PUBLIC'S HEALTH

Part 1 sets the foundation for the field of public health law. Part 2 explores the application of law based on this foundation, particularly concerning how law can be used effectively as a tool to prevent or control identified threats to the health of populations. Inexorable trade-offs between communal and individual interests in the theory and practice of public health law are discussed in key contexts. These include critical assessments of the role of law to (a) authorize voluntary, mandatory, and compulsory public health powers; (b) allow government to tax, spend, and regulate within limits to further community health; and (c) mitigate harms from injuries and deaths through tort and criminal laws.

Not every issue in public health law, however, centers on addressing or controlling some known threat to the health of the community. Building on themes framed in prior chapters, Part 3 examines the scope and limits of law in promoting health outcomes in 4 areas. Chapter 7 explores the influence of law in managing public health information. Law is pivotal to privacy and security protections of modern public health surveillance, reporting, and data use practices. Chapter 8 lays out a series of legal issues that stem from government's role to regulate public and private

communications within society. How law impacts
the built environment and use of private property is
the focus of Chapter 9. Lastly, in Chapter 10, some
of the most controversial and dynamic modern
issues in public health law are analyzed related to
public health emergency legal preparedness and
response.

CHAPTER 7

PUBLIC HEALTH INFORMATION MANAGEMENT, PRIVACY & SECURITY

Data are the lifeblood of public health practice. Public health agencies gather and use an array of data for surveillance, epidemiologic investigations, and research. For decades, these practices have provided essential population-based information about the prevalence of communicable and chronic conditions, limited outbreaks of infectious diseases, and the rise of epidemics. Accurate public health data justify government interventions and support allocations of limited public health personnel, resources, and funds.

Sophisticated surveillance and other activities rely on data generated through legal reporting requirements. These laws obligate medical professionals and others to provide data to government based on tests, screens, diagnoses, treatments, or other findings about individuals. Such efforts are essential to monitoring the public's health, but can be controversial. Much of the data collected via government are identifiable and often sensitive, including information about persons' sexual diseases (e.g., HIV/AIDS), genetic make-up (e.g., Phenylketonuria), mental health status (e.g., Alzheimer disease), and personal profile (e.g., domestic violence). Their acquisition, use, and disclosure via public health agencies raise significant health information privacy and security concerns, all of which must be balanced with public health purposes to achieve key communal objectives. Striking this chord is complicated by a legal patchwork of privacy laws and policy, public perceptions of the need for strong privacy protections, and politicized instances of privacy abuses that question whether public health agencies handle private data securely in all instances.

A.   SURVEILLANCE & REPORTING

Public health surveillance is defined as the "systematic and continuous collection, analysis, and interpretation of data, closely integrated with the timely and coherent dissemination ... and assessment to those who have the right to know so that action can be taken." DICTIONARY OF EPIDEMIOLOGY 239 (Miquel Porta ed., 5th ed. 2008). Public health agencies conduct surveillance largely at the state and local levels. Key information, sometimes in statistical form, is also shared with federal authorities like CDC to ascertain national or regional trends. Each state maintains public health surveillance systems to monitor notifiable disease conditions (e.g., measles, syphilis, cryptosporidium), noninfectious conditions (e.g., injuries, cancers) and public health indicators (e.g., behavioral risk factors). Together with additional governmental collections of vital records (e.g., birth and death records), federal, state, and local surveillance not only helps identify public health threats and trends, it furthers nearly every other intervention in public health practice or research. *See* Stephen B. Thacker,

Surveillance, in FIELD EPIDEMIOLOGY 16–32 (Michael B. Gregg et al. eds., 1996).

Methods of surveillance include:

(1)   Monitoring available data related to health risk behaviors (e.g., tobacco or alcohol use);

(2)   Use of telephone or web-based surveys;

(3)   Development of data registries for cancers or birth defects based on screening programs, hospital discharges, worker compensation claims, and other sources; and

(4)   Assessment of syndromic data, such as spikes in 9-1-1 calls, emergency room visits, or purchases of over-the-counter medications which may precipitate outbreaks of infectious or food-borne illnesses, or even acts of bioterrorism. *See, e.g.,* Wilfredo Lopez, *New York City and State Legal Authorities Related to Syndromic Surveillance*, 80 J. URB. HEALTH i23 (Supp. 1 2003).

The predominant mode of collecting surveillance data is through state-based reporting of identifiable health information about varied conditions. *See, e.g.,* Terence L. Chorba et al., *Mandatory Reporting of Infectious Diseases by Clinicians*, 262 JAMA 3018 (1989). Legal reporting requirements vary across jurisdictions in relation to:

a.   *the type and number of conditions required for reporting.*   Many   states   follow   annual recommendations concerning the approximately 100 reportable conditions from the Council of State and Territorial Epidemiologists (CSTE) and employ modern case definitions set forth by CDC and CSTE. CDC, *Case Definitions for Infectious Conditions under Public Health Surveillance*, 46 MMWR 1 (May 2, 1997); CSTE, *CSTE List of Nationally Notifiable Conditions* (2013);

b. *persons or entities required to report.* In addition to doctors, nurses, and pharmacists, reporters may include diagnostic laboratories, schools, law enforcement agencies, and others. Hospitals and other health entities, for example, are required to report health-care associated infections (HAIs) like Methicillin-resistant Staphylococcus aureus (MRSA) in over half the states. *See* David A. Hyman & Bernard Black, *Public Reporting of Hospital Infection Rates: Not All Change Is Progress*, 53 JURIMETRICS J. 327 (2013);

c. *time periods for reporting conditions.* Persons or entities may be required to share information about a specific condition. In cases of active surveillance, reports may be legally required immediately upon detection (e.g., for bioterrorism agents). For some chronic or other conditions subject to more passive surveillance practices involving routine collections of data to observe public health trends, reports may be requested bi-weekly or monthly;

d. *agencies that receive reports.* Not all public health reports are collected by public health agencies. Departments of consumer safety, education, emergency management, environment, housing, and transportation, among others, may actively receive and process these data; and

e. *penalties for failure to report conditions.* While most state reporting laws include explicit sanctions like fines or licensure revocations for failure to report, they are rarely invoked in modern times absent potential, significant public health consequences. California's medical board temporarily revoked the license of a doctor who neglected to report a food handler with a clear case of hepatitis. A community outbreak of hepatitis associated with the handler arose, resulting in 62 cases and a death. David P. Fidler et al., *Emerging and Reemerging Infectious Diseases: Challenges for International, National, and State Law*, 31 INT'L LAW. 773 (1997).

Rates of compliance fluctuate depending on the type of condition, need for rapid public health responses, and other factors. Reporting of diseases like human rabies capture close to 100% of known cases, due in part to the need for quick interventions to prevent further significant harms to affected individuals. Actual reporting of Chlamydia, gonorrhea, or other STIs (*see* Chapter 4) might include fewer than 10% of actual cases. For these types of conditions, epidemiologists conduct periodic studies to help validate the estimates of the completeness of reporting and better calculate actual disease prevalence across the population. *See* Verla S. Neslund et al., *Legal Considerations in Public Health Surveillance in the U.S.*, *in*

PRINCIPLES AND PRACTICE OF PUBLIC HEALTH
SURVEILLANCE (Lisa M. Lee et al. eds., 2010).

B. BALANCING INDIVIDUAL PRIVACY & COMMUNAL INTERESTS

Collecting some data for public health surveillance through ongoing lawful activities raises few objections. For example, gathering information about how many bottles of antacid are sold in a given day at local drug store may help unveil the presence of a potential outbreak of food- or water-borne illness, but hardly invokes major privacy concerns among individuals so long as purchasers' names are not shared with local government officials. Significant interests arise, however, when names or other identifiers are communicated as per many reporting requirements.

Gathering identifiable heath data through surveillance allows public health officials to assess the accuracy of the information and facilitate specific interventions like treatment or partner notification. It also implicates privacy concerns. Government wants access to identifiable health data to further its mission to protect the public's health. Individuals seek to maintain the privacy of their sensitive health information or claim a "right to know" of additional data (such as their exposure to infectious diseases) that may impact their own health.

While these respective interests may seem inapposite, they are actually synergistic. Government must respect individual privacy interests when it acquires and uses identifiable data for public health purposes. Otherwise, people will evade health services such as testing, screening, partner notification, and even treatment. Prior to the advent of anonymous testing for HIV in the 1980s, many at-risk adults would not be tested for fear of privacy invasions. *See, e.g.,* Carla Markhof Obermeyer & Michelle Osborn, *The Utilization of Testing and Counseling for HIV: A Review of the Social and Behavioral Evidence*, 97 AM. J. PUB. HEALTH 1762–74 (2007). Alternatively, individuals must allow public health authorities some reasonable access to their identifiable health data to protect the community's health (which, as noted in Chapter 1, is by definition a communal objective).

This synergy between respecting individual privacy interests and promoting the public's health via surveillance and other activities helps explain the extant legal environment underlying public health information management. Most reporting laws do not require individuals' consent or authorization to share their identifiable health data with public health officials. Thus, a doctor who diagnoses a patient with TB does not need the patient's permission to report this case to the local health department. Nor does the issuance of a named report by the doctor to a public health agency constitute a breach of the doctor's typical duty of confidentiality. As discussed below, public health reporting requirements represent an exception (among others) to a doctor's legal and ethical duty to maintain patient confidentiality.

Conversely, just because a public health agency may lawfully acquire identifiable health information about individuals does not allow for unrestricted uses of the data. Consistent with privacy and security laws and policies (as noted below), public health agencies are limited in how they can use or disclose identifiable data. These limitations reflect principles of public health ethics supporting the confidentiality of identifiable health data (except in rare instances). Respecting the privacy of public health information is not only good practice, it is essential to accomplishing communal health objectives.

C. PRIVACY, CONFIDENTIALITY & SECURITY

Protecting the privacy, confidentiality, and security of public health data is core to responsible data collection and sharing practices. Though sometimes used interchangeably, these terms have distinct legal and ethical meanings. Health information *privacy* refers broadly to the rights of individuals to control acquisitions, uses, or disclosures of their identifiable health data. The related concept of *confidentiality* denotes the obligations of those who receive such information, often through some legally-recognized relationship (e.g., doctor/patient), to respect individual privacy interests.

Security is different. It concerns technologic or administrative safeguards or tools to protect identifiable health data from unwarranted access, use, or disclosure. Maintaining information security is challenging in an era of digital exchanges within large electronic health databases and biobanks that can be hacked or infiltrated. Peter D. Jacobson et al., *Risk Governance and Population Health*, 53 JURIMETRICS J. 279 (2013). Conversely, e-surveillance systems also facilitate the use of sophisticated techniques to thwart unwarranted access. James G. Hodge, Jr., *Health Information Privacy and Public Health*, 31 J.L. MED. & ETHICS 663 (2004).

Various privacy and security laws and policies governing health data uses and disclosures reflect the fragmented nature of health information privacy protections. As noted in Chapter 3, neither constitutional principles nor common law concepts of duties of confidentiality support broad individual expectations of health information privacy.

In *Whalen v. Roe*, 429 U.S. 589 (1977), the U.S. Supreme Court considered a constitutional challenge to a New York state reporting requirement related to prescriptions of controlled substances (e.g., morphine). To avert known abuses of unscrupulous physicians providing excessive prescriptions for these drugs to patients, which resulted in illegal street sales of the drugs, New York's legislature mandated that all prescriptions for controlled substances be reported to the state health department. Such data were used to monitor potential public health abuses and kept offline in locked facilities. Still, doctors and patients sued, alleging violations of constitutional decisional privacy interests grounded largely from due process principles of liberty under the 14th Amendment. Rejecting their claims, the Court noted that so long as government shares "a proper concern with, and protection of, the individual's interest in privacy," including reasonable security measures, public health reporting requirements are constitutional. *Id.* at 605.

Lacking stronger constitutional and common law protections, a bevy of federal and state statutes and regulations comprises the dominant basis for health information privacy protections across the U.S. These laws, discussed briefly below, safeguard health information privacy while accommodating government interests in accessing identifiable data for public health purposes.

1.   FEDERAL PRIVACY LAWS

Numerous federal laws protecting the privacy of health and other data apply to different types of information, persons, and entities. The Privacy Act of 1974, 5 U.S.C. § 552(a) (2012), governs collections of identifiable information, including medical data, by federal agencies. It protects individual privacy by (a) specifying when one's health information can be disclosed with (or without) consent; (b) prohibiting government maintenance of identifiable data that are irrelevant and unnecessary to accomplish agency purposes; (c) requiring agencies to publish a notice about the purpose of each record system and disclosures outside the agency; and (d) mandating agencies inform individuals of the statutory basis for collecting data, as well as consequences for not supplying the information.

The Freedom of Information Act (FOIA) of 1966, 5 U.S.C. § 552 (2012) requires federal agency records to be open and available to the public. On its face, FOIA seems to be the antithesis to assuring privacy, but its open door provisions are subject to several exceptions. Relevant examples include the Act's exemption for "personnel and medical files and similar files the disclosure of which would constitute a clearly unwarranted invasion of personal privacy." *Id.* at § 552(b)(6).

Additional federal privacy protections apply to research and other health data. The Public Health Service Act (PHSA), 42 U.S.C. §§ 201–300 (2012), protects identifiable information collected respectively by CDC's National Center for Health Statistics (*id.* at § 242m(d)) and DHHS' Agency for Healthcare Research and Quality (*id.* at § 299c-3). Federal agencies can issue "assurances of confidentiality" to individuals and institutions that: "[n]o [identifiable] information . . . may be used for any purpose other than . . . for which it was supplied," absent consent. *Id.* at § 242m(d). DHHS may also grant "certificates of confidentiality" to researchers to protect participants from legally compelled disclosures of identifiable health information. *Id.* at § 241(d). Researchers generally seek these certificates when health data collected are so sensitive (e.g., related to sexual practices, mental health, or illegal conduct) that their subjects might not participate or may otherwise give false information.

Provisions of the E-Government Act of 2002, Pub. L. No. 107–347, 116 Stat. 2899 (2002), protect the confidentiality of federal government statistical collections of health or other identifiable information. The act restricts statistical data uses to the purposes for which they are gathered, penalizes unauthorized disclosures, and requires federal agencies to conduct privacy assessments before developing or procuring information technology.

The HITECH Act of 2009, Pub. L. No. 111–5, 123 Stat. 226, 467 (codified as amended in scattered sections of 42 U.S.C.) authorizes DHHS to establish programs to promote the public's health through electronic health records (EHRs). OFFICE OF THE NAT'L COORDINATOR FOR HEALTH INFO. TECH., EHR ADOPTION & UTILIZATION: 2012 HIGHLIGHTS AND ACCOMPLISHMENTS 1 (2012). Hospitals and other health care providers may receive monetary incentives to follow regulations, including demonstrating that they are putting EHRs to "meaningful use." Over a series of stages beginning in 2011, meaningful use requirements include initially:

- Electronically capturing health data in a standardized format;

- Using EHRs to track key clinical conditions; and

- Initiating the reporting of health quality measures and public health information.

By 2014, providers are expected to participate in a national health information exchange (HIE) and use data efficiently to improve patient quality and safety (leading to better health outcomes). Uptake of electronic data systems, however, has been plagued by multiple issues included industry failures to align systems, lending to profound interoperability gaps. Robert Pear, *Tech Rivalries Impede Digital Medical Record Sharing*, N.Y. TIMES, May 27, 2015, at A13. A lack of standardized policies and practices have further impeded HIE initiatives. However, federal and state authorities are formulating solutions to address these practice, policy, and regulatory issues. Health Information Exchange Policy Issues, DHHS: AGENCY HEALTHCARE RES. & QUALITY (Apr. 2015). Privacy-related issues are addressed through requirements to use advanced software systems, as well as through existing provisions of the HIPAA Privacy Rule, discussed below.

2.   HIPAA PRIVACY RULE

Pursuant to the Health Insurance Portability and Accountability Act (HIPAA), Pub. L. No. 104–191, 110 Stat. 1936 (1996), Congress authorized DHHS to create national standards for health information privacy protections. After years of drafting and significant compromises, the resulting regulations, known as the HIPAA Privacy Rule (or the Rule), 45 C.F.R. pts. 160, 164 (2004), took full effect on April 14, 2004. It was later altered by the Genetic Information Nondiscrimination Act (GINA), Pub. L. No. 110–223, 122 Stat. 881 (2008), and the HITECH

Act (noted above), and subsequently revised in 2013. 78 Fed. Reg. 5566–5702 (Jan. 25, 2013), amending 45 C.F.R. pts. 160, 164; *see* Mark A. Rothstein, *HIPAA Privacy Rule 2.0*, J.L. MED. & ETHICS (Summer) 525 (2013).

The Privacy Rule bestows individuals with greater control over their health information; sets boundaries on the acquisition, use, and disclosure of "protected health information" (PHI); and establishes privacy and security safeguards that covered entities (e.g., health care providers, insurers, and data clearinghouses), their business associates, and others must follow. This includes guidance on how to keep electronic PHI secure against reasonably anticipated threats or hazards (e.g., hacking), as well as unwarranted uses and disclosures by health personnel. 45 C.F.R. pt. 164, at § 164.306(a) (2004).

Although the Privacy Rule sets a national floor of health privacy protections, it does not preempt all state/local privacy laws. Salvatore Lucido et al., *HIPAA Privacy Rule and Public Health: Guidance from CDC and DHHS*, 52 MMWR 1 (May 2, 2003). State or local laws that protect the privacy of PHI to a lesser degree than the Rule are overridden, but those that provide greater coverage are not. These may include, for example, state-based genetics, mental health, cancer, or HIV-specific privacy laws that confer enhanced protections for what some policymakers view as "super-sensitive" data. The Privacy Rule draws no such distinctions among health data; it applies to all identifiable health information regardless of its content.

Under the Privacy Rule, in general, a covered entity must seek a written authorization from an individual to acquire, use, or disclose his or her PHI. As with many privacy laws, this requirement is subject to several exceptions. 45 C.F.R. § 164.508(a)(1) (2013). One exception concerns "standard transactions," or those exchanges of health data between covered entities needed to treat, pay, or reimburse for care. Thus, a hospital need not obtain a patient's written authorization to share her PHI with her health insurance company to seek reimbursement. These sort of transactions are fundamental to the delivery of health services, and thus do not generally require individuals to consent (unless they pay for health care in full out of pocket).

Concerning the public's health, the Rule also allows covered entities to disclose PHI to a "public health authority" (PHA) without individual authorization. A PHA is any governmental agency, as well as entities working under a grant of authority from such agency, that is "responsible for public health matters as part of its official mandate." *Id.* at § 164.501. PHAs include public health agencies like DHHS, CDC, FDA, and tribal, state, or local public health departments. They also include entities under contract with such agencies, such as universities, data processing companies, or hospitals running chronic disease registries.

By design, the Privacy Rule allows covered entities to disclose PHI to PHAs pursuant to state or local reporting requirements without individual consent. The Rule also allows additional disclosures without authorization for specific public health purposes including to:

- maintain the quality, safety, or effectiveness of FDA-approved products;

- notify persons exposed to communicable diseases (a.k.a. partner notification);

- track work-related injuries;

- report victims of abuse, neglect, or domestic violence;

- conduct health oversight activities;

- share school immunization information (resolving prior prohibitions of such data sharing stemming from the Family Educational Rights and Privacy Act (FERPA), 20 U.S.C. § 1232(g) (2012); 34 C.F.R. pt. 99 (2012), applying to student educational records); and

- prevent serious threats to persons or the public, or during emergencies.

In most cases, the Rule requires covered entities to limit the amount of information disclosed to the "minimum necessary" to achieve a specified goal. 45 C.F.R. § 164.514(d)(1). This requirement does not apply to disclosures to PHAs pursuant to reporting laws. Covered entities can reasonably rely on a

PHA's determination that the amount of PHI requested is the minimum needed for a public health purpose. Salvatore Lucido et al., *HIPAA Privacy Rule and Public Health: Guidance from CDC and DHHS*, 52 MMWR 1 (May 2, 2003).

So what is the impact of the Privacy Rule on public health surveillance and reporting practices? The answer is simple in theory. PHAs performing public health activities are not covered by the Rule. Reporting laws authorizing PHAs to collect data remain intact. As a result, covered entities must continue to supply identifiable health data to PHAs without individual authorization just the same as they did prior to the Privacy Rule.

In practice, however, the Privacy Rule impacts PHAs in external and internal ways. *Externally*, the Rule can stymie the flow of some data to PHAs. Despite the allowance for public health disclosures without individual written authorization, some covered entities continue to battle PHAs on whether they can provide PHI without individual consent. *Internally*, while the Rule does not apply to PHAs engaged in public health activities, it may apply when they perform "covered functions," that is, those functions that assimilate what covered entities do.

By way of an example, a local public health clinic may occasionally provide flu vaccines or other health services to the public for a minimal charge (for which it bills electronically). Concerning this activity, it may be engaged in a covered function and thus has to adhere to the Rule. This is true even if the PHA's underlying goal is not so much to provide individual health services (a covered function), but rather to assure vaccination rates remain high in the community (a public health objective). To separate their public health and covered functions for the purpose of compliance, most PHAs declare themselves to be "hybrid entities" through DHHS under the Rule. *Id.* at 9–10. Once approved, only that portion of the PHA which is engaged in covered functions needs to adhere to the Privacy Rule; other parts or divisions of the PHA do not have to follow its provisions so long as adequate safeguards are in place.

3.   STATE & LOCAL PRIVACY LAWS

Many states' statutory, regulatory, and judicial privacy laws share similar protections provided at the federal level. A few states' laws reflect nearly the same broad themes of the HIPAA Privacy Rule. Most state privacy laws, however, do not. Instead, they tend to be more specific, applying to select data recipients (e.g., public health agencies, health insurers); certain medical tests, diseases, or conditions (e.g., genetic tests, HIV status, mental disorders); or particular data sources (e.g., nursing or health care facilities). *See* James G. Hodge, Jr., *Health Information Privacy and Public Health*, 31 J.L. MED. & ETHICS 663 (2004).

As a result, state and local public health agencies are governed by multiple, inconsistent, and fragmented privacy provisions that differ (or are relatively silent) in the degree of privacy protections afforded, allow disclosures outside PHAs, or are unclear about when disclosures may be made. While state and local PHAs excel at assuring the confidentiality of their identifiable health records (despite sometimes limited guidance from antiquated legal provisions), well-publicized breaches of privacy can erode public confidence in public health data practices. In a notorious case in Pinellas County, Florida in 1997, a local public health official caused the names of 4,000 AIDS patients to be leaked to 2 newspapers and was accused of spreading the lists around gay bars. *Man Who Leaked AIDS List Gets 60 Days*, OCALA STAR-BANNER, May 15, 1997, at 2B.

Developed under the auspices of the CDC, the MODEL STATE PUBLIC HEALTH PRIVACY ACT of 1999 (MSPHPA) (which was later incorporated into the TURNING POINT MODEL STATE PUBLIC HEALTH ACT of 2003) provides affirmative privacy provisions for state and local public health agencies. Lawrence O. Gostin et al., *Informational Privacy and the Public's Health: The Model State Public Health Privacy Act*, 91 AM. J. PUB. HEALTH 1388 (2001). These model acts combine clear privacy safeguards for public health data with sufficient authority of health departments to acquire and use identifiable health information for legitimate purposes. Several states have incorporated privacy provisions of these model acts into their statutory or regulatory public health laws. *Id.*

D. PRIVACY & THE RIGHT TO KNOW

Protecting privacy is synergistic with accomplishing public health objectives, but sometimes privacy laws can impair public health efforts. Overly-strict disclosure provisions impinge legitimate exchanges of identifiable data between PHAs (e.g., sharing data about a person with TB who crosses state borders). After the Virginia Tech shooting tragedy (noted in Chapter 6) involving the actions of a lone gunman with a prior mental health history, considerable attention fell on how mental health privacy laws (as well as FERPA) may have resulted in withholding key data from public health and law enforcement personnel. James G. Hodge, Jr., *Protecting the Public's Health Following the Virginia Tech Tragedy: Issues of Law and Policy*, 1 DISASTER MED. & PUB. HEALTH PREPAREDNESS S43 (Supp. 1 2007).

Failure to share related mental health data is at the center of the oft-cited case, *Tarasoff v. Regents of the Univ. of Cal.*, 551 P.2d 334 (Cal.1976). Prosenjitt Poddar told his psychotherapist, Dr. Lawrence Moore, at the University of California that he intended to kill his former girlfriend, Tatiana Tarasoff. Dr. Moore did not warn Tarasoff or her parents about the threat, but he did tell police. They detained Poddar, advised him to stay away from Tarasoff, and released him. Two months later, Poddar murdered her. *Id.* at 340–41. After her parents filed suit, the California Supreme Court held that mental health professionals have a "duty to warn" third parties of known, serious threats of violence by the professional's patients. *Id.* at 334.

Many courts initially accepted the *Tarasoff* decision. *See, e.g., Schuster v. Altenberg*, 424 N.W.2d 159 (Wis. 1988) (physician's duty is established when it is foreseeable that his patient may cause harm to another); *contra Alberts v. Devine*, 479 N.E.2d 113 (Mass. 1985) (absent serious danger to patients or others, a physician owes his patient a duty not to disclose medical information without patient consent). State legislatures have since statutorily converted this judicial duty to warn into a legal privilege (and also extended the privilege to other HCWs). Legislatures not only recognized a chilling effect of duties to warn on the doctor/patient relationship, but also sought to respect traditional duties of confidentiality doctors owe to patients. As a result, a HCW who is aware of a foreseeable danger posed by a patient may lawfully warn persons at risk, but does not have to do so in most states. *See, e.g.,* Lawrence O. Gostin & James G. Hodge, Jr., *Piercing the Veil of Secrecy in HIV/AIDS and Other STDs: Theories of Privacy and Disclosure in Partner Notification*, 5 DUKE J. GENDER L. & POL'Y 9 (1998).

State-recognized duties or privileges to warn in support of an individual's "right to know" extend beyond mental health contexts. One's right to know legally supports individuals' knowledge of their exposure to infectious diseases through:

(1)   an infected individual (i.e., such persons are legally-obligated to disclose their

infectious condition to others at risk. *See, e.g., People v. Jensen,* 586 N.W.2d 748 (Mich. Ct. App. 1998) (state statute requiring HIV+ status persons to disclose their status to all sexual partners does not violate constitutional free speech or privacy concerns));

(2) a medical professional (i.e., a doctor who unintentionally exposes a patient to a blood-borne pathogen. *See, e.g., Brzoska v. Olson,* 668 A.2d 1355 (Del. 1995) (dentist who intentionally lied to patients about his HIV+ status faces fraudulent misrepresentation charges));

(3) a public health agent (i.e., via partner notification, discussed in Chapter 4); or

(4) a health provider (as seen in *Tarasoff*). In respect to the right to know, a HCW may also be legally obligated to instruct a patient on how to limit the spread of the patient's infectious disease. *See, e.g., Reisner v. Regents of the Univ. of Cal.,* 37 Cal. Rptr. 2d 518, 523 (Ca. Ct. App. 1995) ("a doctor who knows he is dealing with the '20th Century version of Typhoid Mary' should inform the patient "what she ought to do and not do and how she ought to comport herself in order to prevent the spread of [HIV].").

E.   DISTINGUISHING PRACTICE & RESEARCH

Public health agencies need identifiable health data primarily for practice activities, including surveillance, epidemiological investigations, and evaluation and monitoring. Yet, other public health activities involving identifiable information may constitute research. *See, e.g.,* WILLIAM W. LOWRANCE, PRIVACY, CONFIDENTIALITY, AND HEALTH RESEARCH (2012). "Human subjects research" is defined in the federal Common Rule (governing federally-conducted or supported research) as "a systematic investigation, including research development, testing, and evaluation, designed to develop or contribute to generalizable knowledge" (32 C.F.R. § 219 (1991)), involving living humans or their private data. For example, a PHA may conduct a double-blinded, controlled study to assess the efficacy of a new treatment among a randomly-selected group of persons. This research requires adherence to a series of research protections (e.g., individual informed consent absent a waiver) and procedures (e.g., review by an institutional review board (IRB)) to help maintain the health and safety of human subjects.

Privately-funded research may not have to meet these specific oversights, leading at times to controversial issues related to the publication of their results (e.g., concerning pandemic influenza or bioterrorism agents). *See, e.g.,* Vickie J. Williams, *The "Jurassic Park" Problem—Dual Use Research of*

Concern, Privately Funded Research and Protecting Public Health, 53 JURIMETRICS J. 361 (2013).

Between clear practice and research activities is an array of public health acts that are not so neatly characterized. Philip Amoroso & John Middaugh, *Research vs. Public Health Practice: When Does a Study Require IRB Review?,* 35 PREVENTIVE MED. 250 (2003). Distinguishing between these activities is critical because:

(1)   federal, state, and local laws and ethical principles governing human subjects research often require extensive and burdensome procedures that can delay or derail activities;

(2)   the HIPAA Privacy Rule (and other privacy laws) employ different standards for the disclosure of PHI to PHAs depending on whether the underlying activity is public health practice or research. In general, it is more difficult to acquire PHI under the Privacy Rule for research purposes without individual authorization (although a combined authorization may be allowed); and

(3)   widespread methodological variations in distinctions between public health practice and research have led to inefficient and duplicative reviews among IRBs and PHAs.

There is no national consensus on how to distinguish public health practice and research activities. Even though the Common Rule, HIPAA Privacy Rule, and other laws require these distinctions to be made, they provide little direct guidance on how to do so. The federal Office for Human Research Protections (OHRP), CDC, and others offer varied approaches that collectively lack coherence, consistency, and coordination. James G. Hodge, Jr., *An Enhanced Approach to Distinguishing Public Health Practice and Human Subjects Research*, 33 J.L. MED. & ETHICS 125 (2005).

In 2004, CSTE proposed a comprehensive approach for distinguishing public health practice and research activities. CSTE, PUBLIC HEALTH PRACTICE V. RESEARCH: A REPORT FOR PUBLIC HEALTH PRACTITIONERS 1–61 (2004). *Public health practice* is defined as "the collection and analysis of identifiable health data by a PHA [to protect] the health of a particular community, where the benefits and risks are primarily designed to accrue to the participating community." *Id.* at 16. Conversely, *public health research* is defined as "the collection and analysis of identifiable health data by a PHA [to generate] knowledge that will primarily benefit those beyond the participating community who bear the risks of participation." *Id.* at 15.

Based on these core definitions, CSTE prescribed a dual-stage process for drawing distinctions. The initial stage begins with an assessment of foundational principles (to classify and dispense with the relatively easy cases). In cases where these principles do not distinguish a specific activity, the following enhanced criteria should be considered during a 2nd stage for each part of a multi-faceted activity.

General Legal Authority. Sometimes specific legal authority exists for a public health practice activity (which often typifies it as practice). In other instances, PHAs may conduct activities pursuant to more general legal authorization. The TURNING POINT ACT, for example, authorizes state or local PHAs to "collect, analyze, and maintain [information to] . . . accomplish or further the mission or goals of public health, or provide essential public health services and functions." TURNING POINT ACT, § 5–102(A). Absent other criteria favoring a research classification, the activity is likely practice and not research.

Specific Intent. CDC and others have historically focused on intent underlying data collection as a distinguishing factor, but proffered over-generalized conceptions of intent that could apply to either practice or research. Revised guidance issued by CDC in 2010 continues to rely on generalized notions of the underlying "purpose of the project," determined on a case-by-case basis, to make distinctions. CDC, DISTINGUISHING PUBLIC HEALTH RESEARCH AND PUBLIC HEALTH NONRESEARCH (2010).

In its report, CSTE specified the underlying intent of *research* is "to test a hypothesis and seek to generalize the findings or acquired knowledge beyond the activity's participants." The intent of *public health practice* is "to assure the conditions in which people can be healthy through public health efforts that are primarily aimed at preventing known or suspected injuries, diseases, or other conditions, or promoting the health of a particular community." CSTE, PUBLIC HEALTH PRACTICE V. RESEARCH, at 15.

Responsibility. In research, responsibility for the health, safety, and welfare of individual participants falls on specific individuals, typically the principal investigators (PIs). With public health practice, responsibility for individuals' well-being is held by government entities in extension of their legal and ethical duties.

Participant Benefits. Research is designed primarily to advance scientific knowledge. Participants may not only fail to receive any direct benefit from the activity, they may even be harmed by it. Whenever risks are imposed on participants to generalize the results, the activity is research. Conversely, public health practice activities are premised on providing some known or expected benefit to participants or the population of which they are members.

Experimentation. Research has an experimental quality that public health practice does not always share. Research may involve introducing something non-standard or unproven to subjects or to their identifiable health data. Although innovations are also part of public health practice, it is dominated by the use of standard, accepted, and proven interventions to address a known or suspected public health problem. Any activity that introduces experimental procedures is more likely research than public health practice.

Subject Selection. Human subjects research is largely (though not exclusively) driven by the researcher's desire to test an underlying hypothesis. To reduce the possibility of bias, the PI may select human subjects randomly so that the results may apply to a larger group. Participants for practice activities are selected because they have, or are at risk of, a particular condition and can likely benefit from the activity. Thus, if an activity utilizes control groups to garner generalizable information or randomly selects its participants to eliminate bias, the activity is likely research rather than practice.

Utilization of CSTE's process may help improve uniformity concerning difficult cases if applied across PHAs and IRBs at various levels of government. Ultimately, clarifying these distinctions supports the overriding objective to perform public health activities that respect and protect the privacy rights and interests of individuals while improving or promoting the public's health.

———————

Significant legal interests arise related to how government acquires and uses health information about individuals. Balancing individual privacy and communal health objectives throughout the management of identifiable health data is essential to the advancement of the public's health.

Other times, government seeks to manage information that is not about individuals, but is rather directed toward them in the greater marketplace of ideas. In these cases, the legal focus shifts from protecting privacy to protecting free speech. And yet, as explored in Chapter 8, the central legal question remains largely the same: when and how can government regulate information in the interests of promoting the health of populations?

CHAPTER 8

REGULATING COMMUNICATIONS

Identifiable health data may be the lifeblood of public health surveillance, but information of another type is also at the core of public health interventions. Through public health education, required disclosures, and communications, information is wielded to apprise individuals and groups of key public health issues, change specific behaviors to ameliorate health outcomes, and avert or correct potentially misleading, deceptive, or fraudulent statements made in the marketplace. Regulating communications to promote positive messages (e.g., eating healthy) and diminish negative ones (e.g., tobacco use) is fundamental to the health of communities. *See, e.g.,* Harvey V. Fineberg, *Editorial: Public Health in a Time of Government Austerity*, 103 AM. J. PUB. HEALTH 47 (2013). Unfortunately, it can also be highly contentious.

Governmental public health education efforts raise sensitive issues surrounding politically hot topics like sex, drugs, guns, and junk foods that sometimes trigger legal or political responses. Required disclosures in the form of product labels, warnings, or advisories lead to industry backlash. Freedoms of speech (noted briefly in Chapter 3) are implicated when government attempts to control commercial marketing or advertising. *See, e.g.,* Micah L. Berman, *Manipulative Marketing and the First Amendment*, 103 GEORGETOWN L. J. 497

(2015). Hurdling these and other legal issues is a major challenge any time public health messages conflict with individual, commercial, or societal interests or expectations about the role of government in the larger marketplace of ideas.

A. PUBLIC HEALTH EDUCATION

Public health education conducted by public or private entities is widespread and varied. It may entail notices of information to at-risk individuals or their parents (e.g., annual school vaccination announcements); use of imagery (e.g., the effects of methamphetamine) or symbols (pink ribbons for breast cancer awareness); as well as systematic, ongoing health campaigns. For example, each year WHO recognizes "World TB Day" in March to marshal educational and other efforts towards the eradication of the disease. CDC annually promotes "STD Awareness Month" in April to highlight information on the prevalence and spread of these diseases. The Utah Department of Health's "Got Vaxed?" campaign targets adolescents to remind them to get vaccinated for measles, rubella, varicella, and other diseases. Local public health officials in St. Louis conducted their "No Flu For You" campaign to increase influenza vaccination among HCWs. The National Institute of Neurological Disorders and Stroke (NINDS) promotes its "Know Stroke" messaging to help educate the public about warning symptoms. Risks and prevention of heart disease among women are the targets of the "Heart Truth" campaign sponsored by the National Heart, Lung, and Blood Institute (NHLBI).

Other governmental entities and private sector companies engage in public health education. The "Click It or Ticket" campaign, sponsored in part by the National Highway Traffic Safety Administration (NHTSA), encourages drivers to wear seatbelts to reduce vehicular injuries and deaths. In 2013, several national cellular providers promoted the slogan, "It Can Wait," suggesting that young drivers refrain from using their cellular devices due to the dangers of distracted driving. Pharmaceutical companies and other medical providers' marketing campaigns can also highlight public health issues. In 2013, Merck & Company ran its "One Less" advertisements promoting Gardasil shots to prevent HPV (discussed in Chapter 4). Many educational campaigns, such as "2min2x" (brush for 2 minutes twice a day) campaign to promote oral health in children, include public service announcements. AD COUNCIL, PUB. SERVICE ANNOUNCEMENTS CATALOG (Q3 2013).

Collectively, public health education is thought to increase individuals' knowledge of conditions or risks resulting in changes in individual behaviors or choices to reduce harms. After 2 years of CDC's "VERB" campaign (encouraging children ages 9–13 to be physically active everyday), researchers in 1 study positively correlated children who saw the campaign with improved cognitive and behavioral outcomes related to physical activity. *See* Marian E. Muhman et al., *Evaluation of a National Physical*

Activity Intervention for Children: VERB Campaign, 2002–2004, 32 AM. J. PREVENTATIVE MED. 38, 42 (2007). As well, population-based communications aimed at preventing cardiovascular disease in the U.S. and abroad from the 1970s through the 1990s have been shown to heighten awareness and improve risk-reducing behaviors, including dietary changes and lowering weight. *See* Melanie A. Wakefield et al., *Use of Mass Media Campaigns to Change Health Behavior*, 376 LANCET 1261, 1265 (2010).

Not all public health education efforts are known and proven to be effective. Some may even offend affected groups or the public. A 2013 anti-pregnancy campaign in Chicago featured mock images of pregnant boys and the slogan, "Unexpected? Most teen pregnancies are." The campaign, aimed at reducing teen pregnancy and STD transmissions through sex education, was objected to by the transgender community. Rheana Murray, *Boys, Not Girls, Are Pregnant in Chicago's Shocking Campaign to Reduce Teen Pregnancy*, N.Y. DAILY NEWS, June 10, 2013.

An anti-obesity campaign in Atlanta ("Stop Sugarcoating It, Georgia") used billboard and television ads to portray overweight children asking "Mom, why am I fat?" and stating, "Being fat takes the fun out of being a kid." Potential stigmatization of obese children and adults led some to criticize the campaign and question its effectiveness. Carrie Teegardin, *Grim Childhood Obesity Ads Stir Critics,*

ATLANTA J. CONST., Dec. 21, 2011; *see also* Chapter 3 for discussion of ADA-related concerns.

New York City's former Mayor, Michael Bloomberg, and the City's Health Department's campaign against the sale of large SSBs was meant to deter their consumption through education and restricted portion controls. On March 11, 2013, a local court blocked implementation of the City's portion size proposal, which was affirmed on appeal on July 30, 2013. *New York Statewide Coal. of Hispanic Chambers of Commerce v. N.Y. Dep't of Health & Mental Hygiene*, 110 A.D.3d 1 (N.Y. App. Div. 2013). In Mississippi, the state legislature passed what it called its "Anti-Bloomberg" bill to circumvent public health efforts there, including educations campaigns, to limit soda intake. Kim Severson, *'Anti-Bloomberg Bill' in Mississippi Bars Local Restrictions on Food and Drink*, N.Y. TIMES, Mar. 14, 2013, at A16.

Public health supported efforts to restrict soda consumption, particularly among minors, extend further. In May 2015, the city of Davis, California ordained that milk and water become the "default choices" for kids' meals offered in restaurants. *See* Claire Doan, *Davis Makes Water, Milk Default in Kids' Meals,* KCRA.COM (May 28, 2015); Jane E. Brody, *Prudent Ways to Fight Childhood Obesity*, N.Y. TIMES, June 23, 2015, at D7. San Francisco's City Council approved ordinances in 2015 designed to curb soda consumption through warning labels on soft drink advertisements, advertisement bans on city-owned property, and prohibition of purchases of soft drinks with city funds. Tamara Audi & Mike Esterl, *Soda's New Enemy: San Francisco,* WALL ST. J. (June 9, 2015). A resulting lawsuit challenging the constitutionality of the measures under First Amendment principles was filed by the American Beverage Association. Sam Frizell, *Big Soda Sues San Francisco Over Beverage Warnings*, TIME (July 27, 2015).

Public health education may help inform the populace of health risks, but it can also lead to public distrust when it lacks transparency. Examples include stealthy attempts via government to manipulate messages in the private sector, compensate people or programs to issue specific information favorable to the public's health, or promote information that is inconsistent with or poorly-supported by scientific data. *See* LAWRENCE O. GOSTIN, PUBLIC HEALTH LAW: POWER, DUTY, RESTRAINT 340–41 (2d ed. 2008).

B.   REQUIRED DISCLOSURES OF PUBLIC HEALTH INFORMATION

Government does not have to rely solely on education and positive messaging to counteract negative societal behaviors or trends. It can also require disclosures of information regarding products or services in the public or private sphere. Two prominent examples of government's ability to mandate disclosures of public health information include (1) mandated warnings or advisories on products and services and (2) posting of calories (and potentially other data) on menus.

1.   WARNINGS & ADVISORIES

Product or service information conducive to the public's health may be voluntarily provided via industry practices or stem from tort-related claims (discussed in Chapter 6). Federal and state public health agencies are also legally authorized to require manufacturers and service providers to label products or services with warnings, advisories, or other messages. Some of this information is designed to equip consumers with adequate data to make healthy choices (e.g., low-fat products), avoid use of specific products (e.g., tobacco), or understand the hazards of certain services (e.g., potential for injury related to recreational activities or amusement rides). Other mandated information is designed to relay accurate data (e.g., contents of food) so consumers can properly assess risks unique to their consumption of products or use of services.

At the federal level, the Consumer Product Safety Commission (CPSC) was established in 1972 to "assist consumers in evaluating the comparative safety of . . . products." Consumer Product Safety Act (CPSA), 15 U.S.C. §§ 2051–2089, at § 2051(b)(2) (2012). CPSC is authorized to investigate potentially-dangerous products. In May 2015, the Commission launched an investigation of the national chain Lumber Liquidators, which allegedly sold flooring with excessive levels of the carcinogen, formaldehyde. Rachel Abrams, *Lumber Liquidators' Founder Steps In as Chief Resigns*, N.Y. TIMES, May 22, 2015, at B3. Lumber Liquidators later agreed to stop selling these products in question, largely imported from China.

CPSC can also require warnings or instructions for various products (except food, drugs, cosmetics, tobacco, and alcohol, which are covered under different federal laws). *Id.* at § 2052(a)(5). For example, CPSC requires manufacturers of portable generators to note on their labels, "Danger: Using a generator indoors CAN KILL YOU IN MINUTES." With some exceptions, packaging of any toy with small parts for children between the ages of 3–6 must feature the following information: "WARNING: CHOKING HAZARD—Small parts. Not for children under 3 yrs." CPSC also regulates toxic, corrosive, flammable, or other hazardous products via the Federal Hazardous Substances Act, 15 U.S.C. §§ 1261–1278 (2012). Labels on such materials feature words like DANGER, WARNING, or CAUTION, precautionary measures, and instructions on how to deliver first aid treatment. *Id.* at § 1261(p)(1).

The Consumer Product Safety Improvement Act of 2008, Pub. L. No. 110–314, 122 Stat. 3016, authorizes CPSC to re-examine the effectiveness of existing warning labels particularly for children's products. 15 U.S.C. § 2056b (2012). In November 2012, CPSC recalled an inflatable children's waterslide and ordered its manufacturer to update the warning labels to include age and weight restrictions. CPSC, Sportspower Recalls Children's Waterslides Due to Injury Hazard; Sold Exclusively at Menards (Recall 13-502) (2012).

FDA is empowered to regulate what it defines as food, drugs, and cosmetics, including by requiring appropriate warning labels or other information. The Food, Drug, & Cosmetic Act of 1938, Pub. L. No. 75–717, 52 Stat. 1040. FDA may consider any such products misbranded if they fail to include material information on their use (21 U.S.C. § 321(n)), and consequently require warning labels through regulation. Cosmetics are subject to several warning requirements including that they have not been properly tested for all uses. 21 U.S.C. § 740.10 (2012). FDA concerns related to the presence of Bisphenol A (BPA) in babies' plastic bottles led the industry to abandon its inclusion in their manufacture. *See* Leila Barraza, *A New Approach for Regulating BPA for the Protection of the Public's Health*, 41 J.L. MED. & ETHICS 9 (Supp. 2013).

FDA's oversight of prescription and over-the-counter drugs entails extensive required disclosures. Aspirin labels must state the following: "It is especially important not to use aspirin during the last 3 months of pregnancy unless definitely directed to do so by a doctor because it may cause problems in the unborn child or complications during delivery." 21 C.F.R. § 201.63 (2012). Following testing and approval, most prescription drugs carry a consumer warning of their unintended uses or potential side effects, which may be summarized in commercial advertisements. This does not include nutritional supplements, like herbal remedies, because they are not defined as "drugs." *See* Peter Goldman, *Herbal Medicines*

Today and the Roots of Modern Pharmacology, 135
ANNALS INTERNAL MED. 594, 598 (2001).

Most packaged foods for direct sale to consumers
are clearly labeled with basic information pursuant
to the Nutrition Labeling and Education Act of 1990
(NLEA), 21 U.S.C. § 343 (1990). Foods generally do
not require warnings *per se*, but there are notable
exceptions. *See, e.g.,* Noah Lars, *The Imperative to
Warn: Disentangling the "Right to Know" from the
"Need to Know" About Consumer Products*, 11 YALE
J. ON REG. 293, 315 (1994). Since 1974, package
labels of the sweetener, aspartame, have warned
about 1 of its ingredients, phenylalanine, which
some persons cannot metabolize resulting in direct
harms. 21 C.F.R. § 172.804; *see also* Harriet H.
Butchko & W. Wayne Stargel, *Aspartame: Scientific
Evaluation in the Postmarketing Period*, 34 REG.
TOXICOLOGY & PHARMACOLOGY 221, 222 (2001).

Dietary supplements containing iron warn
against its accidental overdose, which "is a leading
cause of fatal poisoning in children under 6." 21
C.F.R. at § 101.17(e)(1). Caffeinated products have
recently received additional attention. FDA has long
recognized the safety of caffeine as an additive to
carbonated soft drinks (*id.* at § 182.1180(c)), but its
presence in other products (e.g., ice cream, yogurt,
gum, candies, syrup, bottled water) present new and
under-studied risks. *See* Brady Dennis, *Slew of New
Caffeinated Food Products Has FDA Jittery*, WASH.
POST, June 1, 2013. Caffeine sold in a powdered
form in the U.S. has led to deaths due to unintended
overdoses and calls for stronger FDA regulations.

Murray Carpenter, *Caffeine Powder Poses Deadly Risks*, N.Y. TIMES (May 18, 2015).

The sale and marketing of energy drinks, once classified as "nutritional supplements" by manufacturers, to children led San Francisco to sue a producer to stop its advertising and promotions tailored to kids. Complaint, *.California v. Monster Beverage Corp*, 2013 WL 4573959 (S.F. Super. Ct. 2013); *see also* Barry Meier, *Suit Claims Monster Markets to Children*, N.Y. TIMES, May 7, 2013, at B1. FDA is investigating whether new safety standards regarding caffeinated products should be issued. Consumer Update, FDA, FDA to Investigate Added Caffeine (May 3, 2013).

The Federal Trade Commission (FTC) supplements FDA regulation of tobacco products through its enforcement of the Federal Cigarette Labeling and Advertising Act of 1965, 15 U.S.C. §§ 1331–1340 (2012). Government regulation and industry acquiescence have resulted in progressively stronger warnings on tobacco products, notably cigarettes. What was once a fairly non-specific warning (e.g., "Caution: Cigarette Smoking May Be Hazardous to Your Health") has evolved into clearer warnings such as "Smoking can kill you." *Id*. at § 1333(a)(1). In 2015, a manufacturer of snus, a small pouch of tobacco used between the teeth and gums, asked FDA to consider allowing a significantly reduced warning on the dangers of its product, suggesting its product is a safer alternative for smokers. Sabrina Tavernise, *A Bid for Relief on Tobacco Warning*, N.Y. TIMES, Apr. 9, 2015, at A21.

In 2011, FDA called for new graphic warnings on cigarette packaging (like those featured in Australia and other countries). Required Warnings for Cigarette Packages and Advertisements, 76 Fed. Reg. 36628–01 (June 22, 2011). As discussed in section D below, however, FDA's regulation was struck down by at least 1 federal court. *See R.J. Reynolds Tobacco Co. v. FDA*, 696 F.3d 1205 (D.C. Cir. 2012).

The Alcoholic Beverage Labeling Act (ABLA) of 1988, 27 U.S.C. §§ 213–219 (2012), addresses "health hazards that may result from the consumption or abuse of alcoholic beverages." *Id.* at § 213. All alcoholic beverage containers must include the following: "GOVERNMENT WARNING: (1) According to the Surgeon General, women should not drink alcoholic beverages during pregnancy because of the risk of birth defects. (2) Consumption of alcoholic beverages impairs your ability to drive a car or operate machinery, and may cause health problems." *Id.* at § 215(a). Beyond this warning, the Act may allow additional state-based requirements on the labeling of alcoholic beverages. *See, e.g., Bronco Wine Co. v. Jolly*, 95 P.3d 422 (Cal. 2004). In 2013, the federal Alcohol and Tobacco Trade and Tax Bureau approved voluntary use of nutrition-like labels on all packaged alcohol products. *See* Mary Clare Jalonick, *Nutritional Labels May Be Coming on Some Alcoholic Drinks*, WASH. POST, June 4, 2013.

2.   MENU LABELING

For years, select state and local governments including New York City (2008), Seattle-King County (2009), California (2009), and Massachusetts (2009) required restaurants and other vendors to post calorie data about their products on menus. The overriding public health goal of menu labeling is to help people make healthier choices when they eat out to reduce their calorie intake and improve health outcomes. Together with increased physical activity and other measures, reducing the amount of calories Americans consume is central to addressing the obesity epidemic.

In 2010, FDA was required pursuant to the ACA to issue regulations to implement menu labeling nationally. ACA, Pub. L. No. 111–148, 124 Stat. 119 § 4205 (2010). On December 1, 2014, FDA published a final rule requiring covered establishments to list calorie information for standard menu items. Food Labeling; Nutrition Labeling of Standard Menu Items in Restaurants and Similar Retail Food Establishments, 79 Fed. Reg. 71155 (Dec. 1, 2014) (to be codified at 21 C.F.R. pts. 11, 101). The effective date for the rule's implementation is projected to be December 1, 2016. Sabrina Tavernise, *F.D.A. Extends Deadline for Calorie Counts on Menus*, N.Y. TIMES (July 9, 2015). A separate final rule requires vendors owning or operating 20 or more vending machines to disclose calorie information on the products they sell. Food Labeling; Calorie Labeling of Articles of Food in

Vending Machines, 79 Fed. Reg. 71259 (Dec. 1, 2014) (to be codified at 21 C.F.R. pts. 11, 101).

FDA's regulations will require restaurants or other retail food establishments with more than 20 locations to post caloric information on menus, menu boards, and drive-thrus. Posted data must be in a similar font, size, and color as used to describe menu items and their prices. Variable menu items offering different choices or size options, like combination meals, must include an accurate calorie range (e.g., 500–650 calories).

Though extensive, FDA's proposed regulations are limited in their coverage. They do not apply to foods intended for consumption by more than 1 person purchased in grocery stores or other retail food establishments. *Id.* Nearly 75% of the nation's restaurants are not covered (because they are not chains), nor does the rule apply to hotels, movie theaters, convenience stores, or other entities whose primary business is not food service (even though they often sell foods similar to those sold in restaurants).

Even among the chain restaurants that are covered by the rule, only standard menu items prepared on site, as well as self-serve salad bars and beverage dispensers, must feature posted calories. Posting of calories is not required for condiments, alcoholic beverages, pre-packaged foods (e.g., salad dressing), or temporary or "test" items that appear on the menu for 90 days or less per year (e.g., specialty drinks or appetizers). Due to purported space limits on menus and boards more extensive nutritional data (e.g., fat and salt content) are not required. Menus may include brief statements about the U.S. Department of Agriculture's (USDA) daily calorie standard and how consumers can access additional nutritional data.

State and local efforts to require menu labeling were initially litigated based on several grounds, including that they were preempted by the NLEA. *See* Lainie Rutkow et al., *Preemption and the Obesity Epidemic*, 36 J.L. MED. & ETHICS 772 (2008). Though once opposed, the National Restaurant Association now endorses FDA's forthcoming regulations due in part to their preemptive effect. Press Release, National Restaurant Association Statement on Proposed Menu Labeling Regulations (Apr. 1, 2011). FDA regulations will likely preempt contrary state and local rules applying to covered restaurants, but not rules applying to other restaurants or entities exempt under the ACA.

Even as menu labeling practices go national, their efficacy as a public health preventive measure is debated. Some data suggest that posting calories positively alters consumer habits and vendor practices. *See* Mary T. Bassett et al., *Purchasing Behavior and Calorie Information at Fast-Food Chains in New York City*, 98 AM. J. PUB. HEALTH 1457 (2008) (sandwich shop patrons who saw menu calorie information purchased on average 52 fewer calories per order than those who did not). Calorie postings on menus increase transparency and may heighten restaurants' accountability for the foods they serve.

Other researchers suggest that menu labeling has no or negligible effects on consumers' behaviors. Adults and children dining at fast food restaurants with calorie-labeled menus consume similar amounts of calories as patrons of the same restaurants without them. Tara Parker-Pope, *After Menu Labels, Parents and Kids Order Same Foods,* N.Y. TIMES, Feb. 16, 2011. Menu labels have no effect on calorie consumption even when they include recommendations for calorie consumption per meal in addition to the calorie count of the particular menu item. Melissa Dahl, *Who Cares About Calories? Restaurant Menu Labels Don't Work, Study Shows,* TODAY.COM (July 18, 2013) (citing Julie S. Downs et al., *Supplementing Menu Labeling With Calorie Recommendations to Test for Facilitation Effects,* 103 AM. J. OF PUB. HEALTH 1604 (2013)).

Conversely, a menu's inclusion of an interpretative symbol, such as a traffic light, may have a small but significant effect in reducing consumer calorie selection and consumption. Brenna Ellison et al., *The Effect of Calorie Labels on Caloric Intake and Restaurant Revenue: Evidence from Two Full-Service Restaurants,* 46 J. AGRIC. & APPLIED ECON. 173 (2014); Susan E. Sinclair et al., *The Influence of Menu Labeling on Calories Selected or Consumed: A Systematic Review and Meta-Analysis,* 114 J. ACAD. NUTRITION & DIETETICS 1375 (2014). In 1 study, a high percentage of women report that nutritional labels significantly affect their menu choices, but their consumer behaviors do not necessarily match. Bethany Schornack & Susan Rozensher, *The Effects Of Menu Calorie Labeling On Consumer Food Choice Behavior*, 5 AM. J. HEALTH SCI. 29 (2014).

In recognition of these limits, as well as the preemptive effect of FDA's regulations, some support alternative models of menu labeling nationally or at least allowing greater experimentation at the state or local levels. Peggy J. Liu et al., *A Test of Different Menu Labeling Presentations*, 59 APPETITE 770 (2012); James G. Hodge, Jr. & Lexi C. White, *Supplementing National Menu Labeling,* 102 AM. J. PUB. HEALTH e11 (2012).

C.   CONTROLLING COMMERCIAL COMMUNICATIONS

Government efforts to conduct or fund public health education campaigns sometimes raise political debates and arguments. Still, whether government is empowered legally to speak directly on public health issues is fairly well-settled. It can issue its own messages, even if the citizenry does not always like their content. Less clear is government's power to restrict when, where, and how individuals and companies market their products. Micah L. Berman, *Manipulative Marketing and the First Amendment*, 103 GEORGETOWN L. J. 497 (2015). Government interference with the advertising, marketing, or promotion of products or services ignites allegations of infringement of freedoms of speech, specifically commercial speech, under the 1st Amendment.

Public health agencies can proscribe advertising of illegal products (e.g., cocaine) or services (e.g., prostitution). They can also prohibit advertising of information about lawful products that is false (e.g., medications claiming to cure HIV/AIDS) or misleading (e.g., "low tar cigarettes are better for your health"). As explained below, none of these forms of commercial speech is entitled to any protection under the 1st Amendment. While there is no inherent legal right to sell dangerous or harmful products in the private marketplace, government's ability to restrict the sale of products must be divorced from its interference with commercial expressions about lawful products or services. For example, government may be able to ban the sale of highly-caffeinated beverages to minors, but not prohibit their advertising generally so long as the product remains lawful for other consumers.

Furthermore, public health agencies can set reasonable, "content neutral" limits on commercial (or other) speech. In *Ward v. Rock Against Racism*, 491 U.S. 781 (1989), the Court observed that "government may impose reasonable restrictions on the time, place, or manner of protected speech provided restrictions are 'justified without reference to the content of the regulated speech, that they are narrowly tailored to serve a significant governmental interest, and that they leave open ample alternative channels for communication of the information.'" *Id.* at 791 (citing *Clark v. Community for Creative Non-Violence*, 468 U.S. 288, 293 (1984)).

As a result, public health measures that restrict the *time* (i.e., when a message may be displayed, such as outside the hours of children's broadcast programming), *place* (i.e., where it may be displayed, such as within or near schools), and *manner* (i.e., how it is displayed, such as billboard ads vs. at the point of sale) of commercial advertisements may be lawful so long as alternative channels for communication are available. LAWRENCE O. GOSTIN, PUBLIC HEALTH LAW: POWER, DUTY, RESTRAINT 357 (2d ed. 2008).

Since 1975 when the Supreme Court first recognized commercial speech protections, governmental attempts to (1) restrict advertising of legal products, or (2) require commercial entities to provide truthful information through warnings or counter information may raise constitutional arguments. In the former case, government may be limiting truthful speech (which the Court tends to disdain). In the latter case, government is forcing an entity to speak through compelled warnings or data postings which it might not otherwise choose to state. The freedom to speak under the 1st Amendment also includes the freedom not to speak (*see, e.g., Wooley v. Maynard*, 430 U.S. 705 (1977)) or subsidize speech with which one does not agree, other than through general taxes (*see, e.g., United States v. United Foods*, 533 U.S. 405 (2001) (federal act mandating assessments on handlers of fresh mushrooms to fund advertising and other initiatives violated freedom of speech)).

In *Central Hudson Gas & Elec. Corp. v. Public Serv. Comm'n of N.Y.*, 447 U.S. 557, 566 (1980), the Court set forth a 4-step test to assess potential infringements of commercial speech. Courts must ask whether:

1. the speech concerns lawful activity and is not misleading; *and*

2. the asserted government interest is substantial; *if so, then whether*

3. the law directly advances the governmental interest asserted; *and*

4. it is not more extensive than is necessary to serve that interest.

Step 1 of the *Central Hudson* test is largely a perfunctory assessment affirming points noted above. If commercial speech concerns an unlawful activity (e.g., the sale of illicit drugs) or is patently misleading (e.g., "eating sugared candy is good for your teeth"), government can restrict it because the speech is unprotected. More nuanced issues arise related to commercial speech that intimates behaviors contrary to the public's health, but is not directly misleading. Ohio State University professor Micah L. Berman refers to these sort of communications as "manipulative marketing." Micah L. Berman, *Manipulative Marketing and the First Amendment*, 103 GEORGETOWN L. J. 497 (2015) (suggesting further that these types of noninformational marketing practices are not entitled to any 1st Amendment protection). While industry ads depicting healthy people smoking cigarettes, consuming hard or soft liquor, eating fast food, or driving carelessly may all invoke negative behaviors that impact morbidity and mortality, the ads are not considered misleading or deceptive under current jurisprudence.

Provided the commercial speech subject to regulation survives inquiry under the 1st step, the 2nd part asks whether government's interest is substantial. Government cannot simply restrict commercial speech because it does not like a product, service, or corresponding message. It must have some basis for so doing. Protection of the public's health, especially minors, is routinely agreed by courts to qualify as a substantial governmental interest, particularly when state or local government acts to curtail commercial speech.

The more difficult assessments arise in steps 3 and 4 of the *Central Hudson* test. To survive scrutiny, government's interests in protecting the public's health must be directly advanced by its chosen intervention and be no more extensive than necessary. Early in its commercial speech jurisprudence, the Supreme Court generally accepted government arguments that its interventions directly advanced public health interests consistent with judicial deference of legislative findings under separation of powers (discussed in Chapter 2). This is no longer the case. The Court has clarified that government must demonstrate a strong nexus between its restriction of commercial speech and its public health objective. Increasingly, this means public health agencies must produce evidence of efficacy for a specific intervention that negatively impacts commercial speech.

In *44 Liquormart, Inc. v. Rhode Island*, 517 U.S. 484 (1996), the Court struck down Rhode Island's attempt to ban advertising of the price of alcohol (other than at the point of sale) to help lower alcohol consumption. Concerned about significant limitations of otherwise truthful advertising of the price of alcoholic products, Justice Stevens clarified that the state must show that its restriction will advance its public health interest "to a material degree." *Id.* at 505. The Court concluded:

(1) there was no "reasonable fit" between Rhode Island's abridgement of speech and the reduction in alcohol consumption. *Id.* at 507;

(2) just because the state could ban the sale of alcohol altogether does not mean it can restrict truthful advertising about such products; and

(3) application of lesser standards for protections of commercial speech related to "vice" products like alcohol is unwarranted. *Id.* at 513–14.

D.   COMMERCIAL SPEECH & TOBACCO

Restrictions on commercial advertisements of tobacco products are central to governmental efforts to reduce consumption of products that collectively remain the leading cause of preventable deaths in the U.S. (*see* Chapter 5). Some restrictions are authorized via federal statute. The Family Smoking Prevention and Tobacco Control Act (FSPTCA) of 2009, 21 U.S.C. § 387 (2009), allows states and localities to regulate the time, place, and manner of tobacco promotion or advertising, but not the content. Prior to this Act, state-based regulations on cigarette advertisement were preempted largely by the Federal Cigarette Labeling and Advertising Act, 15 U.S.C. §§ 1331–1341 (1984).

Other advertising limitations were negotiated as part of the Master Tobacco Settlement Agreement of 1998 between big tobacco companies and 46 states and 6 U.S. territories. NAT'L ASS'N OF ATTORNEYS GEN., MASTER SETTLEMENT AGREEMENT (1998). In addition to paying hundreds of billions of dollars to the jurisdictions through 2025, tobacco companies agreed to restrict large outdoor ads such as billboards and use of cartoon characters (e.g., Joe Camel™), as well as limit merchandising and sponsorship of sporting venues (which the aforementioned Tobacco Control Act expressly prohibits).

Some states have sought additional tobacco advertising restrictions. In *Lorillard Tobacco Co. v. Reilly*, 533 U.S. 525 (2001), Justice Sandra Day O'Connor applied the *Central Hudson* test to a series of restrictions on tobacco ads proffered by the Massachusetts Attorney General. Of particular concern was the attempt to prohibit outdoor ads of smokeless tobacco products and cigars within 1,000 feet of any school or playground. While each of the 3 initial prongs of the *Central Hudson* test were satisfied, Justice O'Connor found the regulation failed the final element because it was more extensive than necessary to advance governments' interest in reducing tobacco use. Implementation of the outdoor ban would have broadly curtailed multiple forms and types of speech, including in-store ads and oral communications. As well, there was no attempt, alleged the Court, to tailor the prohibition to different settings in urban, suburban, or rural communities.

The Court also invalidated Massachusetts' requirement that no advertisements of smokeless tobacco or cigars be placed lower than 5 feet from the floor in establishments within the same 1,000 feet radius of schools and parks. Designed to limit kids' exposure to these ads, Justice O'Connor rejected the measure as failing to advance the Commonwealth's interests. "Not all children are less than 5 feet tall. . . ," she noted, and others can simply look up. *Id.* at 566. The Court did allow restrictions on the use of self-service displays and placement of such products outside the reach of minors. Both of these interventions were not considered advertisements under the *Central Hudson* standards. They were approved because they were narrowly tailored to limiting access to children and left open other channels of communication about such products between sellers and adult consumers.

Undecided in *Lorillard* is whether the Court would approve a ban on prominent, behind-the-counter tobacco displays, known as "power walls." These displays tend to sit directly behind counters at convenience stores or other locales, feature dozens of brands of cigarettes or other tobacco products, and often contain large print displays of specific brands (e.g., Marlboro™). At least 2 local governments in New York have considered bans on these displays, and several foreign countries have implemented them. *See* Anemona Hartocollis, *Bloomberg's Plan Would Make Stores Conceal Cigarettes*, N.Y. TIMES, Mar. 19, 2013, at A20; Sarah Boseley, *Cigarettes and Tobacco Displays Banned in Supermarkets*, GUARDIAN, Apr. 5, 2012.

Tobacco advertisements remain a divisive area of Supreme Court jurisprudence with many lessons applying to other commercial speech restrictions in the interests of the public's health. Authorized by the passage of the FSPTCA, noted above, FDA proposed a series of additional anti-tobacco initiatives in 2011, including a requirement that the fronts of cigarette packs feature graphic color depictions of the negative health impacts of smoking. Required Warnings for Cigarette Packages and Advertisements, 76 Fed. Reg. 36628–01 (June 22, 2011). Soon after reviewing FDA's proposed images (some of which were visually disturbing in their depiction of the harms of tobacco use), several tobacco companies challenged FDA's regulations in federal court on 1st Amendment (and other) grounds.

In *Discount Tobacco City & Lottery, Inc. v. U.S.*, 674 F.3d 509 (6th Cir. 2012), *cert. denied*, 133 S. Ct. 1996 (2013), the 6th Circuit Court of Appeals upheld the constitutionality of FDA's proposed graphic warnings for cigarette packs (but rejected a restriction that tobacco advertising be produced only in black and white). Largely bypassing application of the *Central Hudson* test, the court found "[a]mple evidence establishes that current warnings do not effectively inform consumers of the health risks of tobacco use and that consumers do not understand these risks." *Id.* at 569. To the extent FDA's regulations require graphic and textual warnings that convey the "factual health risks of smoking," the court held they were "reasonably related to the government's interest in preventing consumer deception and are therefore constitutional." *Id.*

Six months later in 2012, another federal court of appeals found inapposite to the 6th Circuit decision. In *R.J. Reynolds Tobacco Co. v. FDA*, 696 F.3d 1205 (D.C. Cir. 2012), the D.C. Circuit Court of Appeals held that FDA's proposed graphic images failed to meet the 3rd prong of *Central Hudson*. Although the 6th Circuit found "ample evidence," this court suggested FDA completely lacked any evidentiary support linking use of graphic imagery with lowering tobacco use. "FDA has not provided a shred of evidence—much less the 'substantial evidence' required by the [Administrative Procedures Act]— showing that the graphic warnings will 'directly advance' its interest in reducing the number of Americans who smoke." *Id.* at 1219. FDA's evidence relying on use of similar imagery in other countries was rejected on the basis that it showed only that consumers thought more about the health implications of smoking, but generally did not quit. *Id.* at 1220. Since FDA could not present substantial evidence that its proposal would directly advance the interest of reducing smoking rates, the court struck it down.

These divergent cases have left FDA in a legal quandary. An appeal of the 6th Circuit decision in *Discount Tobacco* was rejected by the U.S. Supreme Court. FDA chose not to appeal the *R.J. Reynolds* decision. Tom Schoenberg & Phil Mattingly, *Cigarette Warning-Label Ruling Won't Be Appealed by U.S.*, BLOOMBERG, Mar. 19, 2013. What remains is a split between federal circuit courts of appeal. As a result, FDA plans tentatively to proceed with implementation of proposed graphic warnings with potentially new images. Matthew Mientka, *FDA Preparing to Relaunch Graphic Tobacco Warning Labels*, MED. DAILY, June 18, 2013. It does so, however, against a backdrop of competing constitutional analyses that reflect disagreement on (1) the need for stronger evidence of efficacy in support of the graphic warnings as well as (2) the full application of commercial speech protections.

———————————

Judicial decisions in tobacco advertisement and other modern commercial speech cases have the potential to set a dangerous threshold for government regulation of communications in the interests of health promotion. Insisting that government unequivocally link proposed regulations of commercial speech to success in accomplishing public health objectives may protect commercial speech interests against unwarranted restrictions, but at what costs?

In furtherance of commercial speech interests, courts may stop public health agencies from restricting negative commercial messages or requiring mandatory product or service disclosures unless they have a strong evidentiary basis of efficacy. Unfortunately, this basis may simply not exist until an implementation is tried and assessed. Requiring high levels of proof of effectiveness for public health entities to intervene dampens the sharing of truthful, positive messaging on the potential harms of commercial products and services for which the public may be largely unaware. One need only revisit the unscrupulous tobacco ads of the 1950s–1970s to understand the potential harms of unregulated commercial advertisements, which the Court (and nearly everyone else) recognizes as a social failure. In response to current political and judicial trends, public health authorities and scholars are strategizing on how to alter the existing legal environment that favors commercial enterprise over communal health as related to commercial speech protections.

CHAPTER 9

MONITORING PROPERTY & THE BUILT ENVIRONMENT

Interventions to ameliorate health risks stemming from uses of public and private property and the built environment proliferate across all levels of government. Its extensive authority to inspect real property (e.g., land and improvements) helps protect public health and safety. Overseeing the production and shipment of foods, drugs, and other consumables is the mission of thousands of governmental and private sector actors. Abating nuisances through regulatory actions as well as private litigation can negate general or particular risks to the community's health.

Altering the built environment to promote safer, healthier communities is supported by federal conditional grants and state legal requirements requiring quality construction of buildings, schools, and playgrounds. Through zoning laws, local officials separate industrial and residential areas, encourage inclusion of biking or walking trails in modern urban and suburban developments, and even restrict the types and numbers of businesses (e.g., alcohol or tobacco outlets, fast food restaurants) that may locate in specific areas such as near schools.

All of these measures (plus other environmental laws related to clean air, water, and land covered outside this text) rely on public health legal authority balanced with individual and corporate property interests. As discussed below, these governmental interventions raise constitutional issues, principally concerning searches (via the 4th Amendment) and takings (via the 5th Amendment), as discussed initially in Chapter 3.

A. INSPECTIONS & OVERSIGHT

Government agencies are empowered to conduct inspections to ensure the safety, health, and welfare of the public. Federal statutes authorize USDA's Food Safety and Inspection Service and FDA to inspect businesses' premises, facilities, inventories, operations, and records. Federal agents inspect domestic and foreign facilities producing meat, poultry, and eggs via a slate of Congressional legislation focused on addressing proper sanitation. Federal Meat Inspection Act of 1906, 21 U.S.C. §§ 601–625 (2013); Poultry Products Inspection Act of 1957, 21 U.S.C. §§ 451–472 (2013); Egg Products Inspection Act of 1970, 21 U.S.C. §§ 1031–1056 (2013).

Pursuant to the Food, Drug, and Cosmetic Act, 21 U.S.C.S. §§ 301–399 (2013), DHHS must prioritize inspections and other efforts concerning "high risk facilities" with known safety risks, negative compliance histories (e.g., food recalls, outbreaks of foodborne illness, or violations of food safety standards) or other criteria. *Id.* at § 350j(a)(1). In 2010, the Food Safety Modernization Act, 21 U.S.C. §§ 2201–2252 (2013), called for DHHS to increase the frequency of all inspections. In 2013, FDA issued new regulations requiring food importers to assure the safety of products they receive from abroad following multiple outbreaks stemming from contaminants in produce and other foods. *See, e.g.,* Mary Clare Jalonick, *FDA Plan Would Put Food Safety on U.S. Importers*, ARIZ. REP., July 27, 2013, at D4. Importers must assure their foreign food suppliers have adequate safety measures. Imported foods with known safety risks must be certified consistent with known safety standards. FDA, INTERNATIONAL FOOD SAFETY CAPACITY-BUILDING PLAN 4 (2013).

States and localities authorize other types of public health inspections of public buildings, private residences, and businesses through statute or regulation. For example, Baltimore's city code provides that the health commissioner may enter "at all reasonable times . . . any structure or premises within the City ... whenever the Commissioner has reason to believe that a health hazard [or] nuisance [or any other violation]" has occurred on the property. BALTIMORE, MD., HEALTH CODE, tit. 2, sub. 1, § 2–107 (2013). In many cases, inspectors arrive without advance notice and search any public spaces (e.g., restaurant or business lobbies or service areas) directly or based on available surveillance. *L.R. Willson & Sons v. OSHRC*, 134 F.3d 1235 (4th Cir. 1998) (surveillance videotape of common areas in hotels can be used for inspection purposes by OSHA).

Public health authorities in many states are explicitly directed to inspect public eating establishments, particularly restaurants, on a regular basis. In New York City, each violation earns a certain number of points. Grades for each establishment are assessed based on the total points (A is 0–14, B is 14–27, and C is 28 or more). N.Y.C., N.Y., R.C.N.Y. tit. 24, ch. 23, § 23–03 (2013). Some states like South Carolina also require the prominent posting of inspection grades at the premises, online, or in print media. 38 S.C. CODE. REGS. 61-25 (2014).

While many states' laws grant extensive authority to inspect premises, there are legal limits. Texas state law prohibits health inspections at private residences without permission from an adult occupant or an authorization by a magistrate or court finding a "probable violation of a state health law, a control measure . . . or a health ordinance." TEX. HEALTH & SAFETY CODE ANN. § 161.011 (2013). Pennsylvania statutes and other states' laws limit the time in which commercial inspections may be conducted to "hours of operation and other reasonable times." PA. FOOD CODE § 46.1101 (2013).

B.   SEARCH & SEIZURE

Public health inspections and property oversight are essential environmental health interventions, but they have the potential for abuse, particularly related to the privacy of one's residence or economic interests related to conducting lawful businesses. To protect against unwarranted privacy invasions, the 4th Amendment of the U.S. Constitution prohibits "unreasonable searches and seizures." As discussed in Chapters 3 and 4, while these privacy protections cover bodily searches of blood or other tests, they traditionally apply to physical searches of one's personal effects, residences, businesses, or other real property. RUSSELL L. WEAVER ET AL., PRINCIPLES OF CRIMINAL PROCEDURE 92–100 (4th ed. 2012).

For decades leading up to the late 1960s, governments conducted routine public health inspections of commercial and private premises without much, if any, advance warning to occupants. Courts tended to approve these unannounced inspections, except in truly egregious scenarios, on the premise that such intrusions were temporary and necessary to accomplish legitimate, public health ends. LAWRENCE O. GOSTIN, PUBLIC HEALTH LAW AND ETHICS: A READER 445 (2002).

However, in 2 companion cases, *Camara v. Municipal Court of the City & Cnty. of S.F.*, 387 U.S. 523 (1967), and *See v. City of Seattle*, 387 U.S. 541 (1967), the U.S. Supreme Court rejected long-standing arguments that government interests in public health inspections automatically outweigh privacy concerns. It determined that the 4th Amendment requires advance warrants for even purely administrative (i.e., non-criminal) inspections.

Camara faced criminal charges for failing to allow San Francisco health authorities to inspect his house without a warrant (in violation of local housing code). He argued that such charges could not be brought because government sought to conduct an unconstitutional search. The Court held that while public health inspections are less intrusive than typical police searches, both searches require advance warrants pursuant to the 4th Amendment. *Camara*, 387 U.S. at 530. San Francisco's concerns about existing safeguards, the functionality of warrants, and the public health need for such inspections, were largely dismissed. In *See v. City of Seattle*, the Court applied similar analyses to fire inspections of commercial property. *See*, 387 U.S. at 543. Following these 2 cases, only under special exceptions would warrantless searches for public health purposes be allowed.

Twenty years later, the Supreme Court reconsidered its application of the warrant requirement to public health inspections. In *New York v. Burger*, 482 U.S. 691 (1987), it held that warrantless searches of businesses were permissible provided there is sufficient statutory authority and oversight. Burger ran a vehicle junkyard and dismantling business in Brooklyn. After he was charged with possession of stolen property, he sought to exclude key evidence based on a warrantless search of his property by officials acting under New York state law. The Court disagreed, upholding the statutory authority for administrative warrantless searches concerning businesses operating in "closely regulated industries." *Id*. at 700. Noted the Court, businesses that are engaged in dangerous activities (e.g., ballistics plants) or are traditionally heavily regulated (e.g., health care facilities) have reduced expectations of privacy related to their operations. As a result, regulatory schemes allowing inspections of commercial establishments without a warrant may be constitutional so long as (1) government's interests are substantial; (2) warrantless inspections are "necessary to further [that] regulatory scheme;" and (3) the inspection program has a "constitutionally adequate substitute for a warrant." *Id.* at 692.

In *Players, Inc. v. City of New York*, 371 F. Supp. 2d 522 (S.D.N.Y. 2005), each of these 3 requirements was considered regarding warrantless public health inspections concerning tobacco use. Players, Inc., a private social club, challenged a New York state law allowing warrantless searches of commercial premises to enforce smoking bans. A federal district court upheld New York's statutory authority for these inspections because:

(1) government has a substantial interest in ensuring the health and safety of restaurants against the risks of exposure to tobacco smoke;

(2) warrantless inspections are necessary since advance knowledge of the date, time, and purpose of the inspection may allow restaurateurs to hide or mask violations; and

(3) the state-based regulatory scheme provided sufficient notice to business owners that they are subject to inspections.

Additional applications of the Court's standards in *Burger* authorize warrantless inspections and searches for public health purposes of private residences and various businesses including:

- restaurants (*Contreras v. City of Chicago.*, 119 F.3d 1286, 1288 (7th Cir. 1997));

- pawn shops (*S&S Pawn Shop Inc. v. City of Del City*, 947 F.2d 432 (10th Cir. 1991));

- adult stores (*Allno Enters., Inc. v. Baltimore Cnty.*, 10 F. App'x 197, 200 (4th Cir. 2001));

- animal dealers (*Hodgins v. USDA*, 238 F.3d 421 (6th Cir. Nov. 20, 2000));

- nursing homes (*Blue v. Koren*, 72 F.3d 1075, 1079 (2d Cir. 1995)); and

- day care centers (*Rush v. Obledo*, 756 F.2d 713 (9th Cir. 1985)).

Still not all warrantless public health inspections pass constitutional muster. In *Gordon v. City of Moreno Valley*, 687 F. Supp. 2d 930 (C.D. Cal. 2009), a federal district court invalidated "raid" style inspections of African-American barber shops by the Moreno Valley health department and city police. The searches were unreasonable because the officers entered establishments brandishing weapons, explored non-public areas, and directly questioned customers. In *Tucson Woman's Clinic v. Eden*, 379 F.3d 531, 538 (9th Cir. 2004), the 9th Circuit Court of Appeals invalidated Arizona's law requiring abortion clinics to submit to unannounced, warrantless searches of the facilities, physicians' offices, and patients' medical records.

C. NUISANCE ABATEMENT

Nuisance law arises from the legal adage that "every person should use [one's] property as not to injure the property of another." *Pendergrast v. Aiken*, 236 S.E.2d 787, 798 (N.C. 1977). In the realm of public health law, nuisance has distinct meanings. The aforementioned TURNING POINT ACT (*see* Chapter 7) defines nuisance as "a condition, act, or failure to act that unreasonably interferes with the health or safety of the community by endangering life, generating or spreading infectious diseases, or otherwise injuriously affecting the public's health." TURNING POINT ACT § 1–102(36) (2003).

Nuisances may take on many forms and impact the public's health in different ways. They may be public or private by nature. Government tends to intervene to abate public nuisances, while individuals or corporate entities litigate to address private ones. As discussed below, laws supporting the abatement of public and private nuisances authorize direct interventions in typical and atypical cases to mitigate health-related harms to the public.

1. PUBLIC NUISANCE

In its broadest conception, a public nuisance is "an unreasonable interference with a right common to the general public." RESTATEMENT (2ND) OF TORTS § 821B (1979). State and local public health agencies' long-standing powers to abate public nuisances are often applied in cases where uses of one's property (e.g., accumulation of trash, creation of noxious smells, operation of industrial equipment in residential areas) produce clear and obvious health risks for others.

In *Summit Cnty. Bd. of Health v. Pearson*, 809 N.E.2d 80 (Ohio Ct. App. 2004), the Pearson family kept lions, tigers, leopards, bears, foxes, pigeons, dogs, and an alligator on its property in Copley Township, Ohio. When the local health department inspected the property following complaints of foul odors, it found unsanitary collections of blood, feces, urine, and decomposing animal bones. Among other potential sanctions, it issued an advisory to the family to remove offending materials. After the Pearsons failed to comply, the property was found to be a public nuisance via an administrative hearing. Following their unsuccessful appeal, the Pearsons were required to abate the nuisance by cleaning the property at their own cost.

As per the *Pearson* case, so long as government follows statutory or regulatory procedures it may abate these acts in the interests of protecting the community's health. Under § 5–11 of the TURNING POINT ACT, state or local public health agencies may immediately and thoroughly investigate any suspected nuisance upon receipt of a complaint or when there is probable cause to believe that a nuisance exists within the agency's jurisdiction. If confirmed, the agency may issue an order to "avoid, correct, or remove, at the owner's expense" any property or condition that constitutes a nuisance.

Nuisance abatement orders may direct a property owner to close, evacuate, or decontaminate any real property, or remove or destroy offending personal property, within a reasonable period of time. Noncompliance with such orders allows the public health agency to remove or abate the nuisance at the owner or occupant's expense. In cases of real property, abatement expenses may be attached to the property through a court-ordered lien. *See, e.g., City of Bellingham v. Chin*, 988 P.2d 479 (Wash. Ct. App. 1999) (abatement expenses attached as lien to tavern that constituted a drug-dealing nuisance). In other instances, judgments may be entered against offending persons for the costs entailed by government in abating the nuisance directly.

Outside traditional uses of nuisance abatement laws to clean up real property or destroy contaminated personal property is the potential to address multiple, other types of offenses. In *City of New York v. Milhelm Attea & Bros., Inc.*, 550 F. Supp. 2d 332 (E.D.N.Y. 2008), New York City brought a public nuisance action against tobacco wholesalers who sold untaxed cigarettes to reservation retailers. The City claimed these cigarettes were being resold at prices lower than the typical market to the detriment of the public's health. In allowing the City's claim to proceed, the court acknowledged a broad conception of public nuisance as "conduct or omissions which offend, interfere with or cause damage to the public in the exercise of rights common to all. . . ." *Id.* at 349–50 (citing *Copart Indus. Inc. v. Consolidated Edison Co.*, 41 N.Y.2d 564, 568 (N.Y. 1977)). The City's nuisance claim was later dropped when the parties settled.

Consistent with other local government suits, the City of Chicago sued the gun manufacturer, Beretta, claiming its weapons were a public nuisance because they led to the deaths and injuries of police, medical personnel, and residents. *City of Chicago v. Beretta U.S.A.,* 821 N.E.2d 1099 (Ill. 2004). The City alleged that Beretta "intentionally and recklessly" designed, marketed, distributed, and sold firearms that it "should know" would be used illegally with direct harms to the community. *Id.* at 361–62. The Illinois Supreme Court affirmed the dismissal of the claim for failure to state a cause of action, finding there was no legal duty applicable to Beretta, as well as a corresponding lack of proximate cause for gun-related injuries or deaths in the community. *See also* Chapter 6.B. for additional discussion of gun-related litigation and the PLCAA.

Additional actions in public health nuisance have been brought to:

• control the gathering of street gangs in California (*see People ex rel. Gallo v. Acuna,* 929 P.2d 596 (Cal. 1997));

• limit emissions among power plants and automobiles in Connecticut (*see American Elec. Power Co. v. Connecticut,* 131 S. Ct. 2527 (2011));

• stymie drug-related activities in Ohio (*see State ex rel. Rothal v. Smith,* 783 N.E.2d 1001 (Ohio Ct. App. 2002));

- recoup damages from exposure to lead paint in Rhode Island (*see State v. Lead Indus. Ass'n*, 951 A.2d 429 (R.I. 2008)); and

- eliminate offensive chili odor and irritants causing physical harm and discomfort (*see People ex rel. City of Irwindale v. Huy Fong Foods, Inc.*, No. BC525856, 2013 WL 5813088 (C.D. Cal. Oct. 28, 2013)).

2. PRIVATE NUISANCE

Unlike public nuisances, a private nuisance refers to the nontrespassory invasion of another's use and enjoyment of land. RESTATEMENT (2ND) OF TORTS § 821D (1979). Private nuisances may arise out of facts similar to traditional public nuisance cases, but entail private rights of action usually through tort litigation to correct the offense (other than physical trespassing, which is addressed under different legal theories).

As in *Pearson* above, odor is the main source of the nuisance in *Pestey v. Cushman*, 788 A.2d 496 (Conn. 2002). After years of tolerating increasingly offensive odors, the Pesteys brought a private nuisance claim against their neighbors, the Cushmans, who operated a dairy farm. In many cases, farmers are allowed greater leeway regarding natural odors from their crop or livestock production. In this case, however, the Pesteys claimed successfully at trial that the odor stemmed from the Cushmans' negligent operations of the farm. On appeal, the Connecticut Supreme Court considered whether: (a) the condition had a "natural

tendency to create danger and inflict injury upon
person or property;" (b) resulting harms were
continuous; (c) the Cushman's use of the land was
unreasonable or unlawful; and (d) the nuisance was
the proximate cause of injuries and damages. *Id.* at
504 (citing *Walsh v. Stonington Water Pollution
Control Auth.*, 736 A.2d 811, 815–16 (Conn. 1999)).
It ruled in favor of the Pesteys consistent with the
jury's prior determination and required the
Cushmans to pay $100,000 in damages.

Consider alternatively the case of *Hale v. Ward
Cnty.*, 818 N.W.2d 697 (N.D. 2012). The Hales
owned land outside Minot, North Dakota, near
Ward County's shooting range used to train law
enforcement officers. They brought a private
nuisance claim against the County, alleging hazards
from the shooting range in proximity to their land.
The North Dakota Supreme Court assessed the
Hales' claims under very different standards than
those applied in *Pestey*. The court (a) asked whether
the Hales came to the nuisance because they knew
or should have known about the activity when they
purchased the land; (b) balanced the utility of the
shooting range conduct against the harm to the
Hales; (c) queried how the Hales attempted to
accommodate Ward County's use of the land; and (d)
looked into whether they were diligent in seeking
relief. *Id.* at 703 (citing *Rassier v. Houim*, 488
N.W.2d 635, 638 (N.D. 1992)). Finding in favor of
the Hales only on the final factor, the court
dismissed their claim.

Another type of interference on the use of private property was litigated in *Lucero v. Trosch*, 121 F.3d 591 (11th Cir. 1997). Dr. Lucero performed abortions at a clinic in Birmingham, Alabama. Anti-abortion protestors outside of the clinic shouted loud enough to disturb activities within the clinic, as well as intimidated patients and medical staff. Dr. Lucero sought to enjoin the protesters' activities via a private nuisance claim. The 11th Circuit Court of Appeals weighed the protesters' freedoms of speech under the 1st Amendment with the interests of Dr. Lucero, his staff, and patients to engage in lawful activity without excessive interference. The court affirmed the lower court's injunction against the protesters. Not only did the protesters interfere with Dr. Lucero's business, noted the court, they also infringed on government's interests to allow patients to seek abortions, ensure public safety and order, respect residential privacy, and protect "captive" audiences from targeted picketing. *Id.* at 602 (citing *Madsen v. Women's Health Ctr., Inc.*, 512 U.S. 753 (1994)).

D. TAKINGS

The power to abate nuisances includes the ability to shutter or evacuate residences or businesses temporarily or permanently. Most of the time the exclusion is not physical *per se* (i.e., an individual is not forcibly removed from the premises), but rather a person or corporation may be required to obviate conditions (at their own expense) or be prevented from engaging in activities on the premises that resulted in a nuisance. In the cases above, for example, the Pearsons were required to clean up the nuisance created by housing animals on their property and the Cushmans had to alter their dairy farm practices (and compensate their neighbors).

Application of nuisance laws that negatively impact property owners' possession, use, or commercial interests raises questions related to whether government has taken private property without just compensation in violation of the 5th Amendment of the U.S. Constitution. As discussed initially in Chapter 3, a taking may occur whenever government (1) physically occupies a premises to the exclusion of a private owner or (2) permanently deprives a property owner of all economic value via regulation or other intervention.

Establishing a taking under the former instance is relatively easy. If government takes a person's land for public purposes (e.g., to build a highway) pursuant to its power of eminent domain, it must provide just compensation. However, as per the *Kelo* case (545 U.S. 469 (2005)) noted in Chapter 3, determining what constitutes a legitimate public purpose can be tricky.

Under the latter instance, proving what is known as a "regulatory taking" is more difficult because there is almost always some economic value left in the property affected by the law or regulation. *See Lucas v. South Carolina Coastal Council*, 505 U.S. 1003 (1992) (property owner who lost the entire economic use of only part of his land still retained some value).

The predominant approach in assessing when regulatory takings require compensation examines 3 factors: (1) the economic impact on the property owner, (2) the "character of the governmental action," and (3) "interference with distinct investment-backed expectations." *Penn Central Trans. Co. v. New York City*, 438 U.S. 104, 124 (1978). For example, in *Rose Acre Farms, Inc. v. United States*, 559 F.3d 1260 (Fed. Cir. 2009), USDA implemented regulations to control the spread of salmonella on poultry farms. These included restrictions on the interstate sale of poultry and eggs and allowing the confiscation, killing, and testing of some chickens on farms with a history of positive salmonella tests. After salmonella outbreaks were traced back to Indiana-based Rose Acre Farms, USDA restricted several of its properties and removed large numbers of potentially infected hens. Rose Acre Farms alleged that application of the regulations effected a taking of its property. The court found that:

- the economic impact was not severe;

- the character of the regulations directly advanced public health and safety; and

- to the extent the regulations were based on new science, Rose Acre Farms could not have reasonably expected changes to its farming practice.

Still, on balance the court concluded that the regulations did not constitute a taking.

At first glimpse, the Takings Clause seems to have the potential to require government to compensate owners for the use or occupation of their property or deprivation of their economic interests to further the public's health. However, compensation is not required when government exercises its power to abate public health nuisances for the benefit of the community. *See, e.g., Harms v. City of Sibley*, 702 N.W.2d 91, 95 (Iowa 2005) (abatement of a nuisance created by dust, noise, traffic, and lighting issues at a concrete plant does not constitute a taking). When private uses of land or other property offend the public's health, as per the cases above, government may enter and inspect the property, remove the offending issues (or require the owner to remove them), or condemn the property. *Lawton v. Steele*, 152 U.S. 133, 136 (1894); *Arcara v. Cloud Books, Inc.*, 478 U.S. 697 (1986). Not only does government not have to pay property owners for such entry, it may attach fines, or levies, to the property (as previously noted).

E. ZONING & THE BUILT ENVIRONMENT

An emerging focus of public health officials is how the built environment impacts the health of communities. New research illustrates how decisions related to the (1) creation and layout of neighborhoods, (2) engineering and building of houses and commercial structures, and (3) design of communities can impact the public's health, both positively and negatively. *See* Shobha Srinivasan et al., *Creating Healthy Communities, Healthy Homes, Healthy People: Initiating a Research Agenda on the*

Built Environment and Public Health, 93 AM. J. PUB. HEALTH 1446 (2003). In an era of global climate change and significant shifts in migration, development of sustainable communities is garnering legal and funding support at the federal, state, and local levels. U.S. DEP'T OF HOUS. & URBAN DEV. ET AL., PARTNERSHIP FOR SUSTAINABLE COMMUNITIES, 3 YEARS OF HELPING COMMUNITIES ACHIEVE THEIR VISIONS FOR GROWTH AND PROSPERITY (2012).

Public health interventions, including a focus on HiAP and increased uses of HIAs (noted in Chapter 1), help to assess potential or actual negative impacts of community design and other factors within the built environment. *See, e.g.,* Joe Gose, *Construction That Focuses on Health of Residents*, N.Y. TIMES, Mar. 6, 2013, at B8 (use of HIAs in developing or revitalizing housing districts in California, Colorado, and Washington). Many municipalities are also harnessing their local zoning authority to effectuate changes in furtherance of the public's health.

Zoning refers generally to a local government's ability to set conditions on the use of public or private property within its jurisdiction. Zoning laws authorize local governments to (1) create various districts for industrial, commercial, residential, and farming uses; and (2) set specifications for density of buildings and lot sizes, with reasonable variances for different uses within each district. Variances may be "grandfathered" in (because the use pre-existed implementation of the zoning requirement), or allowed in some specific applications. Osborne M. Reynolds, Jr., *The "Unique Circumstances" Rule in Zoning Variances—An Aid in Achieving Greater Prudence and Less Leniency*, 31 URB. LAW. 127 (1999).

One of the historic foundations for zoning laws, dating back to their origination in large U.S. cities, relates to protecting the public's health. Joseph Schilling et al., *The Public Health Roots of Zoning: In Search of Active Living's Legal Genealogy*, 28 AM. J. PREVENTIVE MED. 96, 99 (2005). In 1926, the U.S. Supreme Court affirmed not only that comprehensive zoning laws were a permissible via police powers, but also that protecting the public's health was legitimate bases for zoning measures. *Village of Euclid v. Ambler Realty*, 272 U.S. 365 (1926) (approving zoning ordinance preventing a landowner from using his land for industry). For decades, public health zoning measures, coupled with building and fire codes, have:

- separated industrial uses from residential areas;

- required sufficient distance between built structures;

- mandated mixed-use developments; and

- assured adequate egress in the interests of public safety.

As suburban sprawl crept across the U.S., local governments began to require developers to set aside space for parks and community recreation.

Sidewalks, playgrounds, and running trails that encourage outdoor activity consistent with a "complete streets" foci are commonly featured in zoning applications for new projects or revitalization efforts.

To the extent aggressive uses of zoning to alter the built environment limit land uses or add costs for developers and owners, legal challenges inevitably surface. In *Dolan v. City of Tigard*, 512 U.S. 374 (1994), Tigard (Oregon) considered the issuance of a zoning permit to a business owner, Florence Dolan, who sought to redevelop her plumbing/electrical supply store. The City sought to condition the permit on Dolan's agreement to allow space for a greenway that would assist in water drainage and provide a bike/pedestrian pathway. Following a series of legal challenges, the U.S. Supreme Court found that the City did not adequately prove that the exaction was reasonably related to the public purposes of improved drainage and decreased vehicle traffic.

In addition to creating recreational spaces and safer neighborhoods, some local communities are experimenting with their use of zoning to change consumer behaviors in other ways. Their primary target is to restrict access to unhealthy foods by limiting the number, placement, or design of fast food and other restaurants. JULIE SAMIA MAIR ET AL., THE USE OF ZONING TO RESTRICT FAST FOOD OUTLETS: A POTENTIAL STRATEGY TO COMBAT OBESITY (2005). Local zoning laws can be used to help create a healthier retail food marketplace by:

- banning the placement of new fast food, or "formula" (i.e., franchised or chain) restaurants;

- rezoning residential areas to restrict developments of fast food restaurants;

- limiting the density of fast food restaurants or convenience stores, especially near elementary or secondary schools;

- providing incentives for developers to offer healthy food outlets in commercial settings; or

- requiring restaurants to offer a minimum number of healthy choices. *Id.*

In 1 of its historic districts, San Francisco prohibited "formula retail uses" (including franchised fast food restaurants). *Id.* Detroit proposed that certain fast food restaurants may not be built within 500 feet of a school. Seattle restricts the placement of mobile food trucks within its borders through zoning. Other communities have relied on their local zoning ordinances to restrict the number or placement of fast food outlets for aesthetic reasons or limit the installation of drive-thrus in the interests of public safety. *Id.*

A local zoning ordinance in Concord, Massachusetts defines a "drive-in or fast-food restaurant" as:

any establishment whose principal business is the sale of foods or beverages in a ready-to-consume state, for consumption within the building or off-premises, and whose principal method of operation includes: (1) sale of foods and beverages in paper, plastic or other disposable containers; or (2) service of food and beverages directly to a customer in a motor vehicle.

CONCORD, MASS., ZONING BYLAW § 4.7.1 (2002); *see also* CHANGE LAB SOLUTIONS AND NATIONAL POLICY & LEGAL ANALYSIS NETWORK TO PREVENT CHILDHOOD OBESITY, MODEL HEALTHY FOOD ZONING ORDINANCE (2013).

In Los Angeles, a zoning law prohibited the opening and remodeling of stand-alone fast food restaurants beginning in 2008. L.A., CAL. ORDINANCE 180103 (July 29, 2008). It was accompanied by financial incentives to increase South L.A.'s produce markets and sit-down restaurants. COMMUNITY HEALTH COUNCILS, INC., FAST FOOD RESTAURANT REPORT (2011). However, between 2007 and 2012, researchers determined that the prevalence of obese or overweight in the area increased at a faster rate than the rest of L.A. Fast food consumption increased as well. Roland Sturm & Aiko Hattori, *Diet and Obesity in L.A. County 2007–2012: Is There a Measurable Effect of the 2008 Fast-Food Ban?,* 133 SOCIAL SCI. & MED. 205, 205–11 (2015). These discouraging findings may be due to the limited number of fast food restaurants affected by the ban or delays in environmental changes.

Courts typically uphold such exercises of zoning laws on varied grounds so long as government has a rational basis for its measure or decision (and there are no other invidious foundations for the measures). For example, in *Bellas v. Planning Bd. of Weymouth*, 778 N.E.2d 30 (Mass. App. Ct. 2002), a Massachusetts appellate court approved the denial of a zoning permit to a franchised doughnut shop that sought to include a drive-thru window on its premises. The drive thru, observed the court, would generate increased traffic that could negatively affect the safety of school children or others. *See also Bess Eaton Donut Flour Co., Inc. v. Zoning Bd. of Review of Town of Westerly*, No. 99–0209, 2000 WL 276818, at 1 (R.I. Super. Feb. 15, 2000) (approving zoning denial of a bake shop with drive-thru because it would adversely impact the neighborhood); *contra In re Westbury Trombo, Inc. v. Board of Trs.*, 763 N.Y.S.2d 674 (N.Y. App. Div. 2003) (invalidating local zoning law restricting fast food businesses from operating during certain hours).

———————————

Public health powers to monitor property and alter the built environment are limited. Fourth Amendment privacy protections and 5th Amendment requirements to compensate for takings of private property necessitate careful implementation of laws authorizing public health agents to inspect property and abate nuisances. Creation of healthier communities can run counter to some commercial interests and lead to related, economic objections. Whether grounded in constitutional law or local politics, arguments against property-based interventions to advance the public's health reflect the type of tradeoffs that must be accommodated with sufficient guidance and planning.

CHAPTER 10

PUBLIC HEALTH EMERGENCY LEGAL PREPAREDNESS & RESPONSE

One of the most dynamic and difficult areas of public health practice is emergency preparedness and response. During pandemics, acts of bioterrorism, natural disasters, or other major public health crises, public and private sector entities and individuals must make critical choices in real-time that can affect the lives and health of entire populations. In making these choices they must adapt to a new (albeit temporary) paradigm that prioritizes the health of the community (versus the health of the individual) as the consummate goal. James G. Hodge, Jr. et al., *Practical, Ethical, and Legal Challenges Underlying Crisis Standards of Care*, J.L. MED. & ETHICS 50 (2013).

The law adapts as well. By design, emergency declarations at all levels of government change the legal landscape to further the public's health. Following the terrorist attacks on September 11, 2001 and ensuing anthrax incidents, a series of significant legal reforms:

- retooled government organization and efforts to improve response efforts;

- created new preparedness classifications centered on the declaration of "public health emergencies;" and

- revamped existing legal norms to clarify roles and responsibilities of public and private actors in emergency response efforts.

The role of law in emergencies is critical to obviating public health harms, but it can also be contentious. Additional public health emergency threats since 9/11, notably SARS (2003), H1N1 flu (2009/2010), EVD (2014), and Hurricanes Katrina (2005), Isaac (2012), and Sandy (2012), have revealed legal pitfalls and myths in diverse areas of law, including: (1) duplicative roles of federal, state, and local governments, (2) real-time legal decision-making, and (3) liability protections for emergency responders and entities. This chapter lays out core theories and applications of emergency legal preparedness and response, beginning with the scope and definition of public health emergencies.

A. DEFINING PUBLIC HEALTH EMERGENCIES

Traditionally, frontline preparedness and response efforts have largely been the responsibility of state and local governments pursuant to their police powers (discussed initially in Chapter 2). Federal public health agencies like DHHS and CDC provided national guidance and resources, but lacked extensive legal authority or manpower to address specific local public health needs in mass casualty events.

The terrorist attacks and anthrax exposures in 2001 changed everything. Thousands were killed on

9/11, and over 15 people were infected with anthrax and 5 died later that Fall. The source of this bioterrorism attack remains uncertain. The Federal Bureau of Investigation (FBI) alleges that Army microbiologist Dr. Bruce Ivins, who took his own life in 2008, is the lead culprit. However, at least 1 former FBI agent, Richard Lambert, has sued FBI alleging potential discrepancies in its investigation of Dr. Ivins, leading to significant questions as to whether Dr. Ivins was in fact the lead or only bioterrorist. Scott Shane, *Former FBI Agent Sues, Claiming Retaliation Over Misgivings in Anthrax Case*, N.Y. TIMES, Apr. 9, 2015, at A20.

National security concerns arising from these events revolutionized federal preparedness and response efforts. The federal government alone is constitutionally vested with supreme authority to act in defense of the nation. U.S. CONST. art. 4, § 4. Federal efforts to investigate criminal acts of terrorism intersected with state and local efforts to protect the public's health from known or potential anthrax exposures. Significant questions constantly surfaced as to who exactly is in charge of controlling the bioterrorism threats and on what legal basis.

Federalism questions like these in public health have arisen routinely over decades, but the stakes were never higher in the post 9/11 era. As President Obama noted a decade later, integrated, interjurisdictional coordination across all levels of government is essential to effective emergency responses. National Preparedness, 8 PRES. POL'Y DIRECTIVE (Mar. 30, 2011).

Even as federal efforts focused on investigating the perpetrators of the 9/11 terrorist acts, state and local preparedness officials and leaders were concerned about a new type of bioterrorism emergency stemming from the anthrax exposures. Long-standing, existing state-based "emergency" or "disaster" declarations were traditionally crafted to address "all hazards" (including epidemics), but used typically in response to natural disasters (e.g., fire, floods, earthquakes, hurricanes). Unlike these disasters, bioterrorism events had an unpredictable potential for systemic and widespread disability and death in the population for months on end. Searching for new legal responses to address public health threats, state and local policymakers called for legal reforms in late 2001.

With support from leading national public health associations and CDC, the Centers for Law and the Public's Health at Georgetown and Johns Hopkins Universities developed the MODEL STATE EMERGENCY HEALTH POWERS ACT (MSEHPA) in December 2001. Based in part on previously-identified core principles and guided by national input, MSEHPA features a cohesive series of model provisions for state, tribal, and local governments considering how to respond to bioterrorism or other public health threats. Lawrence O. Gostin et al., *The MSEHPA: Planning and Response to Bioterrorism and Naturally Occurring Infectious Diseases*, 288 JAMA 622 (2002). The Act balances individual and communal interests underlying modern responses to a "public health emergency," defined as:

an occurrence or imminent threat of an illness
or health condition that: (1) is believed to be
caused by . . . bioterrorism; the appearance of a
novel or previously controlled or eradicated
infectious agent or biological toxin [or other
causes]; . . . and (2) poses a high probability of
. . . a large number of deaths . . . ; a large
number of serious or long-term disabilities . . . ;
or widespread exposure to an infectious or toxic
agent that poses a significant risk of
substantial future harm to a large number of
people in the affected population. MSEHPA
§ 104(m) (Ctrs. for Law & the Public's Health
2001).

Though this definition was criticized by some as
overly-broad, the scope of what constitutes a PHE is
considerably more limited than most existing state-
based definitions of emergency or disaster (which
are sometimes used to respond to public health
crises). Under MSEHPA, a PHE declaration may be
issued only when it can be shown that an act of
bioterrorism or other public health threat poses a
"high probability" of a large number of deaths,
disabilities, or exposures to agents that could cause
future harms. These limits are designed to confine
PHE declarations to instances necessitating rapid
and effective public health responses like SARS or
smallpox, but not so much the slow, global spread of
conditions like obesity (for which rapid legal
responses may not be efficacious).

Since the introduction and passage of MSEPHA,
however, some states and localities have declared

PHEs to address an array of threats well outside the initial context of pandemic illness or bioterrorism. For example, in 2013, the City of Boston and New York State issued separate declarations of PHEs for short periods in response to annual flu outbreaks. *See* James G. Hodge, Jr., *The Changing Nature and Scope of PHEs and Response to Annual Flu,* 11 BIOSECURITY & BIOTERRORISM 142 (2013).

In March 2015, Indiana's Governor declared a state of PHE to respond to a localized spike in the numbers of HIV infections in rural Scott County, across the Ohio River from Louisville, Kentucky. Tribune Wire Reports, *Indiana to Declare Public Health Emergency over HIV Outbreak*, CHI. TRIB., Mar. 26, 2015. Governor Pence's declaration authorized the temporary implementation of a needle exchange program (NEP) to counter the spread of HIV to over 160 people largely infected through intravenous drug use of the prescription opioid, Opana. Massimo Calabresi, *The Price of Relief*, TIME, June 15, 2015, at 26. Indiana's health commissioner Dr. Jerome Adams noted "[IDUs are] addicted, and [are] getting HIV because they're addicted." Alan Schwartz & Mitch Smith, *Needle Exchange Is Allowed After HIV Outbreak in an Indiana County*, N.Y. TIMES, March 27, 2015, at A13. The Governor extended the PHE until mid-May 2016 to continue to authorize the operation of the NEP.

Since 2001 additional declarations of PHE have been issued for a variety of other conditions including:

- Contamination of public water supplies (Alamosa County, CO);

- Localized measles outbreaks (Pima County, AZ);

- Release (and potential further release) of amphibole asbestos (Libby and Troy, MT);

- Drinking water contamination (Black Falls and Grand Falls, Navajo Nation);

- Dramatic increases in reports of domestic violence (Nassau County, NY);

- Shortages of affordable, safe medical cannabis (Oakland, CA);

- Severe storms and tornadoes (MO);

- Food insecurity (County of Hawai'i, HI); and

- West Nile Virus outbreaks (Dallas County, TX).

For more information, see table and accompanying information in JAMES G. HODGE, JR. ET AL., EMERGENCY MEDICAL SERVICES AND MEDICAL SURGE: ESSENTIAL LEGAL ISSUES 1–83 (ASTHO 2015).

B.   STATE & LOCAL PUBLIC HEALTH EMERGENCY POWERS

Following the completion of MSEHPA, state legislatures or agencies in well over ½ the states and D.C. introduced legislative bills or regulations based in whole or part on the Act. By 2006, 39 states' legislatures passed bills related to MSEHPA. CTRS. FOR LAW & THE PUBLIC'S HEALTH, MSEHPA: STATE LEGISLATIVE ACTIVITY 2–20 (2006). According to the Network for Public Health Law 33 states and D.C. have legislatively built PHE, or like terms, into their laws. NETWORK FOR PUB. HEALTH LAW, MSEHPA: SUMMARY MATRIX 7 (2014). In addition, several MSEHPA provisions are reflected in other model public health acts, including the TURNING POINT ACT and UNIFORM EMERGENCY VOLUNTEER HEALTH PRACTITIONERS ACT (Unif. Law Comm'n 2007) (focused on the deployment and use of volunteer health providers in emergencies).

Through these and other legislative or regulatory reforms, a more consistent legal platform for PHE response efforts has emerged, particularly at the state and local levels. A declaration of PHE triggers a series of optional, expedited public health powers for governmental public health agents to respond in concert with public safety and emergency management actors. While these powers still vary across jurisdictions, state and local public health officials are authorized generally during PHEs to expeditiously:

- Abate public health nuisances and destroy dangerous or contaminated materials;

- Take private property with just compensation as needed to care for patients or protection of the public's health;

- Close roads, implement curfews, and evacuate at risk places or populations where justified;

- Collect specimens and implement safe handling procedures for the disposal of human remains or infectious wastes;

- Test, screen, vaccinate, and treat exposed or infected persons;

- Separate individuals exposed (via quarantine) or infected (via isolation) with communicable conditions from others to prevent further transmission;

- Seek assistance from out-of-state health care volunteers through licensure reciprocity (recognizing the license of an out-of-state volunteer in good standing as if it were issued in-state during the PHE);

- Immunize select public and private actors (including volunteers) from legal claims grounded in negligence (discussed further in section D, below);

- Reimburse private sector contributors to emergency response efforts; and

- Inform the population of public health threats in accessible, understandable, and culturally-relevant ways.

In many states, the Governor (or other politically-appointed actor such as a state health commissioner) may waive specific statutory or regulatory laws that impede response efforts for the duration of a PHE (e.g., licensure regulations, scope of practice limitations, or procurement codes that may hamper resource acquisitions). *See* Daniel G. Orenstein, *When Law Is Not Law: Setting Aside Legal Provisions During Declared Emergencies*, 41 J.L. MED. & ETHICS 73 (Supp. 2013). Concerning the emergence of HIV cases in Scott County, Indiana, noted above, the Governor's PHE declaration waives state laws otherwise prohibiting the implementation of NEPs. Shari Rudavsky, *Scott County, Health Department Working on NEP*, INDYSTAR (Mar. 27, 2015).

The Governor or other state officials may also:

- coordinate services among public health and emergency actors (e.g., authorizing state public health departments to work closely with emergency management and law enforcement personnel);

- allocate state resources (e.g., state agents, supplies, drugs, equipment); and

- expend finances as needed to effectuate emergency response efforts (with opportunities later for a full accounting).

See James G. Hodge, Jr., *The Evolution of Law in Biopreparedness*, 10 BIOSECURITY & BIOTERRORISM 38 (2012).

C. FEDERAL PUBLIC HEALTH EMERGENCY POWERS

While much of the action in PHE preparedness is exerted by state and local actors on the frontlines of response efforts, the federal government is deeply embedded in preparedness through multiple legislative reforms and related programs arising after 9/11. The dense slate of federal emergency preparedness laws include:

- The Federal Public Health Security and Bioterrorism Preparedness and Response Act of 2002, Pub. L. No. 107–188, 116 Stat. 594 (2002). This Act (1) authorizes the implementation of the National Disaster Medical System (NDMS) to coordinate rapid deployment of specialized response teams; and (2) establishes CDC's Strategic National Stockpile (SNS) to distribute pre-stocked essential medicines and supplies within hours of an event anywhere nationally.

- The Project BioShield Act of 2004, Pub. L. No. 108–276, 118 Stat. 835 (2004), which allows FDA to issue emergency use authorizations (EUAs) during declared chemical, biological, radiologic, or nuclear (CBRN) emergencies. 21 U.S.C. § 360bbb–3(a)(1) (2013).

- The Homeland Security Act of 2002, Pub. L. No. 107–296, 116 Stat. 2135 (2002), and Public Health Threats and Emergencies

Act of 2000, Pub. L. No. 106–505, 114 Stat. 2314 (2000), which create and empower the Department of Homeland Security (DHS).

• Additional federal reforms authorize emergency waivers of provisions of the Emergency Medical Treatment and Active Labor Act (EMTALA), 42 U.S.C. § 1320b–5 (2008). EMTALA typically requires hospitals to provide emergency care to persons seeking treatment. In addition, through what is known as "§ 1135 waivers," CMS eligibility requirements for Medicaid and Medicare programs can be temporarily suspended. 42 U.S.C. § 1320b–2 (2013). Meeting EMTALA or CMS requirements can be difficult in real-time PHEs, necessitating their temporary suspension.

Many federal emergency powers are concentrated in the:

(1) Robert T. Stafford Disaster Relief and Emergency Assistance Act (Stafford Act), 42 U.S.C. §§ 5121–5205 (2008);

(2) National Emergencies Act, 50 U.S.C. §§ 1601, 1621, 1622, 1631, 1641, 1651 (2008);

(3) Public Health Service Act (PHSA), 42 U.S.C. § 201 (2000); and

(4)   Pandemic and All-Hazards Preparedness Act (PAHPA), Pub. L. No. 109–417, 120 Stat. 2831 (2006), reauthorized via Pub. L. No. 113–5, 127 Stat. 161 (2013).

Collectively, these laws authorize the federal government to declare states of general emergency, disaster, and PHE. Emergency and disaster declarations may be made by the President via the Stafford Act or the National Emergencies Act. Such declarations are issued following a request of a state Governor for federal assistance following natural disasters (e.g., tornados, ice storms, floods, forest fires, or hurricanes) or man-made emergencies (e.g., civil unrest, oil or chemical spills, bombings, explosions, bridge collapses, or blackouts).

While corresponding federal emergency or disaster powers are broad, they are not tailored *per se* to PHEs involving the spread of infectious diseases or bioterrorism agents. *See, e.g.,* EDWARD C. LIU, CONG. RESEARCH SERV., RL34724, WOULD AN INFLUENZA PANDEMIC QUALIFY AS A MAJOR DISASTER UNDER THE STAFFORD ACT? (2008). As a result, the PHSA authorizes DHHS' Secretary to declare a PHE in response to "significant outbreaks of infectious diseases or bioterrorist attacks." 42 U.S.C. § 247d (2008). Federal PHE declarations allow DHHS to:

• rapidly execute grants or contracts;

• award expenses from existing federal funds;

- investigate the cause, treatment, or prevention of a disease or disorder; and

- waive certain federal laws (including provisions of the HIPAA Privacy Rule (discussed in Chapter 7).

Congressional reauthorization of PAHPA in 2013 significantly facilitated the use of medical countermeasures for various public health threats and enhanced FDA's ability to issue EUAs. As noted above, EUAs allow use of unapproved medical products or unapproved uses of approved products leading up to or during an emergency in the absence of adequate and available alternatives. 21 U.S.C. § 360bbb–3 (2013). FDA can issue EUAs prior to a PHE involving a CBRN agent based on any of the following:

- Determination by DHHS' Secretary of a PHE (or its significant potential) that may affect national security or the health and security of U.S. citizens living abroad;

- Determination by the Secretary of the Department of Defense of a military emergency (or its significant potential) involving a heightened risk of attack;

- Determination by DHS' Secretary of a domestic emergency (or its significant potential) involving a heightened risk of attack; or

- Identification of a material threat by DHS' Secretary sufficient to affect national security or the health and security of U.S. citizens living abroad.

In 2013, FDA relied on its new authority pursuant to PAHPRA to issue EUAs for the use of certain in vitro diagnostics for preparedness purposes in response to the threat of Middle East Respiratory Syndrome Coronavirus (MERS-CoV) and the novel influenza A(H7N9) virus. *See* EUA of an In Vitro Diagnostic for Detection of MERS Coronavirus; Availability, 78 Fed. Reg. 42,779 (July 17, 2013); Authorization of Emergency Use of an In Vitro Diagnostic Detection of the Novel Avian Influenza (H7N9) Virus; Availability, 78 Fed. Reg. 38,044 (June 25, 2013).

In 2014, FDA issued several EUAs related to the use of assay tests in the field to detect EVD. Authorization of Emergency Use of an In Vitro Diagnostic Device for Detection of Ebola Zaire Virus; Availability, 79 Fed. Reg. 55,804 (Sept. 17, 2014). An Enterovirus D68 (EV-D68) outbreak in late 2014 prompted FDA to issue an EUA for limited use of an assay by qualified laboratories to detect strains of EV-D68 in at risk individuals exhibiting symptoms. EUA of an In Vitro Diagnostic Device for Detection of EV-D68; Availability, 80 Fed. Reg. 37625–33 (July 1, 2015).

D. THE EVOLVING EMERGENCY LEGAL ENVIRONMENT

Substantial legal reforms have altered the emergency legal environment, but significant law and policy conflicts remain. Three premier challenges in emergency legal preparedness, discussed below, include (1) assessing the respective roles of federal, state, and local governments arising from multiple emergency declarations and response efforts; (2) engaging in "legal triage" during real-time emergencies; and (3) protecting practitioners and entities from liability during crises.

1.   INTERJURISDICTIONAL ROLES IN PREPAREDNESS

The extensive array of emergency laws at all levels of government leads to the potential for overlapping emergency declarations and authorities. In response to Hurricane Katrina, for example, federal states of emergency and major disaster were initially declared pursuant to the Stafford Act on August 27, 2005 and August 29, 2005, respectively. DHHS' Secretary also declared a PHE for Louisiana on August 29 as flood waters rose in New Orleans.

Responding to multiple declarations, DHS' officials were unsure how best to deploy their resources. Major gaps in services resulted from a lack of inter-agency collaboration, leading to additional legislative reforms. As noted above, PAHPA stripped DHS from its primary role in PHEs, replacing it with DHHS. SARAH A. LISTER, CONG. RESEARCH SERV., RL33579, THE PUBLIC HEALTH AND MEDICAL RESPONSE TO DISASTERS: FEDERAL AUTHORITY AND FUNDING 6 (2007).

State and local emergency declarations can also overlap. PHE reforms based on MSEHPA, for example, are layered on top of existing "emergency" and "disaster" frameworks. Like federal authorities, states sometimes issue dual declarations for the same event. In 2005, Louisiana's Governor issued states of emergency and PHE following Hurricane Katrina. So did Maryland's Governor in response to the H1N1 pandemic in 2009. Duplicate emergency declarations are not only redundant and potentially confusing, they can create legal conflicts. For example, similar emergency powers to evacuate or close premises may be vested in different governmental agents (e.g., departments of health and emergency management), resulting in potentially divergent orders when states of emergency and PHE are simultaneously invoked. *See, e.g.,* James G. Hodge, Jr. & Veda Collmer, *A Legal Duty To Evacuate Health Care Facilities in Emergencies*, 25(3) ABA HEALTH LAWYER 20 (2013).

Coordination breakdowns related to preparedness and response efforts within and across jurisdictions can waste scarce resources through duplicative or conflicting efforts that negatively impact the public's health or erode public confidence in communal safeguards. During the 2014 Ebola outbreak, multiple states (e.g., CA, FL, NJ, NY, TX) refused to follow specific CDC social distancing guidance concerning HCWs returning from "hot zone" clinics in affected West African countries. CDC, EPIDEMIOLOGIC RISK FACTORS TO CONSIDER WHEN EVALUATING A PERSON FOR EXPOSURE TO EBOLA VIRUS (2015). Legally, state and local governments were not required to adhere to CDC's guidance given their sovereign public health legal powers under principles of federalism. James G. Hodge, Jr.,

Legal Myths of Ebola Preparedness and Response, 29 NOTRE DAME J. L., ETHICS & PUB. POL. 355 (2015). Resulting approaches varied across states as to how best to handle risks related to these returning HCWs, as per the isolation case of Maine nurse Kaci Hickox noted in Chapter 4.F.1.

2.   PRACTICING LEGAL TRIAGE

Ideally, emergency laws authorize a clear set of powers to facilitate emergency responses. In actuality, there are real questions as to what public or private actors can do in emergencies pursuant to constitutional, statutory, or regulatory laws, as well as contracts and other agreements. Framed often in sweeping terms and subject to multiple interpretations, emergency laws offer lots of options. Yet, key choices must be made by public health and emergency management leaders and their private sector partners, lending to the need for resiliency-training and preparedness exercises before and after major events.

These and other real-time factors necessitate rapid and substantial legal decision-making in an altered landscape, as well as enhanced public health governance. Lance A. Gable, *Evading Emergency: Strengthening Emergency Responses Through Integrated Pluralistic Governance*, 91 OR. L. REV. 375 (2012). Yet the practice of PHE legal preparedness and response are non-standardized, under-studied, and, at times, poorly executed. Peter D. Jacobsen et al., *The Role of Law in Public Health Preparedness: Opportunities and Challenges*, 37 J.

HEALTH POL. POL'Y & L. 297 (2012) (noting that public health practitioners' frequent misperceptions of emergency laws could implicate morbidity and mortality in emergencies).

Through "legal triage," public and private health practitioners, emergency responders, and their legal counsel must prioritize legal issues and solutions in real-time to facilitate legitimate public health emergency responses. Practicing legal triage entails:

- identification of legal issues that may facilitate or impede public health efforts;

- assessing and monitoring changing legal norms;

- crafting innovative, legally-sound solutions to known or purported barriers to public health responses;

- explicating legal conclusions through effective, tailored communications; and

- Regularly revisiting the utility and efficacy of their legal guidance to improve public health outcomes.

James G. Hodge, Jr. & Evan D. Anderson, *Principles and Practice of Legal Triage During Public Health Emergencies*, 64 N.Y.U. ANN. SURV. AM. L. 429 (2008). These objectives are not easily met, but can be as essential to effective emergency responses as medical or other practices designed to limit public health impacts.

3.   EMERGENCY LIABILITY PROTECTIONS

One of the most contentious issues related to emergency response efforts involves personal and entity liability. Health care and public health practitioners, volunteers, and others fear potential liability for medical malpractice or other claims leading to injuries or deaths during emergencies. Hospitals, clinics, public health agencies, and nonprofits are anxious about their liability for negligent acts or omissions of their staff.

Concerns over liability in emergencies can diminish health care providers' participation in response efforts to the detriment of the public's health. *See* IOM, CRISIS STANDARDS OF CARE: A SYSTEMS FRAMEWORK FOR CATASTROPHIC DISASTER RESPONSE 59 (2012). Such unease can also impact their direct provision of care in emergencies (and non-emergencies). *See, e.g.,* Emily R. Carrier et al., *High Physician Concern About Malpractice Risk Predicts More Aggressive Diagnostic Testing In Office-Based Practice*, 32 HEALTH AFF. 1383 (2013) (physicians worried about malpractice risks are significantly more likely to practice defensive medicine with some patients).

Some suggest these concerns are unwarranted because extensive or unscrupulous liability claims during and after public health crises are uncommon. George J. Annas, *Standard of Care—In Sickness and in Health and in Emergencies*, 362 NEW ENG. J. MED. 2126 (2010). Yet health practitioners and entities point to exceptional liability claims that arise in attempting to handle patients with limited resources in crises. *See* Michelle Carpenter et al., *Deploying and Using Volunteer Health Practitioners in Response to Emergencies: Proposed Uniform State Legislation Provides Liability Protections and Workers' Compensation Coverage*, 3 AM. J. DISASTER MED. 17 (2008).

High profile criminal and civil cases against HCWs or hospitals are illustrative. Following Hurricane Katrina Dr. Anna Pou initially faced multiple criminal charges related to the alleged euthanasia of 4 patients (aged 61–90) by nurses under her supervision at the flooded and largely inoperable Memorial Medical Center in New Orleans. The criminal charges were later dropped, but civil litigation brought by 3 families against Dr. Pou ensued. *Everett v. Tenet Health Sys. Mem'l Med. Ctr., Inc.*, No. 20067948 (La. Orleans Parish Civ. Dist. Ct. Aug. 12, 2010); Christopher Drew & Shaila Dewan, *Louisiana Doctor Said to Have Faced Chaos*, N.Y. TIMES, July 20, 2006. The cases settled for undisclosed terms. SHERI FINK, FIVE DAYS AT MEMORIAL: LIFE AND DEATH IN A STORM-RAVAGED HOSPITAL 467 (v3.1_r6 2013).

In a separate case, Tenet Health Systems, which operated Memorial Medical Center where Dr. Pou was employed, settled claims in 2011 brought by Katrina victims for a reported $25 million. The victims' claims were grounded not only in negligence for Tenet's failure to respond, but also for its failure to properly plan and prepare for the hurricane and city-wide flooding. James G. Hodge, Jr. & Erin F. Brown, *Assessing Liability for Health Care Entities*

That   Insufficiently   Prepare   for   Catastrophic Emergencies, 306 JAMA 308 (2011).

Weeks after Dallas' Texas Presbyterian Hospital admitted that its staffs' failures to properly diagnose and treat Thomas Eric Duncan for EVD, may have contributed to his 2014 death, the hospital settled with his family for an undisclosed amount. The Associated Press, *Texas: Ebola Victim's Family to be Paid by Hospital*, N.Y. TIMES (Nov. 12, 2014). One of 2 nurses, Nina Pham, who became infected with EVD while treating Duncan, separately filed a lawsuit against the hospital for current and future injuries. She alleges in part that the hospital's preparedness failures to safely treat Ebola patients through adequate protections for HCWs led to her own infection and injuries. Jennifer Emily, *Dallas Hospital's Owner Says Ebola Nurse Nina Pham's Lawsuit Should be Dismissed*, THE DALLAS MORNING NEWS (April 3, 2015).

These nationally-publicized cases and other factors affect practitioners' attitudes. Multiple studies attest to the unwillingness of many HCWs to serve during emergencies when faced with the threat of potential liability. *See, e.g.,* Jonathan Ives et al., *Healthcare Workers' Attitudes to Working During Pandemic Influenza: A Qualitative Study*, 9 BMC PUB. HEALTH 56 (2009). As a result, IOM recommended in 2009 that "state and local governments should explicitly tie existing liability protections (e.g., through immunity or indemnification) for health care practitioners and entities to crisis standards of care." IOM, GUIDANCE

FOR ESTABLISHING CRISIS STANDARDS OF CARE FOR USE IN DISASTER SITUATIONS 49 (2009); *see also* IOM, CRISIS STANDARDS OF CARE: A TOOLKIT FOR INDICATORS AND TRIGGERS (2013).

Despite prevalent liability concerns and national recommendations, there is no comprehensive liability protection for HCWs, volunteers, or entities in all emergency settings. Instead, an array of federal and state liability protections apply selectively to practitioners and entities— particularly volunteers and government entities and officials—who act in good faith. Sharona Hoffman, *Responders' Responsibility: Liability and Immunity in Public Health Emergencies*, 96 GEO. L. J. 1913 (2008). These laws immunize or indemnify actors or entities from specific claims or monetary damages.

For example, all states and D.C. have executed the Emergency Management Assistance Compact (EMAC), Pub. L. No. 104–321, 110 Stat. 3877 (1996). EMAC provides strong liability protections for state or local agents (but not private actors) during declared emergencies. Additional protections stem from limited waivers during emergencies of sanctions or fines for failing to comply with certain federal or state statutes.

The Public Readiness and Emergency Preparedness (PREP) Act, 42 U.S.C. § 247d-6d (2012), addresses liability risks in distributing or implementing federally-approved medical countermeasures (e.g., medicines, vaccines, supplies). Upon a PREP Act declaration by DHHS' Secretary, liability immunity is extended to federal officials, manufacturers, drug distributors, pharmacies, and state and local program planners involved in the development, distribution, and administration of medical countermeasures. The PREP Act also creates a compensation fund for individuals injured from the administration or use of covered countermeasures.

Though broad, PREP Act liability protections apply for a limited period of time and only to acts that are negligent in nature, not intentional or criminal. One lower court decision in New York suggested that PREP Act liability protections do not immunize a school system or health practitioner involved in the alleged "bad faith" administration of the H1N1 vaccine to a minor student whose parents did not provide their consent. The case was reversed on appeal. *Parker v. St. Lawrence Cnty. Pub. Health Dep't*, 954 N.Y.S.2d 259 (N.Y. App. Div. 2012); *see also Kehler v. Hood*, 2012 WL 1945952 (E.D. Mo. No. 4:11 CV 1416 FRB, May 30, 2012) (PREP Act barred product liability and failure to warn actions against vaccine manufacturer when employer failed to obtain informed consent prior to administration of the H1N1 vaccine).

Though inconsistent, the collective patchwork of federal, state, and local laws provides a series of liability protections covering hundreds of thousands of practitioners, volunteers, and entities for acts of ordinary negligence under a collective umbrella. Like the PREP Act, virtually no liability protections immunize or indemnify practitioners or entities for acts that constitute gross negligence, willful or wanton misconduct, or crimes. In addition, considerably more limited liability protections cover hospitals, clinics, pharmacies, and other health entities. TFAH, READY OR NOT?: PROTECTING THE PUBLIC'S HEALTH FROM DISEASES, DISASTERS, AND BIOTERRORISM 38–39 (2008).

Existing liability protections have neither satisfied HCWs seeking complete immunity nor dissuaded patient-rights advocates wanting to preserve access to legal remedies for injuries or deaths arising from negligence. HCWs have consistently asked Congress to pass national, uniform liability protections that apply widely in declared emergencies. One example is the Good Samaritan Health Professionals Act, H.R. 1733, 113th Cong. (2013). It was introduced initially on April 25, 2013 and reintroduced as the Good Samaritan Health Professionals Act of 2015, H.R. 865, on February 11, 2015. Among its purposes, the Act would limit the liability of volunteer HCWs responding to a federal disaster, emergency, or PHE if they act in a "good faith belief" that a treated individual is in need of health care.

Conversely, some seek a reversal of existing liability measures to preserve patients' access to courts to litigate prospective claims. On August 6, 2011, ABA's House of Delegates expressed opposition to laws, particularly immunity provisions, that "would alter the legal duty of reasonable care in the circumstances owed to victims of a natural or manmade disaster by relief organizations or health care practitioners." ABA

SECTION OF INDIVIDUAL RIGHTS & RESPONSIBILITIES, REPORT TO HOUSE OF DELEGATES: RESOLUTION 125 (Aug. 8–9, 2011). While the resolution is a mere policy statement without legal effect (and even contradicts prior ABA statements), it reflects the minority view in the larger debate over the breadth of laws designed not only to protect practitioners and entities from liability, but also further the public's health.

In the decade following the terrorist acts on 9/11, biopreparedness legal reforms have transformed how all levels of government and private sector actors prepare for and respond to PHEs. Federal, state, and local governmental agencies reorganized. New classifications of PHE emerged and were put to new uses. Emergency public health powers were clarified. Public health officials, emergency managers, and civil libertarians continue to debate the premises of existing and potential legal reforms. The next decade assuredly will bring new preparedness challenges and answers about how to use law effectively to improve PHE preparedness, eliminate actual and perceived barriers, and build a legal infrastructure that helps prevent injuries and deaths during major catastrophes that impact the population's health.

INDEX

References are to Pages

ABORTION, 166, 236, 243

ADVERTISEMENTS, 15, 121, 158–159, 203, 205, 209, 212, 219, 223–228
Misleading information, 159, 218

AFFORDABLE CARE ACT, 44, 58, 122–124, 127, 130
Federalism, 29–32
Individual mandate, 31
Menu Labeling, 213–215

ALCOHOL, 12, 16, 42, 86, 121, 125, 129–130, 135, 139, 142–143, 154, 160–166, 173, 208, 229
Advertisement, 222
Alcohol Beverage Labeling Act, 212
As a disease factor, 116–118
During prohibition, 166
Taxes, 15

ALZHEIMERS DISEASE, III, 115, 125, 171

AMERICANS WITH DISABILITIES ACT, 133–136, 205

ANTHRAX, 78, 255–258

BILL OF RIGHTS, IV, IX, 2, 47, 51, 54, 65

BIOTERRORISM, III, 78, 93, 108, 173–174, 193, 255, 257–260, 265, 267

BODILY INTEGRITY, 11, 66, 102

BUREAU OF INDIAN AFFAIRS, 44

CAFFEINE, 116, 143, 210–211

CANCER, III, 3, 75–76, 80–81, 111, 113–114, 120, 173, 184, 202

CENTERS FOR DISEASE CONTROL AND PREVENTION,
84, 90–91, 96, 105–106, 116–117, 120, 172, 174, 181, 185, 189, 195–196, 202–203, 256, 258, 265, 271
Statistics, 79–81, 113–115, 118, 141, 145–146

CENTRAL HUDSON, see **FIRST AMENDMENT**

CHRONIC DISEASES, III, 73, 75–76, 121, 171
Causes, 115–119
Costs, 113, 117, 124, 128
Defined, 111–113

CIVIL RIGHTS ACT OF 1964, 57

COMMUNICABLE DISEASES, III, 3, 10, 62, 73, 75–76, 88–91, 96, 101–103, 109, 111, 121, 171, 186
Defined, 77–82

CONFIDENTIALITY, 19, 117, 178–182, 189, 191

CONSUMER PRODUCT SAFETY COMMISSION, 160, 207
Investigation, 207
Recall, 158, 160, 208, 230

CONTROLLED SUBSTANCES, 130, 179

CRIMINAL LAW, 140–141, 147
Addressing injuries with, 162–167

CRUEL AND UNUSUAL PUNISHMENT, see **EIGHTH AMENDMENT**

CULTURE OF HEALTH, 5–6

CURFEW, 64, 102, 106, 121, 263

DEPARTMENT OF AGRICULTURE, 215

DEPARTMENT OF HEALTH AND HUMAN SERVICES, 44, 96, 112, 127, 181–182, 185, 188, 230, 256, 267–268, 277

DIRECTLY-OBSERVED THERAPY, 77, 89–90, 92

DISABILITY PROTECTIONS, see **AMERICANS WITH DISABILITIES ACT**

DOMESTIC VIOLENCE, 145, 164, 171, 186, 261

DRIVING UNDER THE INFLUENCE, 162, 164–165

DRUG
Courts, 16
Possession, 140, 165
Use, 121, 135, 142, 144, 260

DUE PROCESS, 2, 11, 26, 41, 49, 51, 53–56, 58–59, 67, 69, 89, 92, 108, 180
Fifth Amendment, 54, 56, 61, 94, 230, 244, 252
Fourteenth Amendment, IV, 2, 26, 47, 51, 54, 46, 61, 99, 180
Procedural, 41, 54, 89, 108–109, 132
Substantive, 49, 54, 67, 92, 166

EBOLA, 3, 82, 103, 111, 269, 271
Communicable condition, 3, 82, 111
Nina Pham, 276
Quarantine/isolation, 103

EIGHTH AMENDMENT, 25–26, 59–60
Cruel and unusual punishment, 25, 59–60

ELECTRONIC HEALTH RECORDS, 182

EMERGENCY PREPAREDNESS
After 9/11, 256–257
Declarations, 255, 259, 267, 270–271
    Defined, 256–259
    State and local powers during, 261–264
Emergency Use Authorization, 265, 268–269
Epidemics, 106, 171, 258
Laws, 255–256, 267, 270
Legal triage, 270, 272–273
Liability, 256, 270, 277, 279
    Man-made emergencies, 267
Natural disasters, 258, 267, 270–271

EMINENT DOMAIN, see **FIFTH AMENDMENT**

EQUAL PROTECTION, 2, 11, 48–51, 56–57, 67, 99
Fifth Amendment, 56
Fourteenth Amendment, 2, 51, 56, 99

Invocation, 56
Suspect classes, 48–49, 56

EXECUTIVE BRANCH, V, 32–33, 44

EXPEDITED PARTNER THERAPY
Defined, 90
Legal concerns, 90–91

FEDERAL TRADE COMMISSION, 211

FEDERALISM
During the New Deal, 29
New Federalism, 30–31
Principles, 2, 11, 27, 28, 36, 39, 44, 66, 71, 122

FIFTH AMENDMENT
Eminent domain, 61, 244
Equal Protection, 56
Takings, 60–61, 243–246, 252

FIREARMS, 60–61, 162, 240
See also SECOND AMENDMENT

FIRST AMENDMENT, 66, 97, 99–100, 126, 218–219, 226, 243
Central Hudson, 52, 221, 226
Commercial speech, 51–52, 218–221
  Manipulative marketing, 201, 217, 220
Freedom of assembly, 52
Freedom of expression, see FREEDOM OF SPEECH

FOOD AND DRUG ADMINISTRATION, 83, 96, 101, 155, 185–186, 209–217, 225–230, 265, 268–269

FOOD SAFETY, 230–231

FORCED TREATMENT, 91–93

FOURTEENTH AMENDMENT, see **DUE PROCESS AND EQUAL PROTECTION**

FOURTH AMENDMENT, 58, 85–86, 230, 232, 234
In regulated industries, 234
Search of personal residences, 231–236

FREEDOM OF MOVEMENT, 55, 102, 107

FREEDOM OF RELIGION, 11, 51, 53, 97
Establishment Clause, 53, 99
Free Exercise Clause, 53, 99
Vaccination, 53, 97, 99

FREEDOM OF SPEECH, 51, 201, 218, 220, 243
Freedom not to speak, 219
Political speech, 51
Unprotected speech, 220

HEALTH IMPACT ASSESSMENTS, 6, 221

HEALTH IN ALL POLICIES, 5–7, 242

HIPAA PRIVACY RULE, 183–188, 194–195, 268

HIV/AIDS, 3, 64, 78–87, 93–95, 111, 125–126, 164, 171, 177, 184, 188, 191–192, 218, 260, 264

HOME RULE, see **LOCAL GOVERNMENT**

HUMAN PAPILLOMAVIRUS, 80–83, 120, 203

INCORPORATION DOCTRINE, 66

INDIVIDUAL RIGHTS, 2, 9, 11, 17–18, 26–27, 39–40, 46–76, 88, 92, 102, 122, 152, 167, 178, 186, 198, 279–280

INFECTIOUS DISEASES, see **COMMUNICABLE DISEASES**

INFLUENZA, 3, 21, 78–79, 107–108, 193, 202, 267, 269, 276
H1N1, 3, 79, 256, 271, 278
"Spanish flu" pandemic, 79
Vaccine, 96

INJURIES, 3, 16, 26, 73–76, 101, 113, 118, 131–133, 139–169, 172, 186, 197, 203, 240, 242, 274–280
Chronic, 3, 73, 75–76, 113, 118, 131, 133, 139
Prevention of, 139, 145, 148, 153, 162–164
Sources
    Cellular devices, 203
    Drugs, 139–140, 143–144, 158, 162, 164, 166

Poisons, 143
Products, 118, 131, 139–143, 146–148, 153, 155–156, 159–161, 164, 186
Vehicles, 16, 141, 151, 203

INSPECTION, 7, 230–236
Safety standards, 230–231, 235

INTENTIONAL ACTS, 147–148, 151, 158, 164
George Zimmerman, 21, 152, 162

INTERMEDIATE (HEIGHTENED) SCRUTINY, 49

INTERSTATE COMMERCE POWER, 28–32, 36

ISOLATION, 7, 63–64, 72, 77, 88, 102–110, 121, 263, 272
Andrew Speaker, 105

JUDICIAL BRANCH, 32, 44, 70, 72

LABELING, 52, 210–217, 223
Alcohol, 212
Menus, 52, 213, 215–16
    Interpretative symbol, 216
    Vending machines, 213
Tobacco, 52, 211–212, 223
Warnings, 36, 158, 201, 205, 208–210, 212, 227

LEGISLATIVE BRANCH, 32–33, 44, 70

LIABILITY, 38, 91, 101, 148, 151–157, 159–160, 163, 256, 270, 274–280
Compensation, 38, 101, 275, 278
Product, 148, 153–156, 159–160, 278
    Defects, 155
    Failure to warn, 278
    Misrepresentation, 159
Strict, 148, 153–155

LIQUOR, see **ALCOHOL**

LOCAL GOVERNMENT, 1, 7, 10–12, 16, 25–26, 30, 37–39, 41–44, 50, 55–56, 61, 65–66, 70–71, 85–88, 94, 96, 124–125, 128, 131, 160, 162, 172, 176, 185, 202, 213, 217, 221–225, 229–253, 256–258, 262, 265, 270–271, 276–277, 280
Dillon's Rule, 42–43
Home rule, 41–42, 132, 163
Powers, 7, 10–12, 25, 37–44, 50, 61, 65–66, 70–71, 88, 125–128, 131, 162, 221, 237, 248, 256, 262, 280

MEASLES, 2, 82, 98–99, 172, 202, 261

MEDICAID, 30, 125, 127–128, 266

MEDICARE, 30, 127, 266

NATIONAL SECURITY, 37, 52, 175, 181, 183–184, 257, 265–266, 268

NEEDLE EXCHANGE PROGRAM, 260, 264

NEGLIGENCE, 148–151, 153–155, 263, 275, 278–279
Damages, 148, 150–151
Duty of care, 148, 279

NUISANCE, 237–246
Abatement, 7, 161, 237, 239, 246
Private, 61, 229, 231, 237, 241–244, 246, 252, 262
Public, 7, 61, 161, 229, 231, 237–246, 252, 262

OBESITY, 3, 11–12, 15, 124–125, 132, 135–136, 213, 215, 249, 259
Attempts to curb, 11, 24
Childhood, 11, 116, 117, 124, 204–205, 251
Disease, 119, 135, 204
Rates, 116–119

OCCUPATIONAL HAZARDS, 4, 141

PARENS PATRIAE POWERS, 38–40, 65

PARTNER NOTIFICATION, 93–95, 176–177, 186, 191–192
Privacy concerns, 176, 192
Purpose, 177, 186

PATERNALISM, 21

POLICE POWERS, 29, 38–41, 67–72, 162–163, 167, 248, 256

PREEMPTION, 2, 37, 215

PRISONS
Imprisonment, 95, 152
Overcrowding, 26
Prisoners, 25, 40, 55, 60, 65, 90, 92–93

PRIVACY, see **RIGHT TO PRIVACY**

PROPERTY, 26, 39, 54, 60–61, 71, 86, 161–162, 170, 205, 229–253, 262

PROTECTED HEALTH INFORMATION, 94–95, 184, 218
Health Information Exchange, 179, 183, 185

PUBLIC HEALTH
Agencies, 1, 7, 9, 26, 33–34, 39, 41, 49, 77, 107, 128, 131–132, 139, 171–174, 178
Authorities, 11, 17, 28, 32, 39, 42, 66–67, 75–77, 82–85, 96, 102–103, 105, 107, 109, 111, 119, 172–173, 177, 183, 228, 231, 233, 270
Boards of health, 12, 42, 66, 214
Education, 10, 13, 39, 62, 96, 121, 139, 164–65, 175, 186, 201–206, 210, 217
Emergencies, see EMERGENCY PREPAREDNESS
Ethics, 16–23, 63–64, 72, 75, 88, 105, 178–179, 184–188
Information
    Disclosure, 59, 171, 178–182, 184, 186–187, 189–191, 194, 201, 206, 209, 228
    Warnings, 52, 158, 201–202, 205–210, 212, 219, 225–226, 233
Law-defined, 7–13
Powers, 39
    Compulsory, 62–68, 82, 169
    Mandatory, 62–63, 82, 169
    Voluntary, 62–63, 82, 88, 107–109, 169
Practice, 4, 7–11, 15, 17, 20, 23, 41, 43, 47, 51, 63–64, 77, 102, 163, 169, 171–178, 181–189, 207, 215, 221, 244–245, 255, 264, 272–274
Reporting, 85, 125, 169, 171–187
Research
    Defined, 15–16

Versus practice, 193–199
Surveillance, 1, 13, 39–41, 77–81, 125, 146, 169, 171–179, 187, 193, 201, 231

QUARANTINE, 7, 39, 57, 64, 72, 22, 102–110, 121, 263
Andrew Speaker, 105
Kaci Hickox, 103, 272

RATIONAL BASIS SCRUTINY, 50, 56

REGULATORY POWER, 10, 30, 37, 121, 131–132, 147, 244, 262, 272

RELIGIOUS FREEDOM RESTORATION ACT, 100

RIGHT TO BEAR ARMS, see SECOND AMENDMENT

RIGHT TO HEALTH, 25–26

RIGHT TO KNOW, 172, 191

RIGHT TO PRIVACY, 58–59
Bodily, 66
Decisional, 58–59, 66
Informational, 58–59, 85, 94, 169, 176, 178, 198
Laws, 171–172, 179–180, 185–195, 232, 252, 268
Mental health data, 171–172, 181, 184–185, 190, 197–198

RIGHT TO TRAVEL, 54–55
Restrictions, 55, 106

SEARCH AND SEIZURE, see FOURTH AMENDMENT

SEATBELTS, 21, 203

SECOND AMENDMENT, 60, 85

SEPARATION OF POWERS, 2, 11, 27, 32–35, 44, 50, 66, 71–72, 109, 126, 221

SEXUALLY TRANSMITTED DISEASE/INFECTION, 60, 80–81, 90, 191, 202, 204

SMALLPOX, 3, 64, 66, 69, 78, 95, 108, 259
Eradication, 3, 259
Outbreak, 3, 66, 95
Vaccination, 3, 64, 66, 95

SOCIAL COMPACT THEORY, 71

SOCIAL DISTANCING, see also **CLOSURE, CURFEW, ISOLATION, QUARANTINE**
Legality, 64, 101–102, 107, 109, 121, 271

SOCIAL JUSTICE THEORY, 20, 67, 70
Resource allocation, 171

SOVEREIGNTY POWER, see **TENTH AMENDMENT**

SPENDING POWER, 36
Addressing chronic conditions, 125–128

STRICT SCRUTINY, 48–50, 64, 221

SUGAR, 6, 34, 116, 118–119, 123, 143, 204, 220

SUGAR-SWEETENED BEVERAGES, 34, 121, 123, 205

SURVEILLANCE, 1, 12, 39, 41, 77, 79–81, 125, 143, 146, 169, 171–179, 187, 193, 201, 231
Methods, 173

TAKINGS, see **FIFTH AMENDMENT**

TAXING POWER, 122

TENTH AMENDMENT, 28, 29, 31, 38
State sovereignty power, 71

TESTING AND SCREENING, 7, 59, 62–62, 76, 93, 101, 110, 120, 177
Distinguishing, 82–87
Ethics, 83
Legality, 82–87

TOBACCO
Advertisements, 15, 36, 52, 116, 121, 164, 201, 211–212, 223, 224–228
As a disease factor, 116, 118, 121, 134, 173

Discrimination against users, 121, 134
E-cigarettes, 118
Litigation, 140, 160–161
Snus, 211
Taxes, 15, 36, 121–122, 140, 212, 239
Warnings, 52, 201, 207–208, 211–212, 225–227

TORTS, see also **INTENTIONAL ACTS, NEGLIGENCE**
Defined, 140, 147–148
Types, 148–162

TRANSPORTATION, 5, 10, 33, 37, 105, 125, 141, 175

TRIBAL GOVERNMENT, 1, 10, 25, 43–44, 125, 128, 162, 185, 258
Indian Health Service, 44
Move toward self-governance, 44
Snyder Act, 43

TUBERCULOSIS
Andrew Speaker, 105
Control laws, 17
Extreme drug resistant, 79
Multi-drug resistant, 89
Tests, 55, 80, 93, 105
Transmission, 89

VACCINATION, 3, 7, 13–14, 16, 21, 39, 53, 62–64, 66, 68–70, 72, 76, 95–102, 120, 157, 162, 187, 188, 202, 263, 277–278
Ethics, 16, 63–64
Exemptions, 97–100
Schools, 13–14, 21, 72, 96–101, 202, 278

VEHICLE SAFETY, 16, 21, 37, 140, 142, 148, 156, 160
Helmets, 21, 165–166

WRONGFUL DEATH, 151–153

ZONING, 11–13, 229, 246–252
Built environment, 12, 229, 246, 247, 249, 251–252
Complete Streets, 249
Fast-food restaurants, 249, 250
Food trucks, 250